# Secrets of Closing Sales
# Sixth Edition

# OTHER BOOKS BY ROY ALEXANDER

*Climbing the Corporate Matterhorn* (with James A. Newman)
*Direct Salesman's Handbook*
*Nothing Is Impossible*
*Power Speech: Quickest Route to Business and Personal Success*
*Commonsense Time Management*
*Taking Your Company Public* (with Philip W. Taggart)

Charles B. Roth & Roy Alexander

# Secrets of CLOSING SALES

## 6th Edition

**PRENTICE HALL**
Englewood Cliffs, New Jersey 07632

Prentice-Hall International (UK) Limited, *London*
Prentice-Hall of Australia Pty. Limited, *Sydney*
Prentice-Hall Canada, Inc., *Toronto*
Prentice-Hall Hispanoamericana, S.A., *Mexico*
Prentice-Hall of India Private Limited, *New Delhi*
Prentice-Hall of Japan, Inc., *Tokyo*
Simon & Schuster Asia Pte. Ltd., *Singapore*
Editora Prentice-Hall do Brasil, Ltda., *Rio de Janeiro*

© 1993 by
Prentice Hall

**10 9 8 7 6 5 4 3 2 1**

**Library of Congress Cataloging-in-Publication Data**

Roth, Charles B.
   Secrets of Closing Sales /by Charles B. Roth and Roy
Alexander.—6th ed.
      p.  cm.
   Includes biographical references and index.
   ISBN 0-13-799412-5
   1. Selling. I. Alexander, Roy. II. Title.
HF5438.25.R67   1993
658.85—dc20                                      93-6799
                                                     CIP

ISBN 0-13-799412-5

**PRENTICE HALL**
Career & Personal Development
Englewood Cliffs, NJ 07632

Simon & Schuster, A Paramount Communications Company

**Printed in the United States of America**

# DEDICATION

To Constance Jason

# About the Authors

**Charles B. Roth** personally has trained over 30,000 people in closing techniques. As a salesman and sales counselor for 30 years, Roth helped develop selling effectiveness at dozens of leading firms.

**Roy Alexander** operates the Manhattan axis for Taggart & Alexander, a Houston and New York financial relations firm noted for analytical fact-driven selling of public companies to the investor public. He is former editor (for 10 years) of *Marketing Times*, published by Sales and Marketing Executives International, a professional society of 22,000 members. He is a graduate of Northwestern University School of Journalism and has written six other business advisory books, including *Taking Your Company Public* and *Power Speech: Quickest Route to Business & Personal Success*. He lives in a townhouse in Manhattan's historic Kips Bay.

## 2. Related Books/Tapes

- *The Power of Business Rapport* by Dr. Michael Brooks, Harper Collins, New York (1992)
- *Power Speech: Quickest Route to Personal & Business Success*, AMACOM Books, New York (1986)
- *Commonsense Time Management*, AMACOM Books, New York (1992)
- *Secrets of Closing Sales*, the audio/workbook edition of the hardcover book, with Roy Alexander interviewed by Connie Jason. Prentice Hall, Englewood Cliffs, NJ (1989)

## 3. Publications

- *Personal Selling Power*, 1127 International Parkway, Fredericksburg, VA 22405. Eight times per year. Much solid advice and useful selling cases.
- *Sales and Marketing Management*, 633 Third Avenue, New York, NY 10017. The industry standard on sales management; covers personal selling among dozens of disciplines.
- *Agency Sales*, Box 3467, Laguana Hills, CA 92654. Serves manufacturers representatives. Much advice on agency management and selling skills pertinent to independent reps.

## 4. Seminars

- *Seminars for Growing Companies*, including "Closing the Sale" with Arnie Schwartz and others plus how-to sessions on organizing for selling and individual persuasion skills. Seminars are held in four or five U.S. cities each year. Literature is available from Marlene Sholod, American Management Association, 135 W. 50th Street, New York, NY 10020.
- *Dun & Bradstreet's Business Education Services* offers seminars on selling, presenting, and speaking in various cities. List is available from D&B, Box 3734, New York, NY 10008.

## Acknowledgments

5. Contributors I first met as editor of *Marketing Times* are Walter H. Johnson, Jr., William J. Tobin, Samuel S. Susser, Joe Gary,

# Acknowledgments and Recommended Sources

Fundamental acknowledgment, of course, must go to Charles B. Roth, the prime mover for *Secrets of Closing Sales*. His deft hand is still felt throughout.

Other sources recommended for investigation are the following:

## 1. Books on Selling

- *Niche Selling* by William T. Brooks, Business One Irwin, Homewood, IL (1992)
- *Winning Group Sales Presentations* by Linda Richardson, Business One Irwin, Homewood, IL (1990)
- *Complete Workbook for Today's Saleswoman* by Bev Kievman, Prentice Hall, Englewood Cliffs, NJ (1982)
- *Direct Sales* by Joyce M. Ross, Pelican Books, Gretna, LA (1991)
- *Selling* by Lloyd Allard, Pelican Books, Gretna, LA (1991)
- *Subliminal Selling Skills* by Kerry L. Johnson, AMACOM Books, New York (1988)
- *Five Minute Lessons in Successful Selling* by Rodney Young, Prentice Hall, Englewood Cliffs, NJ (1985)
- *The Heart of a Sale* by Garry Mitchell, AMACOM Books, New York (1991)
- *Personal Selling* by Charles Futrell, Business One Irwin Homewood, IL (1992)

Robert Connolly, Mary Kay Ash, Art Harris, Robert Carl, Glenn O. Benz, David Sandler, Don Covington, Kenneth B. Haas, Peter Hockstein, Dr. Vincent S. Flowers, and Dr. Charles C. Hughes.

6. Professionals who invested time and diligence in sharing expertise for *Secrets* include Chuck Meister, Donara Schmidt, O. C. Halyard, D. Bruce Shine, Phil Taggart, Hugh Edwards, Hokan Leo, Clinton Bird, Gregory Jaworowski, Bruce Alexander, Lois Dale, and Lori Farmaghetti.

7. *Hubert Bermont,* Bermont Books, 815 Fifteenth Street, Washington, DC 20005, publishes a series of books particularly valuable to sellers of consulting services. His books are available only by mail.

8. *Dr. Paul Mok,* Paul Mok & Associates, heads a Dallas-based sales and sales management training firm; for details on his "Relationships in Selling Kit" contact him at 14455 Webb Chapel Road, Dallas, TX 75234.

9. *Tom Power* and Roseann Wright at Prentice Hall are rocks of editorial excellence. Eve Mossman is a sterling production editor.

10. *Donald P. Horton* once again weighed in with zest and zeal.

11. As indispensable word processors, **Enrique Pabon** and **David Jackson** get the highest praise. **Gus West** won the even-tempered administrative bulldog award.

At this point, it is customary to thank dozens of other contributors—after carefully absolving them all of blame for errors. That's hogwash. We're all in this together, guys and gals, and if gaucheries have crept in, it's share and share alike!

R.A.

# Introduction:

## How This Sixth Edition of Secrets Will Help You Close Sales and Enhance Your Income

The demand *for*—and the rewards *to*—the achiever in closing sales is today at an all-time high. For ambitious closers at every level, the sixth edition of *Secrets of Closing Sales* stands ready. For nearly 50 years, *Secrets* has helped professionals hone closing skills

Why has this book become a classic? Because, without the close, *there is no sale*. How shattering to invest hours in prospecting, appointment setting, and customer research—only to watch as *the close goes awry*. Clearly, learning new and better ways to close sales is a vital and continuing quest.

In this edition, as in the past, we've gone directly to the firing line to tap into new closing methods effective in meeting emerging challenges.

In this era of millisecond information access, you can get floor plans to Tokyo in two minutes—and so does your competitor. You can access databases thousands of miles away for an obscure SEC release your competitor lacks.

A few years back, who knew the word *fax*? Today fax is standard in all business, particularly in sales quotes and rush spec sheets.

In this data-spewing world, professional closing is more important than ever. One-on-one closing remains the payoff stage in business, the law, government, education, sales and more.

The selling profession is shifting to match global dynamics, industries that weren't here last year, services unheard of three years ago. In the sixth edition of *Secrets,* you'll approach selling as consultative and conversational, empathic, group persuasion, CEO to CEO, unorthodox closing, reverse selling, win/win sign-ups, and from other vantage points. (*Secrets* itself is also now available in audiotape/work book format, see Acknowledgments and Recommended Sources.)

While reading this book, you'll learn how to translate product benefits into closing power phrases (words that move mountains). You'll discover the six most powerful closing words in the American language. Curious about closing sales by saying "nothing" strategically? It's here.

This book is organized first to get you psychologically intimate with closing, then to move inside the buyer's mind, and then to capitalize on your knowledge of self and buyer. You then progress to special sign-ups, graduate-levels closings, and a field trip to audit master closers at work.

You'll learn exactly how to spot *I'm-ready* signals:

- When to let others do your closing
- Why storytelling signs up prospects
- How and when to sell tough in closing
- Assume the no-minded buyer doesn't understand
- When to use shock treatment
- Closing when you've forgotten your sales story

Human relations know-how closes sales. You'll learn to analyze four basic customer types—what to say, to each, and when.

You'll also find:

- How to use The Echo in quashing objections
- Ways to measure buyer weakness to nail down orders
- How to spot attitude shifts that lead to sign-ups
- How to turn on heat with ego-involved prospects

Handling difficult buyers? Find out how to open and then close The Clam, shut down The Chatterbox with a buy order, and bring out dollar signs in The Money-Minded. There's more to make The Contrary sit down and sign, how to sell the prospect whose "health will not permit him to buy," what to say when the buyer says "absolutely not"—and means it.

You'll make calls with masters to learn how to:

- Use one famous saleswoman's enduring secret for closing
- How to close with the dramatic gesture
- Profit from the principle that poker and selling share
- Sell to people who have everything
- Get the *mañana* buyer off the dime
- Use Arnie Schwartz's feel/felt/found closer

You'll also learn how to:

- Match a professional seller and a professional buyer
- Listen for buying signals and then move in for the kill
- Develop empathy so strong the buyer wants to buy now
- Unearth real objections to win the order

You'll discover why the customer isn't always right—and when to tell him or her so to close. Action is a closer: sometimes you take it, sometimes the customer does. You'll learn *which* to do *when*: why you should avoid eye contact while you're writing the order; how to use courage and audacity as heavy mortar fire in signing up customers, and when gratitude and flattery win (and when they do not).

Sometimes asking for a larger order wins. Sometimes you scale down. Each way closes sales, and you'll learn both. You'll learn to pick Ms. Right in a group and play to her—without neglecting the others. Watch a master sell two partners, playing each against the other to his advantage.

For all these reasons, and more, welcome to this closer's database of valuable useful information. You'll find yourself referring, again and again, to the most comprehensive storehouse on prospect signing ever produced. *Secrets* can transform the novice into a full professional, make the seasoned professional's work more productive, and increase income for salespeople in all areas.

The new *Secrets of Closing Sales:* its uncommon benefits are yours for the taking.

Roy Alexander

# Contents

CHAPTER 3   *Building Your Own Powerful Closing Awareness   33*

CHAPTER 4   *How to Close First in Your Own Mind: That Vital Self-Sell   47*

CHAPTER 5   *Capitalize on Buyer Weakness to Nail the Sale   57*

## Part III

## THE MASTER CLOSER IN ACTION   207

CHAPTER 17  *29 Special Closings That Rock Holdouts and Crack Hardcases   209*

CHAPTER 18  *How to Close When All Seems Lost   219*

CHAPTER 19  *Closing on Outrageous Objections   231*

## CHAPTER 20 *Champ Closer As Business Actor*  247

## CHAPTER 21 *Power Words That Close Sales*  267

CHAPTER 25  *Closing Sales to Groups   335*

CHAPTER 26  *The Master Closer in Top Form   351*

## PART ONE

# GETTING PSYCHOLOGICALLY INTIMATE WITH CLOSING

CLOSERS-OF-SALES—company career-climbers, lone professionals, or entrepreneurs in between—share a common need: mastering the psychic nuts and bolts of seller-buyer interaction. In Part I, you'll learn what happens in *your* mind as you attune your objectives with buyer perceptions.

You first review *self*-motivation—then factor that knowledge into *buyer* motivation. (Just as charity begins at *home*, motivation starts with *self*.)

You then move in this order: first the rock-bottom basics of closing as selling's moment of truth, then closing through your CEO's eyes, on to building closing awareness after closing in your own mind first.

Your grasp of *self* intact, you move into understanding the buyer (his or her weakness are your strengths) and how the customer tells you when to close (once you know how to *listen*). Soon you are fine-tuning your closing climate, via tested ways to listen, when to talk, how both words and silence build powerful empathy. You're then equipped to capitalize on your knowledge of self and buyer.

# CHAPTER ONE

# *If* You Can't Close, You Can't Sell

Ever wonder how the upper 20 percent of salespeople close 80 percent of the sales? After all, they're selling the same product or service as the lower 80 percent! They close sales by using one (or more) of the classic keys proved effective in millions of selling situations.

Knowing *when* and *how* to use these keys—that's the *art* that separates the upper 20 percent from the thundering herd. These classic closers are available to all salespeople. Fortunately, applying these classic keys is a science you can learn. To join this elite closing group, start by getting the right mental set.

As her first postcollege job, Chiffon Lanier took an entry-level post in accounting with a computer software manufacturer. One of the first midmonth salesperson payroll checks she processed was for $5,200.

Curious, she asked her supervisor: "The man getting this check—what does he do for the company?"

"He's our top salesperson."

"Does he get a $5,200 check twice a month?"

"Well, not every time. But you'd be surprised at the big checks he does get. It'd knock your socks off."

"It already has," replied Chiffon. "What are the chances of me transferring to the sales department?"

The supervisor was sympathetic though not encouraging. If Chiffon wanted to cut off her secure paycheck and work largely on commission, it could probably be arranged. After two weeks of backing and filling, she arranged a transfer to the sales training program.

The first thing Chiffon did was buttonhole the big earner to ask exactly how he did it.

"It is very easy," the successful salesman said. "All you have to do is to circulate, see the people, tell your story, be pleasant—and always be in there trying to close the sale."

Today, Chiffon Lanier is one of the nation's most successful software salespersons. In fact, her leading competitor's representative quit and went into another field. She literally drove him out of business. Chiffon Lanier is not a miracle. She mastered the most important phase of salesmanship—closing. Learn how to close and the world is yours.

## *B*ASE YOUR ENTIRE APPROACH ON CLOSING

You may wonder how a young person, selling an intricate and sophisticated product, could achieve such a record. It happens in other fields too.

Suppose a salesperson, tired of his retail job, tried a few different slots for size and finally decided on a really tough field—selling encyclopedias.

Suppose in just a few years he succeeded so well that he became the top earner in his division, then in the nation. Suppose he closed five sales out of every six. That person has something every other salesperson needs—don't you think?

There is such a closer: Robert Pachter. For years he has been either first or second in his kind of selling. He's one of the greatest closers of all time. Closing—his not-so-secret weapon—is what he lives for. He sees no sense in making a call without getting the order. "That's why I'm there," he says.

So Pachter bases his entire approach on closing, closing, closing. The only time he fails—one time in six, remember—is when the prospect turns out not to be a prospect in the first place.

"Give me a person who qualifies as a real prospect, and I'll sign him or her," says this ingratiating closer.

He will, too, for if you can't close, you can't sell! Closing is just that last step in your presentation, but it must be paved with effective groundwork. You must *earn* the right to ask for the order! But then you must *ask*!

Let's say you're swimming across Lake Michigan. Even though you make a heroic effort, you fail 10 feet from the dock. Well, you've *failed* indeed (glug, glug, glug). It's that way with closing. The close is everything.

Closing is the pinnacle of selling achievement. Here is where your time/money/effort pays off—or goes down the drain. Effective closing makes the critical difference. Learn from the top producers who *do* close. Most truths are simple. Most sales are closed with a simple key. It's a science you can learn.

In using these classic closers, the real secret is learning *how* they're applied. It's like word choice. After all, the same words are available to the best-selling novelist and the postcard-scribbling vacationer. The *way* they *employ* these words makes a world of difference!

## *T*AILORING YOUR PRODUCT TO YOUR PROSPECT

Many salespeople are very poor closers. Bob Pachter's firm has 5,000 salespeople. Of these, how many are in the money?

"This is going to shock you," said he, "but the answer is only 200 out of 5,000. The rest I don't call salespeople at all. I call them arms and legs. They aren't closers."

Is closing sales so difficult that only 200 out of 5,000 can master it? No. To close isn't difficult. To close is the simplest, most obvious step of the sale. All it requires is, first, the right attitude and, second, the right closing key. Make both these selling principles yours via this book.

But always tailor the tool to the prospect! H.D. Gardner, top salesman and sales counselor, presented a sales promotion service to Carlos Gonzalez, head of a firm that employed 100 driver-salespeople.

Gonzalez said he'd buy if Gardner could convince his two sales managers. Gardner went to the sales managers. They refused to buy because the boss had *secretly* told then to say no. Catch 22!

Gardner, a courageous salesperson, went back to Gonzalez and said: "Am I correct in assuming that even if your sales managers recommend my program, you won't buy it?"

On the spot, Gonzalez said: "I didn't realize how expensive it was. Our budget won't allow it."

Gardner knew the frontal assault wouldn't do—time for a flanking movement. He asked Gonzalez how he had started the business (always a good idea).

Gonzalez came to the United States from Mexico as a young man. He had worked hard. But he never forgot his compatriots across the border. In fact, he'd given many jobs to others from his homeland.

"That's a fascinating story," Gardner said. "But I wonder if you haven't overlooked one thing? You've been good to your countrymen. You've hired many of them. But have you given those that work here all materials they need for success? Have you given them enough help to put them on a *level playing ground* with competitors? That's what they lack!"

Gonzalez said: "Wait a minute. I am going to buy your program."

Gardner dipped into his customer's experience to close. He had put a foundation under his master closing.

## *B*E WILLING TO TAKE A CHANCE

What Lord Chesterfield defined as "a decent boldness" is a priceless ingredient in closing. Arnold Gibb, a seller of religious books, wanted permission to install a book display on church property. Dr. Marble, the pastor, wouldn't say yes. Gibb decided to force the truth.

"Dr. Marble," he said, "pastors refuse to allow a display for one of two reasons. Either they hate to see money for these books leave their congregation. Or they're worried about improper behavior on the part of our salespeople.

"Now you can see I'm a perfect gentleman (pause, with smile). So you have no worries on that score. Further, there won't be more than a couple hundred dollars leaving your congregation. Surely this isn't enough to cause major concern."

He paused and waited. Dr. Marble blinked once and said: "Well, I'm not worried about you. I'm not worried about the money. You can have your display."

Dr. Marble reversed his decision rather than allow Gibb to think his motives were so negative. Courage won the day.

Bob Pachter proved the value of courage a different way in closing on an expensive set of books. The prospect began writing down what Pachter was saying.

"What are you writing?"

"The benefits you're listing."

"Put down your pencil and paper," Pachter advised. "These points are all covered in the order blank. Why not okay it now?"

And the prospect did just that.

Courage implies willingness to risk failure as a condition. Theodore Roosevelt said it this way:

> Far better it is to dare mighty things, to win glorious triumphs, even though checkered by failure, than to take rank with those poor spirits who neither enjoy much nor suffer much, because they live in the gray twilight that knows not victory nor defeat.

## PRO SELLER VERSUS PRO BUYER

Closing requires professional application. You're dealing with sophisticates who know all the tricks and the answers. You must be a better *closer* than they are *evader*.

Charles Mandel, publisher and selling force at *Science Digest*, has been an ace advertising space salesman for years. He still recalls his rocky beginning—and the lesson he learned about matching professional selling to professional buying.

"My first job was selling advertising when I was 18," Mandel relates. "One day I went back to the office and gave my sales manager a long list of excuses about why people weren't buying. The sales manager said: 'They're professional buyers. You're a professional seller. So how come they're not buying and you're not selling?'

"That one remark is the basis for the most constructive attitude I could possibly have. Sales calls to me are an upper. I enjoy them. I enjoy going out and saying, 'Hi, I don't believe you know me. My name is Charlie Mandel. Let me tell you what we're doing today.' That's fun.

"Even if I go out one day and the first six don't buy, I go on the seventh call exactly the same way. I know the averages are working for me. I've been doing it for so long, I know it works.

"There are people who say they wouldn't buy from me, no matter what. They think my product doesn't fit. Or they think I have bad breath. Although I miss more times than I hit, I hit many more times than most closers. In this business, you must be willing to miss in order to hit."

# THE KEY: TRY TO CLOSE EACH SALE

The top secret of closing: be willing to *try* to close all sales. (You'll keep coming back to that principle in this book). Into my office not long ago walked a man selling a product I often buy. His firm was new to me. I listened to him courteously and attentively. I watched him carefully, as I do every salesperson. This man had mastered all phases of his business. He told his story simply, convincingly, succinctly. I liked him.

Then he let me down, drastically and disappointingly. When he reached the closing stage, he did nothing.

"Is there anything else you want to tell me about your products?"

"Why, no, I think not."

"Then it's up to me to buy or not to buy," said I.

"I guess you're right."

He put his fate in my hands. I was judge, jury, arbiter, master of his fate. If I decided to buy, fine. If I didn't, he'd tell his buddies, "You can't trust prospects any more. They are unreliable. Selling is getting tougher every day."

Is this salesperson an exception? *Au contraire.* He is the rule. Most salespeople go about their business hoping for orders and getting some. But they never reach the full potential of what they *could* do.

The plain truth: a salesperson who cannot go out and close sales (which seldom close themselves), who cannot make up customers' minds for them, who cannot overcome their procrastination, and who cannot bring in orders isn't a salesperson at all. He or she is a business visitor or a conversationalist.

You become an ace closer by acquiring practical techniques that cause people to respond instantly and favorably. Practice these methods until they are a part of your persona. Only then do you close easily, naturally, inevitably.

The closing rules in this book come from thousands of interviews and tests by thousands of professionals—a pooling of millions of expert hours. In this book, closers are classified by situation and need, in a form you can make yours and start using right away.

## MANAGING YOURSELF AND YOUR WORK

Before you can close others, you must manage yourself—to many, the thorniest task of all. Scottish poet Robert Burns prayed: "Oh wad some Pow'r the giftie gie us/To see oursels as others see us."

In modern group therapy, the knowledgeable counselor says: "George is much improved over a year ago. Now he has a good idea *who* he is."

These insights are helpful, but the best way to manage yourself is also the simplest: positive thinking. This theory's been with us so long because it's basically true. Recent medical studies indicate that some cancer patients can actually *think* themselves well! Jim Newman's football coach used to say:

> If you think you're beaten, you are.
> If you think you dare not, you don't.
> If you'd like to win, but you think you can't, It's almost a cinch
>     that you won't.
> If you think you'll lose, you're lost.
> If it seem too tough you'll find
> Success begins with a fellow's will.
> It's all in the state of mind.

Newman, who became vice chairman of Booz Allen Hamilton, says: "I believed this then, and I see no reason to disbelieve it now."

## CHARISMA HELPS BUT PERFORMANCE IS VITAL

"It's all well and good for Ethel to preach positive thinking," a disgruntled closer said. "If I had her charisma, I'd be a positive thinker, too."

That brings up the story of the fellow worried about his inferiority. He went to an analyst. After six months of therapy, the doctor said: "We've found the trouble. You really *are* inferior."

But getting back to charisma: *how needed an ingredient?* At one time, this quality was called *personality* or *personal magnetism,* and even *charm.* Sure, if you have *it* (by whatever name), it helps.

If you lucked out with more than your share of charm, add boldness and even *chutzpah*—when the time is right.

Stuart Browne did that when he walked into the *Encyclopaedia Britannica* executive office: "It was plush. The manager had a long oak-paneled room with pile carpet four inches deep. Original paintings on the walls. We had to walk the length of the room to get to his desk. Our high priest was on a throne on a dais under a ceiling spotlight."

Stuart was not intimidated. He walked that long walk holding a long cigar with a long ash. Halfway he stopped and aimed that cigar at a standup ashtray—six feet away. He missed and got ashes all over the floor. He stopped and looked around and said: "Jesus, what a dump!"

His actions were saying: These trappings don't impress me.

It worked. The encyclopedia executive thought: "Anyone this outlandish *must* be good." But remember: Stuart *was* good. If you're going to be outrageous, better be good enough to back it up.

If everywhere you go, people want to do something for you and if you get letters from 50 people signed "your best friend," consider yourself blessed. But don't make the mistake of many charismatics and rely *solely* on charm (going light on work). If you do, you'll be typecast as a matinee idol—not a heavy hitter.

And if you don't have charisma, don't try to create it artificially. Concentrate on performance. It's more important in the long run.

# $T$HE VALUE OF PERSISTENCE

Few training programs talk about the value of keeping everlastingly at it. They should.

A reporter once asked Thomas Edison how it felt to have failed 10,000 times with a new invention. Edison said: "Young man, since you are just starting out in life, I will tell you something of benefit. I have not failed 10,000 times. I have successfully found 10,000 ways that will not work." Edison estimated that he performed more than 14,000 experiments in perfecting the incandescent lamp.

Ray A. Kroc, of McDonald's Corporation, agreed—and posted this maxim on his wall:

Nothing in the world can take the place of persistence.
Talent will not; nothing is more common than unsuccessful men with talent.
Genius will not; unrewarded genius is almost a proverb.
Education will not; the world is full of educated derelicts.
Persistence and determination alone are omnipotent.

Every customer has an element of weakness in his or her makeup. Each can be closed if you have the courage to try once more—sufficient reason to keep on going when the customer tells you he or she's not going to buy.

The buyer's "no" doesn't mean the buyer cannot be sold. It may mean the buyer needs pressure that appeals to weakness—the gentle pushing that's almost irresistible, if properly applied at the proper time. Each good salesperson keeps trying to close the sale long after the customer has announced: "I'm not going to buy."

Great closers always try one more time to close.

# *T*HE NO-WORK RATIONALE

Many salespeople won't pay the price of keeping everlastingly at it. More typical is George Edwards. He closed an important deal. So he took the day off.

"How come you're not hitting the ball, Big G?" his manager asked. "This isn't a holiday, you know."

"I had the biggest day of my life yesterday," George explained. "Closed the Patterson Company for $50,000. I am taking a day to celebrate."

George Edwards just talked himself out of the champion class.

You can always find a reason *not* to work. Most people are adept at it. Wisconsin winters are not exactly Miami Beach. In a week when the temperature didn't rise up to zero, a Wisconsin salesman took a field day. He gloried in an excuse not to work. So he goofed around the house for 13 days and didn't make a call: "Nobody works when it's this cold."

Yet I checked retail sales and bank clearings in his city during that period. No change. Only this salesman showed a drop-off. Like the proud mother said in watching her son's military school drill: "Everyone's out of step except Jim!"

Another reason salespeople find for not closing more: they fancy themselves in a slump. Salespeople almost always cause it themselves. Gene Lewis called it: "Getting nuts in his head!" Don't lose the sale in your mind. Remember Hamlet's advice: "There is nothing either good or bad, but thinking makes it so."

# *S*TRONG DESIRE TO CLOSE: ESSENTIAL!

In this book you'll acquire *substantial knowledge:* how great salespeople close sales. Their experience will become part of you. You will also acquire the first essential to closing sales—confidence—available to you in good times or bad.

There's one other essential you need: the *desire* to close—a desire so strong everything in your life is insignificant in comparison. That desire must be built from the inside. This spirit makes our ace closer say: "There is nothing I'd rather do than sell. The prospect of closing is mother's milk to me."

Even after he had all the money he wanted, all the fame he needed, there was something about closing that still made it the world's most fascinating challenge.

## *B*EWARE OF AIMING TOO LOW

One sales manager gets his people to accomplish more by distributing miniatures of Phillip Sears' striking statue—an Indian brave shooting arrows at the stars.

Each man or woman who comes to work for my friend gets a miniature of this statue. "I tell my people," said he, "this statue is the very essence of success—an aspiration so high, a goal so far away, it's like shooting an arrow at the stars. Believe me, high aim is what breaks sales records."

Walter H. Johnson, Jr., chairman of Quadrant Marketing Counselors, put this skill-acquisition process in this perspective:

> Salespersons are unique in the American business community: the last great unsupervised element of the work force. The salesperson's success depends upon his or her attitude, preparation, skill, and professionalism.

> The American standard of living is, to a high degree, due to the unique concepts of selling—the product of our business system and our buyer's economy.

> All professional salesmanship is built upon a common set of guidelines. Whether the product is highly technical, a major labor saver, or an exciting consumer product, successful presentations follow a logical pattern of persuasion.

> There are no born doctors, dentists, lawyers, accountants, or salespeople. The successful salesperson has studied the craft, understands customers and their needs, and builds a presentation of product/service changes constantly. The salesperson must adjust psychologically and professionally to these changes.

The salesperson lives and works on the edge of change—but through all this changing worlds certain elements of professional principles are common and unchanged.

Most important of all: the salesperson must be familiar with the classic principles of closing sales.

# CHAPTER TWO

# Viewing Closing Through the CEO's Eyes

Business heroes go in and out of fashion. A decade ago, the deal-making CEO was spotlighted. Later in the go-go years, number-crunchers became anointed.

Today the sales-minded CEO has replaced the cost-cutter atop the corporate totem pole. Nothing positive happens in the absence of revenue. Red Motley, the CEO at *Parade* magazine, put it simply: "Nothing happens until somebody sells something." The economy needs *more* opportunities—not *less*—to add jobs. Closing sales brings jobs and prosperity.

In fact, guru Peter Drucker sees all business as two functions: *marketing* or *innovation*. And the *marketer's message* is often his company's *innovation*. Indeed, salespeople today must be informed and sensitive. Buyers today are increasingly aware, can access better information, and are much more skeptical than their counterparts a few years back.

Companies work to develop products and services that bring about change. The closer-of-sales transforms that innovation into a momentum to grow, to push forward—vital to corporate prosperity and life giving to the national economy.

No surprise then that closers are rapid risers to general management. No surprise that many—having risen—keep on closing the big ones from the corner office. No wonder the career-climber sees closing sales as his or her route up the ladder.

You may see your closing expertise as grist for career advancement. Or maybe you plan to get increasingly better at business's most important function—closing sales. *Either way, these days you must learn to view closing sales through CEO eyes.*

In some cases, you are the CEO and thus keep your closing skills honed for the big tickets. You may be the de facto CEO in a territory that requires you to wear many hats. If you're planning big company advancement, what better way to rack up a record? *Act* and *think* like a CEO! It's the quickest and easiest route to more responsibility, bigger assignments, the brass ring.

## *W*HEN LARGE-COMPANY CEOS ARE BOTH CLOSERS AND BUYERS

The catalyst of sales, now more than ever, turns the wheels of business. Without the closing of sales, there is no mobility of capital, no innovation, no enrichment of human opportunity. Those who match need and solution—the professional closers— once again come to the fore. This places the sales-oriented CEO on the front line.

A desire to sell something better to customers is the hallmark of great executives. Think of Edwin Land at Polaroid or John Whitehead at Goldman Sachs. Their organizations flourished through enthusiastic purveying of products and services. They never relaxed their uncommon pride in excellence of products and services.

"We need more of that spirit," *The Wall Street Journal* said recently. "It faces forward. It can provide the soundest spark to get the economy moving upward, the public's pessimism reduced, with new opportunities proliferating."

Often CEO's with "that spirit" are found closing the important sales: "Decisions are of such magnitude and customers so important to the company's long-term health, it's simply too risky to leave the big ones to others," says Louis W. Stern, marketing professor at Northwestern University.

Xerox CEO Paul Allaire agrees. He jumped in the fray to win a $300,000 contract from a division of a southeast food company. Xerox already had a $3 million contract with the parent company. But the sales team struck a snag on the division. So Allaire and two top sales executives visited the food company's chairman.

The summit presentation worked; Xerox won the contract.

"The chairman enabled us to crack the division," recalls Allaire, who told the food company mogul frankly that Xerox was having trouble contacting appropriate division managers. "If I can get $300,000 for a half-hour meeting, that's certainly worth my time."

Allaire personally handles five of the copier company's largest accounts—AT&T, GM, 3M, Honeywell, and United Technologies. "Any time customers are dissatisfied, they're comfortable picking up the phone to call me."

The CEO sits on the buy side of the table, too. Stuart Rose, CEO of Audio/Video Affiliates, Inc., Dayton, Ohio, no longer permits his buyers to make key contracts with suppliers. He takes on the job himself, pivoting on the ever-changing tastes of wholesale customers at his 90 appliance stores.

As CEO, Rose makes snap decisions and finds "suppliers are willing to work a little harder with me." He isn't above nickel-and-diming: "I actually negotiate with the supplier down to the last $2 on a VCR purchase," he says.

Negotiating with a TV vendor, Rose got an extra 90 days to pay bills and shaved 2 percent off the entire order. In exchange, he agreed to carry models he ordinarily wouldn't stock. (If you sense an adroit win-win closer on the sell side, you're right!)

While Rose is happy to negotiate with midlevel sales representatives, CEOs more typically make presentations to fellow CEOs. "Generals like to talk to generals, lieutenants to lieutenants," notes Diane Sanchez, CEO of Miller, Heiman, Inc., West Coast sales management consultant.

As more retailers and manufacturers pare the number of approved vendors, CEOs are increasingly negotiating the minute contract details. "Companies want relationships at the highest levels," says David Cole, chairman of Kurt Salmon Associates, an Atlanta-based corporate consultancy.

# THE GROWING COMPANY'S MANAGEMENT-MINDED CLOSER

Biotechnology is widely regarded as the growth industry of tomorrow. Closers in this field—in Drucker's words—work daily in both *marketing* and *innovation*. Each man and woman on the Biotech firing line must also *think* like a CEO—in their territories they *are* the company, they *are* the industry.

Their assignment: selling today, building toward sales tomorrow, and educating the buying market about developments just out of the lab—well, sometimes not out of the lab but "coming soon."

Listen to J.D. Brooks as he drives south through Virginia's Dismal Swamp region, a cellular telephone and a plastic coffee cup in the front seat, cheerfully explaining how Mycogen's bacteria destroys stomachs of Colorado potato beetles.

Brooks, 42, is the eastern regional sales manager for Mycogen, one of the handful of biotech companies whose representatives are traversing rural America to close sales with the first agricultural products based on gene splicing. *This makes him a missionary-scientist.*

But he also knows a closer must generate $1 million in revenues for the company to cover his or her costs. Mycogen's sales forces should hit that target for the first time in 1993, he adds. *That's the CEO talking.*

Salespeople earn $30,000 to $50,000 a year at Mycogen, depending on experience and ability. Most ag-chem representatives get little or no commission. As for salaries, "Mycogen's are probably 25 percent lower than competitors," Brooks says. "But salesfolk also get stock options that could be lucrative if Mycogen prospers."

"If we are successful, I'll fund two college educations, set aside something for retirement, and have made a difference in the environment," Brooks says. *That's the entrepreneurial manager speaking.*

Brooks also sees his company in context of the biotech industry that ranges from many small start-ups to multinational giants, Monsanto and DuPont, for example. Hundreds of millions of dollars have been plowed into agricultural biotech research. Investors in newly public companies have been lured by visions of super cows, hardier plants, healthier fruits, safer pesticides/fungicides/weed killers.

Now, with a torrent of government-approved products pouring from laboratories and field tests, the selling/buying/trying process has begun to sort out winners and losers. *That's the industry analyst talking.*

Which of these four personas dominates when Brooks closes sales? All work together because of the industry's newness.

To the uninitiated, biological pesticides might seem an easy sell. Farmers want alternatives to synthetic chemicals. They do not like exposing themselves or families to hazardous chemicals. Sure they fret about chemical residues in soil and water. They shrink from tighter regulations that continually make chemicals more expensive. Yet they know consumers are becoming more anxious about residues in food.

Brooks finds farmers happy to *listen*. But they are not rushing to trust part (or all) of a crop to Mycogen's care. Growers must be sold step by step. Their biggest worry: bugs becoming resistant to chemicals. Many accept bacteria and other biologicals not as chemical substitutes but as means to slow the pace of bug's adaptations.

Biologicals work slower than chemical and break down quicker once sprayed and often work most effectively in early stages of an insect's life. Some users cite disappointing results unless they change spraying equipment or techniques regularly.

These job constants dictate Brooks's grueling travel schedule so he can invest time talking high-tech, joining in joshing conversation, and spending hours poking about in fields and warehouses. Brooks closes sales by being one of the boys—pitching in to drive tractors or help bag potatoes at harvest.

Further, farmers tend to hold off pesticide orders until they're ready to spray. Then if the local distributor doesn't have Mycogen in stock, farmers switch to something else rather than wait. Ergo: Brooks spends a chunk of time making sure ag-chem distributors are stocked with Mycogen.

In short, to close the sales that generate the $1 million needed to cover the costs of his one-person business in a growing company, Brooks wears four hats. Or, to put it simply, he *thinks* and *acts* like the CEO in that territory—which he is.

# *W*HEN MIDSIZED COMPANY CEOs HIT THE ROAD

Bernard Marcus, CEO Home Depot, Inc., spends much of his time on the road meeting with vendor CEOs—typically Marshall Hahn, Jr., of Georgia-Pacific Corp., Richard H. Ayers of Stanley Works, and William W. Adams of Armstrong World Industries, Inc. His close ties with these CEOs allow Home Depot to carry low inventories and plan rapid restocking.

"We don't believe in adversarial relationships," he says. "We need one another."

Start talking business travel—a topic known to generate eye rolling among top managers—and Bob Crawford waxes evangelical. Not only does Crawford like spending half of his time on the road, he feels he *has* to be there and he believes other CEOs not so committed are wrong.

Forget the arguments "you're just one person" and "you can't be everywhere" or "the telephone takes you to more people more efficiently."

"I totally reject those," says Crawford, CEO of Brook Furniture Rental, Arlington Heights, Illinois. "It's real hard to listen, get the full content, unless you see the person, feel his or her presence. A telephone gives you only diluted communication."

Others groan and say: "I'm too busy to leave for long periods of time. Too much going on." To which converts riposte: "Just the point! Too much going on—out *there*. A CEO behind a desk attending to today's business is going to miss the business of tomorrow."

In 10 years Bob Crawford has grown Brook Furniture Rental from annual revenues of $480,000 to $50 million. He now has 40 showrooms in 40 states, 55 outside salespeople, and business in both residential and office furniture rentals.

His clients, he says, are under pressure to make decisions more quickly than ever before. His reaction: be *away* from his office more.

"The CEO must sense the marketplace to be confident he's moving in the right direction," Crawford says emphatically. "It's extremely demanding. But it's crucial."

Crawford's personality and training reinforce his commitment. He started as salesman and has kept physical stamina/concentration for constant face-to-face contact with customers. But when out on joint calls with field salesfolk, he takes a back seat.

"We don't confuse things with too many people." he says. "I might jump in occasionally and say, "I hope you don't mind if I ask a question." If the customer starts playing to me, I'll say, "I think Joe has a great response to that."

## *F*RANK PACETTA: GIANT XEROX'S HIGH ROLLER

When Xerox Corp.'s Independence, Ohio, district sales manager left, the office was in disarray. Some employees wondered if anyone would take the job.

But Xerox promoted a can-do whiz kid named Frank Pacetta, who joined as a copier salesman and quickly rose through the ranks. On his first day as district manager, Pacetta vowed before the entire staff: "This district will finish the year No. 1 in the region and No. 4 among Xerox' 65 districts." (No. 1 in the nation that year: midtown Manhattan). Since then, operating profits in Pacetta's district jumped 43 percent. And he has received freedom to set its own deals.

In copiers, high-tech marketshare is determined by foot soldiers in the field. Pacetta, more sports buff than business hound, views closing as parallel to athletics: winners are clearly defined, risk takers reap huge rewards, success requires grit and perseverance.

One customer, OfficeMax, Inc., Cleveland-based office supply company, has 65 stores. Xerox sent in special negotiators to hammer out a multimillion-dollar contract. But OfficeMax founder Michael Feurer wanted special leasing terms. To Feurer's amazement, Pacetta took OfficeMax's side against Xerox, arguing for more favorable terms. Even at lower profit margins, Pacetta argued, the contract would plant seeds for more business.

Pacetta worked to get new terms approved by his superiors. Three levels of management rejected the pact. So Pacetta invited

Xerox finance vice president Philip Fishbach to visit Feurer. Feurer laid out his business plan. OfficeMax got the special terms.

"Pacetta is a street fighter," Feurer says. "He knew how to beat his own system."

---

### Pacetta's Advice for Closers Who Work with CEOs

- Prepare your customer proposals on weekends and evenings.
- Never say no to a customer. Everything is negotiable.
- Make customers feel good about you by sending cards for birthdays and promotions. Take them to lunch and ballgames.
- Meet customer requirements, even if it means fighting your own bureaucracy.
- Do things for your customers you don't get paid for—like solving billing problems.
- Know your competitor's product better than your competitor does.
- Be early for meetings.
- Dress well so "you look like superior product."
- At day end, when it's time to go home, make one more phone call.
- If you stay in the shower a long time in the morning because you don't look forward to your work, get yourself another job.

---

## SMALL BIZ SECRET: DON'T GIVE AWAY THE STORE

Lois Dale, CEO of Barter Advantage, Inc., New York's premier barter exchange, is nationally recognized today as the first lady of barter—her eminence attested by *USA Today, Journal of Commerce,* and *US* magazine. ("She even sold her ob/gyn doctor on delivering her baby on barter!" one editor marveled.)

But when Dale started Barter Advantage in 1981, few prospects knew the business benefits ("you accrue supplementary sales") and didn't care. Dale, a winning salesperson with reserves in articulate charm, was eager to get barter accepted—so eager she made a memorable error.

A travel agent wanted to get a $27,000 printing job done, Dale recalls. He hadn't put any services into the barter system *yet*—but promised to do so. Dale did know her members were eager to get travel on barter.

"Get us the printing we need now, and everything will be all right," the persuasive agent told her.

"It's a big sale," Dale told herself. "Let's do it." She extended him the credit.

The day after the print job was delivered, trouble. The agent didn't return calls. A too-late credit check said: "Beware." The agent went to Brazil. His company went down the drain.

"It was a disaster, but I learned a most instructive lesson," Dale relates. "*No* sale is better than a *bad* sale. I found out how to evaluate a potential customer with a CEO's eyes—and not be just a salesperson seeking another scalp."

"Without this jolt, I'd have never been corner office material," says Dale. "Now I can still *sell* them. But I know when to collect in advance. And when to *reject* them, too."

"Sure, knowing how to close sales is vital and exciting. But knowing how to pick the profitable prospect makes you *promotable*. And your ability to close sales continues to be valuable at *every* level."

Epilog: Lois's daughter Jordana is already bartering "closed-out dolls" for new toys with her kindergarten schoolmates. As the twig is bent so goes the tree.

## *T*OP SIGN—LLOYD ALLAIRE'S ONE-CALL CLOSES

Lloyd Allaire (no relation to Xerox's Paul Allaire) is a sign seller par excellence. He gets through to CEOs all the time. But sometimes the CEO bucks the decision *downstairs*.

John Downey liked the sign plan but "our 12-member board—maker of all major purchasing decisions—meets only on Wednesday evenings." It was Friday. Lloyd's plane left Saturday.

"Sorry," Downey said, "rules are rules. We'll just have to wait 'til Wednesday for a decision on this."

After a short pause, Allaire said: "I understand. I wish we could have done business."

When Allaire finished packing, he added wistfully, "You know sometimes we give discounts to small businesses for doing business with us on one call. Now, I'm sure a big company like you wouldn't be interested, but let's figure it out, anyway." With flourishes of the pen, he hummed Custer's old calvary tune *Garry Owen* as he figured out his "one-call discount." When he finished he looked at the figures and said: "Wow, that's a lot of money!"

Allaire showed Downey the work sheet and said: "Now this is next Wednesday's price. However, if you hand me a check for $2000—outside that door in the next 15 minutes—this'll be today's price" (it was much lower). "Anyway, thanks for your time." Allaire stepped out the door into the coffee shop.

After a few minutes, the door opened Downey handed Lloyd a check for $2,000, winked, and said: "We know what you did in there. You weren't fooling anybody. But what the heck. We wanted that sign, so you made our job easier."

Allaire has sold churches that needed a consensus of deacons and the opinion of the congregation. He's sold lodges that said they had to poll membership. *He does it all on one call.* It can be done! "Think it through," he says, "work up the courage. You'll usually find a way."

# *T*HE PERDUE TECHNIQUE IN CLOSING SERVICES

Before Frank Perdue, people bought generic chicken. Perdue's genius: create a brand in a commodity field. Jack C. Davis, regional manager for First American Title Insurance, St. Louis, does the same thing with a commodity *service.* For his clients, local real estate agents using First American's title insurance services, Davis created a club:

an effective inexpensive way to differentiate his firm from all the others.

In mid-December Davis mailed a postcard to CEOs of St. Louis real estate firms. On the front, over an attractive white eagle on a silver background, the headline said only, "The Eagle Is Coming!" No indication of card sender. A second card, mailed in early January used the same format to say: "The Eagle Is Coming *Soon!*"

A third mailing brought a brochure headlined: "The Eagle has Arrived!" Inside, facts on First American Title's Silver Eagle Service Club plus services and benefits for members. A reply card (postage required) urged readers to request more information.

From the 9,000 names mailed, Davis signed up 380 new agents and did as much business during the first five months as the first nine months of the previous year.

The heart of the service-branding idea: the official-looking enrollment form. It asks prospects: (1) do you want First American to contact buyers and sellers directly, or (2) always go through you, and (3) when and how do you want closing statements sent.

"Finally, somebody is asking *me* what *I* want," says Joann Britton Gundaker, Better Homes and Gardens brokerage, St. Louis. She's a new First American client and club member.

"It's mostly what we were doing before," says Davis, "but now we've packaged these services and given them a name. When I proposed it, my boss said: 'It's the stupidest thing I've ever heard.' I said: 'I know. That's why it'll work.' "

Note to closers: "stupid" innovations often ring the bell.

"You can't leave all big-ticket selling to salespeople anymore," say other CEOs turning commodities into value-added products or services. If you make that move, customers insist on dealing with top management. A value-added business is based on relationships, whereas a commodity business involves only transactions. When you start selling value added, you're asking customers to invest in your company.

"I once thought the road to quality began and ended on the manufacturing floor," one value-added CEO says. "Three years later I'd reduced my sales force by a third, completely retrained the other two-thirds and redefined my own job in the process."

# Lessons in Closing from Hollywood

CEOs "meet to test topside chemistry." Seasoned closers "make presentations to get agreements." None of that dignity for Hollywood. Closing is simply called "making a pitch." When you see *how* it works, you'll agree: a toner description would be pretentious.

Pitching—verbal presentation of a movie story of idea in hopes of getting financing before actually doing the work—is a high-stakes crapshoot. It does not always make sense. But it *is* the vital starting point for much of the content on the large and small screen.

A pitch is as much a part of the film industry as Armani suits, cellular phones, and car-to-car fax memos. Who's the pitcher? A screen writer, an independent producer, a director, or an actor. The pitcher's common need: financing for a film idea.

In a tight market, pitching (a hit-and-miss proposition in the best of times) is riskier than ever. To succeed, both pitcher and catcher must dazzle. Pitches have even been made with puppets—an eager boomlet after the NBC series character "Alf" (the title character, an alien) was a puppet.

Pitching, as in all Hollywood encounters, has its unwritten rules:

- When you go in, never sit on the couch. Then the buyer sits on the chair and he's higher than you.

- When the secretary asks if you want something to drink, always say yes. You're conditioning the buyer into giving you what you want. Don't say you'll take anything; say, "A *Coke* in a *glass* with *ice* please." Be specific. That tells them you know what you're doing. Set the tone. After all, you hope to work for a couple of hundred grand by meeting end.

- Never let the pitch run more than five minutes, counsels Roger L. Simon, co-screenwriter of *Enemies* and *Scenes from a Mall*. That's about the average person's attention span. *Ars longa, pitch breve*.

Says Brandon Tartikoff, former head of Paramount, "if you've got the goods, you can grab people in a minute."

- Roger Birnbaum, at 20th Century Fox, believes a good pitch resonates immediately. "Once I hear it, I can't forget it," he says, "and I can't wait to pass it on." That was his experience when writer Barry Morrow first pitched him *Rain Man*. "I couldn't wait to get home and tell my wife," he says.
- Adapt quickly. "When their eyes go dead," warns Simon, "you've got to change your story." Always have a backup.
- Sketch the big picture. "The less you tell the better," insists writer/director Paul Mazursky. "The trick is not to let the listener fall asleep."

A pitch must also be simple enough to be easily remembered and retold to the next executive up the ladder. That's called high concept—reduction of an idea to a quick phrase or a few sentences.

John Hill, writer of *Quigley Down Under* and episodes of "LA Law," once carefully boiled a TV movie idea down to three words: "Haunted White House." One word from the buyer ended the meeting: "Pass."

Get added clout by attaching a major element—a star, director, or producer the studio wants to work with. "Bring in Jack Nicholson and pitch them the telephone book, and they'll tell you it's the best idea they've ever heard," one producer said.

"In many ways, film closing is surprisingly like real life. Weight it as much as you can on your side. Give them the excuse to say yes, says Ron Shelton, writer/director of *Bull Durham*.

"The higher the person you're pitching, the better off you are," says Mazursky. "You want to pitch to the person who can say yes."

Life can be one extended pitch. Tartikoff has been pitched while playing softball, in restaurants, by parking valet, even by the rabbi who performed his grandfather's funeral. His dentist once pitched a TV movie idea during a root canal. "It goes with the territory. I've been a hustler myself," he admits.

If you, like everyone else, have dreamed of putting your idea on film, don't hang back. Make sure you say you've got Jack Nicholson and, of course, sit on the chair. Never the sofa.

# $T$*AGGART 'S PICTURE IS WORTH 1,000 WORDS*

Phil Taggart, chairman of Taggart & Alexander, the Houston and New York financial relations firm, has always believed in the third-party endorsement. So when he moved his office from Dallas to Houston, he carried with him the endorsement of Rauscher, Pierce & Company, North Texas brokerage firm. "Be sure to call Bob Gow, CEO at Stratford of Texas, when you get there," Fritz Burnett advised him. "By all means use my name."

The name got Taggart through to Bob Gow, all right, who was pleasant. But setting a meeting was something else: Gow, highly respected in the business community, was convinced he didn't need financial relations help. After all, he's worked with George Bush at Zapata Corporation on subsea mining and offshore engineering. He knew how to do it all himself. So he kept delaying the meeting.

Taggart, certain that Stratford of Texas needed help in presenting itself to the financial/investor community, kept calling. No stranger to persistence, he called every 6 weeks for 18 months. Gow remained cordial but no meeting. Taggart was sure a meeting would move it forward. He decided it was time for humor.

"If you'll see me for 15 minutes, I'll give you a break and skip the next 6 weeks' call," Taggart told Gow. "How's that for an offer?" Gow agreed. "Get here at 5 P.M. and we'll spend 15 minutes," he said.

En route to Gow's office, Taggart decided 15 minutes of talk wouldn't do it! He'd draw Gow a picture. In the office, Gow repeated: "I can't see what you do that I need."

"I hope you don't mind if I draw you a picture," Taggart said. He drew an egg-shaped oval on the sheet of paper: "This is your company," Gow nodded.

Taggart then drew a box around the egg. "That's your industry."

Then a large box around the box: "That's the national economy."

Finally he added a still larger box around the national box: "That's the world economy."

Taggart then put his pen back on the egg. "What goes on in this egg is the only part you control. So that's where we work."

He drew a vertical line down the center of the egg then labeled the right side *performance* and the left side *communications*. His final line divided the communications part into one-third/two-thirds.

"Two thirds of our communications emphasis is who you talk to. One-third is *what* you say. Now here's where we come in: identifying the *right* audience and *saying* the right things to them. That's how we help you."

Gow, who understood immediately, asked: "*That's what* you *do*. Why didn't you say so?"

They talked until 6:30 P.M. Taggart left with a signed letter of agreement.

"Without the third-party endorsement, I wouldn't have gotten through on the telephone," Taggart believes. "Without persistence, I'd never made the appointment. But without the picture, I wouldn't have made the sale. I finally got down to simple."

He also unearthed a genuine need the client was unaware of—and explained it interestingly (always a good way to go). Proof of value: Taggart's been working with Bob Gow ever since.

## *D*RAWING THE LINE IN CLOSING BIG TICKETS

At the Alamo in 1836, Col. William B. Travis (flanked by Jim Bowie and Davy Crockett) drew a line in the sand as the vastly outnumbered garrison waited for Santa Anna's army. Travis said to each Alamo defender: "Stay with Travis or leave now—get on one side of the line or the other!"

In closing big-ticket sales, Chuck Meister, regional sales manager for Novell, Inc., Rolling Meadows, Illinois, says, "sometimes need to draw the line." Meister did just that in selling networking software to a Big Six accounting firm. He drew the line and closed a $3 million sale. But he had to risk all to gain all. (Novell is an operating systems software company. Its products manage/control the sharing of services/data/applications among computer work groups.)

Meister quarterbacked a massive two-year-long series of product presentations to the accounting firm, including contact with

50 people "from the lower-echelon technical specialists through middle managers up to senior vps and general partners. And all along, we drew on the best tech brains in the industry."

Finally, after 20 months, the prospect eliminated two of the competitors, leaving Novell in the field alone.

"We really thought we had the contract then," Meister said. "But then they told us they wanted a one-on-one summit—one of our top people to sit alone with their senior vp to check topside chemistry."

Meister arranged this tete-à-tete with all the trappings of Henry VIII meeting Francis I of France on a field draped with cloth of gold. Both topsiders assured one another of respect and high confidence (personally and corporately.)

"*Wonderbar,*" said Meister.

But—still no contract!

As the selling effort approached its two-year anniversary, Meister knew it was now or never.

"Our technology was advancing. Our management was changing chairs. The prices we quoted weren't going to hold forever. I'd told my boss it was 99 percent closed, and he'd told *his* boss. Still we didn't have the contract!"

Meister called a meeting of the core group he's worked with at the accounting firm. He took along a box of Swiss army knives, the kind MacGyver (the TV series hero) uses so expertly to get out of caves/warehouses/underwater grottos.

"I've brought everyone here a survivor's knife to commemorate getting through Chicago's Loop water crisis," Meister said. "Congratulations! I'm just sorry I can't join you with my own Swiss Army knife. I haven't been awarded mine yet."

The room became stone silent. Finally, one of the customer group asked: "What do you mean?"

"You gave me a commitment," Meister explained. "I passed it on to my boss and he to *his* boss. It's been relayed to the Novell president. Yet we don't have a contract. Just a knife in the back."

The group looked downcast, scuffed its shoes, muttered.

"Now, I'll tell you where we stand," Meister said. "If we don't do it now, I cannot guarantee what will happen. It may all go back to square one. If that happens—and it may—we'll start all over. New specs. New prices. And much more time. We'll be working with new people. I can't guarantee the outcome. Do you want it to go that way?"

The group shook its heads. Several members said "no" and "not at all" and "not after all this."

Meister then drew the line in the sand.

"Now's the time to do it," he said. "We must have the contract or go back to square one. Now."

Within days, Novell got the signed papers. The customer paid half a million dollars and agreed to pay another $2½ million over the next two years.

Big order. Great teamwork. Outstanding Novell tech backup for two years. Capped off by a master closer, knowing *when* and *how* to draw the line in the sand. And all under that powerful umbrella: viewing closing through the CEO eyes.

# CHAPTER THREE

# Building Your Own
# Powerful Closing Awareness

Rocky Bleier was severely wounded by shrapnel. Doctors said he'd never walk again. Yet he was determined not only to walk but to *play football*.

Bleier, determined, never stopped trying, never stopped thinking about playing football. He played halfback for the Pittsburgh Steelers for 10 years and he was a big factor on the only team to win four Super Bowls.

Rocky grabbed at every chance. He ran while other backs stood still. "The instant before I see light I run," he said.

This same success consciousness is present in great closers. The minute they see light, the slightest chance, they start throwing closing action at the prospect.

While other salespeople are standing on one foot waiting for the prospect to make up his or her mind, champions are in there closing, closing, closing.

## TAPPING THE CARNY PUSH

In your own selling experience, you've probably had buyers on the verge of signing many times, but you didn't know it. They were ready for the close. But your closing awareness wasn't honed sharply enough to respond. If you'd pushed at the right time, you would have bagged the game. But you let up a little and your quarry escaped.

A little more persuasion on your part, a little more drive, a little more insistence, a little more pressure, and you'd have closed many of those sales. Sure, it's human to yield to buyer weakness. But turn the coin over: only a very-strong-willed prospect can resist the gentle but strong persuasion of an articulate salesperson—a closer who knows the product and has strong timing awareness in hand.

Charlie Bigelow, a great salesman and as strong a closer as ever existed, learned a valuable secret from traveling carnivals. You know how persuasive the barkers are, how alluring they depict attractions just on the other side of the canvas.

"I often wondered," said Bigelow, "why—when the barker finished his pitch—it was *easier* to go up to the window and pay than to back out. I felt caught in an irresistible tide that seemed to come from behind. I might be wavering in indecision. But invariably, if I listened to the barker I'd go to his show—whether it interested me or not.

"Later, I found out why. That surge that carried me forward wasn't spontaneous at all. It was engineered. In the back of the crowd were *pushers*—people assigned to push the crowd toward the ticket seller. They shoved you gently forward at the right moment. You didn't know this, of course. You yielded. You moved closer. You bought. That was superb salesmanship, based on the weakness in each of us. We're unable to resist the right kind of push at the moment of buying."

Does Bigelow use the same pusher tactics in closing?

"I don't go around physically pushing my prospects," said he. "But I use the same principle exactly. Realizing it's difficult for a prospect to say *no* to a salesperson who pushes hard for an order, and recognizing the weakness in each of us, I try to close every sale. Not the browbeating tactics of the old-strawhat-era pressure artist. I'm subtle, gracious—but insistent. And it seems to work."

# *H*OW TO DEVELOP CLOSING AWARENESS

George N. Kahn, a Connecticut marketing consultant, believes the salesperson must have a close-the-sale awareness in every waking moment. Its takes time to develop this, of course, but it pays off big. Says Kahn:

> Closing a sale is like the approach of a shy suitor.
>
> He cannot bring himself to pop the question and chatters on about irrelevant matters.
>
> The prospect usually offers no help and often the order is lost because the salesperson simply doesn't know how to close.
>
> Even while a buyer is offering objections, he or she may well be psychologically ready to give you an order. All the buyer needs is assurance from you that he or she is making the right decision.
>
> The buyer has doubts, fears, and apprehensions like anyone else. You must direct his or her thinking into proper buying channels. How? By always being on the offensive. Always think: close the sale. Beat back objections with strong counterarguments until the prospect has exhausted the reasons for not buying. Then move in quickly and close.

Objections are excuses. No professional should be discouraged by a prospect who says he's:

- Bound up with other producers
- Buying from too many different firms now
- Reducing his inventory
- Waiting until business conditions pick up
- Using a product like yours

Turn these negatives into positives with your agile mind and strong belief in superiority of your product.

*When* to close? Some veterans claim there is only one psychological moment. One-chance closing may occur once in 20 interviews. The other 19 offer several opportunities for closing. Always seize your opportunity.

There is nothing wrong in using a little pressure. Often it works. Many prospects, bored by the soft sell, welcome a push. Help them make up their minds. Buyers often toss in objections, not out of conviction, but as a means of obscuring their own doubts and indecision. They're on the fence and waiting for you to knock them off.

> *Prospect:* I don't think I'm ready to buy right now.

> *You:* Mr. Smith, I think you're as ready as you'll ever be. If there is still something you're in doubt about, name it and I'll clear it up. Otherwise, why don't we get on with it?

> *Prospect:* Your company is a little high in price.

> *You:* If that's all that's worrying you, you may as well sign right now. Our prices are competitive. You won't do better anywhere in the industry.

Telling lies to close never pays. Don't say prices are going up if they're not. Don't say your product's raw material is in short supply if it isn't. These tactics will invariably boomerang.

Make a list of stock objections so you can counter them and close more sales in less time. Selling is a game of chess. The more often you counter your opponent's move, the quicker your victory.

Don't sidestep a serious objection. Meet it squarely. But once you answer it, don't belabor the point. Give the buyer a chance to buy.


# $S$URPRISING POWER OF SO-THAT SENTENCES

Phil Taggart, Houston-based seller of financial relations consultation to top management, bases his closing awareness on two simple words: *so that.*

His formula is simple. Each statement made to a prospect is followed by a *so that* sentence detailing client benefit:

- "We'd like to hold the meeting during the 25-day Quiet Period, Mr. Jones, *so that* we'd be all geared to start talking to analysts the moment the restriction's lifted."

- "George, we'd like to make this arrangement now *so that* our New York office can start forwarding business to you in Baltimore on a regular basis."

The simple powerful *so that* not only keeps the seller closing oriented, it constantly reminds the buyer of reasons why prompt action pays off. Start using *so that so that* you'll increase your closing ratio *so that* your stature and income will rise accordingly!

## *T*RAINING YOUR CLOSING CONSCIOUSNESS

You must have closing consciousness to become a great salesperson. Closing awareness rests, of course, upon alertness.

George Handler, a great salesman, consciously exercised day after day to develop alertness. "A salesperson has to think fast and act fast," he said. "I was once a slow thinker. My reflexes were not developed like a featherweight boxer's—the way they are now. So I had to force myself to be alert and to catch signs."

He discovered a close relationship between physical and mental alertness. For weeks he practiced sitting in a chair, standing up swiftly—then bounding up, until his muscles were on edge with alertness.

Then Handler carried the development into the mind. He began paying rapt attention to what everyone was saying, listening to exact shadings of words.

Handler was ahead of his time. Today, expensive alertness seminars attract salesfolk and executives—formal training in alertness. You can also do it yourself, as George Handler did.

## *H*OW TO SELF-START AUTOCONDITIONING

Autoconditioning is another way of developing closing consciousness.

You condition your mind to do what you want it to do—from mastering a new subject to making you more alert to opportunities. Here's how it works:

1. *Define what you want.* You want to develop closing conscious-ness, of course.

2. *Live with the idea.* Think about closing, closing opportunities, closing keys, closing, closing, all the time.

3. *Wait for the breakthrough.* You will gradually develop the alert-ness you seek.

Soon you'll be perceiving closing opportunities you're not aware of now. You'll learn how to detect signs you didn't know existed. Your mind will be conditioned to make the most of every prospect.

Give yourself a cross-exam each night. Carry prospect cards home. Go over your calls. Did certain prospects show signs you didn't perceive at the time? What did the prospect say that should have led you to try to close? How many chances did you muff because you weren't alert?

A salesperson with proper closing consciousness is like a lively thoroughbred at the starting gate. Everything is tuned to get out in front. Think, live, and act *closing* each hour of the day. Soon closing will be part of your *persona* and part of your life.


# $P$LOTTING YOUR CLOSING PROGRESS

So important is closing that apprentice salesfolk sometimes view the sign-up as a separate entity from the rest of the selling conver-sation.

Don't fall into this fallacy. That's following closing conscious-ness right out the window. Would a playwright throw out Act One and two-thirds of Act Two—to present only the major climax of his play, "since that's the most important part?" Certainly not. Neither can you allow your closing awareness to leap over the vital steps that place you in closing position.

To make sure you see closing as one more step, allbeit the *raison d'être* of the exercise, Arnie Schwartz, the Long Island-based sales trainer, has graphed the selling process:

- **Prospecting** — Qualified decision maker agrees to a firm appointment.
- **Precall data gathering and study** — Salesperson gets information on company or individual.
- **Approach** — Prospect gives salesperson undivided attention and interest; is open to answering questions.
- **Questioning** — A definite need is uncovered—prospect acknowledges need and is interested in salesperson's solution.
- **Presentation** — Prospect shows interest, gives buying signals.
- **Handling objections** — Prospect's concern is met, is satisfied with your answer.
- **Trial close** — Prospect agrees with salesperson's claims or assertions about product or answers positively to questions concerning product benefits.
- **Close** — Prospect answers a closing question affirmatively.

During the selling process know where you are at all times and what your next step must be. Plot your progress to assure closing awareness.

## *H*OW TO CREATE OPPORTUNITY AS YOU GO

By training yourself in alertness, you create closing opportunities as you go along. Your prospect may not be aware of these openings, but that doesn't matter. You will be.

A sale is merely a series of opportunities to close. A good salesperson seizes them. An unaware salesperson muffs them, or, worse, is unaware that they exist.

Buyers, if you're alert, will tell you when they're ready to buy. Not in so many words, but by actions. They finger your sample. They tap the table. They lean forward.

If they open their eyes wider, it's almost certain they want to know more.

Buyers may show they're ready by finding fault with your product. Good salesfolk close on resistance. When buyers say they aren't—going to buy, take it as a sign—they will.

Usually buyers aren't conscious of giving themselves away. Sports history gives us a knockout illustration.

Gene Tunney, perhaps the craftiest boxer who ever lived, knocked out Tom Gibbons. Yet Gibbons, a marvelous defensive fighter, was flawless. Jack Dempsey hadn't been able to knock him out in 15 rounds. No one could touch Gibbons. Yet Tunney knocked Gibbons out with a punch to the liver.

Earlier, Tunney had noticed that just before Gibbons threw a punch, he momentarily left his liver unguarded. Tunney watched for the sign. It showed. Whammy—down went Gibbons.

"Tommy never knew he had this weakness," said Tunney later. "But I studied his pictures. I knew it. So I took advantage of it."

The closing-aware seller operates this way all the time.

# CLOSE EARLIER AND MORE

Hugh Bell closed more by closing twice as early. His record proved him right.

When Hugh was young and inexperienced (and a stranger in town), he wasn't making the grade and other salespeople were. In despair, he attended a sales rally.

"If you don't start to close twice as early," the speaker said, "you won't have a chance to close at all."

Afterward, Hugh Bell asked the speaker to explain.

"Train yourself to close twice as early," the old hand said. "Tomorrow, long before you think you are ready to close, try to close anyway."

"I tried it the next day," Hugh said, "and closed two sales I would have missed if I had held back. Ever since then I've tried to close twice as soon. Believe me it works."

Develop your closing consciousness. Try early. Don't be afraid to be turned down.

## $T$WELVE WAYS TO MAKE SURE YOUR BENEFITS OUTWEIGH THE PRICE ISSUE

When a customer complains about price, what is he or she really saying? That in your prospect's mind *price* far outweighs value. The seller with strong closing awareness turns this around until *value* outweighs price.

Here are consultant Carl E. Clayton's suggestions:

- Demonstrate the quality and value of your product. Let the prospect "see" and "feel" whenever possible.
- Show the quality-control measures used in the manufacturing. Show and explain test results.
- Explain benefits. Most people are willing to pay more for quality benefits.
- Provide case histories and testimonials from satisfied customers. Most people are willing to pay more for quality once they see documented benefits.
- Stress this: your service personnel are well trained and certified. Explain what this means to the customer.
- Tell the prospect you use the very best components and how this translates into customer benefits.
- Talk about your company's reputation, its facilities, equipment.
- Illustrate how your company is totally committed to its customers.
- Show your prospect a list of satisfied customers and tell how you helped each.
- Demonstrate genuine interest in your prospect. When your prospect knows you truly care, price becomes less important.

- Always be willing to go the extra mile and never fail to follow through on commitments. The more you serve, the less the emphasis on price.
- Get excited! Your prospect will not be any more excited—or less—about your product than you are.

# $D$EVELOPING CLOSING MOMENTUM

A top Philadelphia salesman developed closing consciousness another way. He had prospects of all shapes and sizes. Yet surprisingly he usually picked a *small* prospect for the day's first presentation. Why not work on the big ones when you are rested and fresh?

"The quicker you launch yourself into sign-ups, the better you'll roll that day," he said. "I try for a sale on my first call. The amount isn't important. The sale is. With that sale on the books, I'm building momentum.

"By midafternoon, I am at my best. I'm self-assured and feeling powerful. My order book is full of sales. I'm loaded for bear."

Ben Sweeney, who sold houses, planned his closing consciousness. In showing a house, Sweeney always unearthed a rusty old horseshoe somewhere on the premises. (Friends claimed he planted the shoe in advance!) He casually showed the horseshoe to the prospect but didn't emphasize it. The prospect's mind was thinking: "Good luck." Usually, without any further help from Sweeney, the prospect would decide on the house.

Another salesman, selling fire extinguishers, set his own car on fire. (He had previously poured a small quantity of gasoline on the block.) After putting out the fire, he said to the prospect: "Lucky I had one of these extinguishers with me. Saved a $15,000 car." You know the rest.

# $W$HAT CLOSING CONSCIOUSNESS IS NOT

Since you're learning what closing consciousness is, it's important to know what it *isn't—simple surface enthusiasm—*when selling the industrial buyer. Samuel S. Susser, a 40-year sales veteran with Ethyl Corporation, says you do not need to "bubble with enthusiasm even on your bad days" and immediately after (if not during) funerals, floods, and disasters.

"You are told if you do not radiate bubbling enthusiasm, you won't be able to sell," Susser says. That a buyer will immediately buy (or not buy) in ratio to the hot glow he feels (or does not feel) oozing from your eyeballs. This presumes the buyer is (1) stupid and that (2) high on his purchasing criteria is the salesperson's childish enthusiasm.

"An intelligent buyer, even one of low I.Q., is often scared to death of an aggressive, enthusiastic seller. Are some products sold that way? Yes, but only to the most unsophisticated consumer of used cars, home repairs, and insurance. Never to a professional industrial buyer."

How come in training films a toothy actor invariably extols *enthusiasm* as the single most desirable asset in a salesperson? On your next call, try pouring it on like that, Susser says. If the purchaser likes you, he may say:

"Look, Joe, I've been buying from you because you're a nice guy to talk to about the product, and you never gave me this high-powered selling. So what's happened—you feeling all right? You always sold me like a pro. Now all of a sudden you're acting like one of these kids I throw out of here twice a day."

Don't try overenthusiasm on an experienced buyer. Susser says, "It could cost you."

## *H*OW TO PATTERN YOURSELF ON SUCCESS

Another way to develop closing consciousness is to pattern yourself on a success. W. Clement Stone, the Chicago insurance tycoon and one of the nation's famous salesmen, put it bluntly: "If you want success, copy from success."

"We all need a model. If we select the right model, nothing can be more helpful. The trouble is, many of us follow false models. Discover the most successful salesperson in your field, the strategic closer. Then discover, if you can, the reason for his or her success.

When you find *how* and *why,* adapt these techniques, and closing becomes much easier."

But don't copy blindly, Stone cautions. Adapt the ace's principles to your personality.

Frank H. Davis, one of the world's greatest insurance salesmen, gladly shared closing principles with everyone who worked for him. They wanted to close like the old man. Vast numbers did.

Bill Goebel had a productive habit of asking himself during presentations: "What would Frank do? How would he bag the sale?"

Learn closing methods of great salesfolk to advance your closing ratio geometrically.

## $U$NCOVERING THE CLIENT'S HIDDEN NEED

The art of closing propels you to learn a number of rules to improve your performance. However, don't be surprised if axiom A contradicts axiom B. Actor Jack Lemmon, in his articulate TV interview on *American Movie Classics,* tells why. Host Richard Brown tried to clarify "contrasting enigmas in acting." Lemmon quoted Camus: "If mankind understood the enigmas of life, there'd be no need for the performing arts."

Ditto with closing. When advice A contrasts with advice B, choose the route that (1) works best for you, and (2) suits the prospect situation the best.

You've heard from Clement Stone on following the tried and true. Now heed Joe Gary on cutting new trails.

In developing your closing orientation—as you must—the tried-and-true path isn't always the answer. Joe Gary, marketing vice president of AECO Products Division, National Services Industries, Atlanta, is himself a crackerjack personal salesman. Says Gary:

> Some salespeople achieve more because they're *not* following the leader. Innovators uncover hidden problems and offer sound solutions. They practice investigative selling.

> You don't become an innovator by chance. Make a conscious effort to sell in depth. Stop trying to get the same order everyone else is after. Go for the creative sale, not the commodity.

The greater the challenge, the greater the reward.

An envelope's an envelope, right? Not hardly. Our customer was using a vinyl envelope with three pockets. The envelope, stored in a file folder, was printed in white on an orange background.

Some salesmen would have said: "That's that!" Our salesman did not. He recommended an envelope made of Polywove, a very strong lightweight material. He recommended two connected envelopes with an index tab on one side.

The buyer liked it. A cost analysis indicated enormous savings.

The salesman presented in detail to the department using the envelope. He wrote a very large order.

He learned the customer's business. He isolated a product he could replace. He conceptualized a product and prepared a prototype.

The sale developed in well-prepared natural sequence. Our salesman got approval at each stage before moving to the next.

Build a profile of each customer's needs. Revise it constantly. Each customer call is a learning experience.

You can develop selling skills, build great prospect lists, work territory efficiently, offer salable products competitively priced, and *still not* reach true potential—unless you realize your product must satisfy customer needs.

Uncover and develop that need. There's more to closing sales than showing wares.

Joe Gary's salesman has closing awareness. His record proves it.

## *T*WENTY EVERYDAY WORDS WITH SUPERB SELLING POWER

One way to ensure your closing consciousness is to immerse yourself in *sign-up words*—money motivators that have proved their mettle via the greatest selling vehicle of the twentieth century: television.

Certain TV commercial-selling words have been tested and rated by hard-nosed marketers charged with putting ad dollars on winners. Here are the 20 most popular adjectives and verbs, in order of frequency:

| ADJECTIVES | VERBS |
|---|---|
| new | make |
| good/better/best | get |
| free | give |
| fresh | have |
| delicious | see |
| full | buy |
| sure | come |
| clean | go |
| wonderful | know |
| special | keep |
| crisp | look |
| fine | need |
| big | love |
| great | use |
| real | feel |
| easy | like |
| bright | choose |
| extra | take |
| safe | start |
| rich | taste |

*Good* and *new* appear twice as often as any other adjective. All these top 20 words look unremarkable, but their selling power is superb! Closers who make these words part of daily presentations are associating with sales-getters.

N.B. Note the simplicity of top 20 words. Hint!

# CHAPTER FOUR

# How to Close First in Your Own Mind: That Vital Self-Sell

"Closing," the crackerjack salesman exclaimed, "is often the easiest part of the sale. Many closers make hard work of it because their concept's not right. They try to close in the prospect's mind, which means struggle. My plan is much simpler. I close the sale in my own mind first. Then the actual closing follows naturally enough."

Such has been Jere Thatcher's approach since—as a young sprout—he interned under veteran Robin Antiquo, who logged a lot of closes but never appeared to be in a hurry.

Jere, full of vinegar, wanted to sell everyone in the world in 10 minutes. He raced from call to call and tried to rush buyers off their feet. He gave every prospect the works, but his closing ratio was low. He was spinning his wheels. Robin took him in hand.

"Take it easier. In Spanish we say: *poco a poco se anda lejos*[1]

"You're *preventing* sales. You are talking to people twice your age. These mature people need to be led. No one can drive them, not even their spouses. So what chance do you have?"

Robin then advised Jere close the sale first in his own mind. "*See* yourself signing the order," Robin said. "*Know* you are going to win. Then when you are with the prospect, act at ease and be patient. Since you can't force him, let him take his time. Hang loose. And why not? You *know* he's going to sign. It's much easier to sell a prospect when you make the sale to yourself first."

The more Jere thought about it, the more right it seemed. Then he dug in and uncovered psychological reason why it works. See them for yourself.

---

[1]Little by little, you travel a far distance.

# How to Sell Yourself First

Through a strange alchemy of mind that no one quite understands (yet most psychologists recognize), we transmit our thoughts, feelings, expectations, exaltations, fears, and doubts to people we talk to. They transmit *their* thoughts, feelings, expectations, exaltations, fears, and doubts to *us*. These emotions go round and round.

If you don't know exactly how these ESP transmissions are made, at least recognize they *do* happen—a real advantage to the astute closer.

One of the best big-ticket sales managers America has known—Barclay Hopkins—believed heartily in closing consciousness. He told his salespeople each day:

"Remember one thing—*expect* success from morning till day-end. You will get it. If you expect failure, failure will come to you just as surely."

Hopkins required his salespeople go through a little ritual prior to each sales call. Each salesperson must tell himself: "I am going to sell this buyer. I know I am."

Naturally, Hopkins's salespeople didn't sell *every* buyer. Who does? But by learning to expect success, they failed in far fewer cases than their competitors.

In Baltimore, John X., the rich and respected CEO of a multinational business, believes this rule goes far deeper than closing sales. It's an entire working philosophy of life. He describes it as "thinking lucky."

In earlier years, John struggled to get a foothold as a salesman. Ill health dogged him. He kept thinking lucky. His best-laid plans went haywire. He kept thinking lucky. His best customers failed him, as they do occasionally with all of us. No matter what happened, John kept thinking lucky.

Today this executive suite salesman traces his success back to always thinking lucky. Everywhere he went, he presented the bearing of a person who knows he's going to win.

"Develop the attitude that you cannot fail," John says today. "Insist on the positive expectation of success. If you have that fundamental, you have it all. If you lack it, you lack everything."

This positive expectation

- Provides you articulate self-confidence that establishes conviction. In closing sales, self-confidence is contagious.

- Transmits assurance to your customer—in the mysterious way we don't understand (but which we surely applaud). The customer is thereby influenced to do what you want him to do. Everyone wants to associate with a winner.

This book provides you many definite and tangible closing techniques—all built on this cornerstone: communicate by everything you *do* or *say* that you *will* close every sale.

When you interrelate with your customer, assume he or she is *going* to buy, *can't help* but buy. Demonstrate it the way you talk, the words you choose ("When you use this product, you will . . ."). If you are positive in your own mind, this positiveness will be apparent. Your attitude will say the customer is going to buy, there is no doubt about it. The only question is when and how much!

# $D$UMP NEGATIVE BAGGAGE NOW

At first, it may be difficult for you to develop and maintain this positive attitude. That's natural enough. Before you call upon a buyer, you decide he or she is the kind you cannot sell. Another, you decide, can't afford it. Running through your mind: unwelcome thoughts that you do not have what it takes to become a great salesperson.

"There's only one way to overcome negative slants on life," said one hard-boiled pragmatist who's clocked 50,000 salespeople in action. "The only way to banish these negatives in your selling life is to just *do it*—get rid of them right now, before they increase."

"Ah," you say, "but how?"

Well, be bold. Drive them from your mind. Put them out of your life for good. In their place, plant the idea you can sell as well as any one alive, that the next prospect you encounter is as good as sold already.

Don't take it too far by saying to yourself: "I am a closing genius. No one can resist me." The closing attitude needs more substantial nourishment: *affirmation.*

Louise L. Hay, the self-help psychologist, says nothing can beat *affirmation.* Start using it right away. When you *affirm,* you repeat a positive word or phrase over and over until it becomes etched in your subconscious mind. If you affirm a positive thought often enough, it works miracles.

Say you recognize negative feelings are holding you back—that optimists achieve and pessimists fail. Say to yourself: "I *really* enjoy being myself. I really enjoy being happy and succeeding."

Take it from the greatest psychologists: if you repeat what you want to believe often enough, it *will* happen. This is not a new idea. It's a greatly *unused* classic idea.

# *H*OW TO AVOID NAY-SAYERS

To banish negative thoughts in selling, your most important step is avoiding nay-sayers. Don't associate with negative people. Remember Gresham's law: bad money drives out the good. O.C. Halyard, dynamic sales trainer in Maitland, Florida, tells his trainees:

> You must learn to overcome fear. We all have fears, some realistic—some not; fear of failure, fear of being a failure, fear of being rejected. Rejection comes in the form of a *no.* You tend to take a *no* as a personal rejection. It hurts the ego.
>
> Consequently, people avoid giving others opportunity to reject them. Unfortunately, when you fail to provide opportunities for a *no,* you also eliminate opportunities to get a *yes.*
>
> The person who rejects your services today may accept what you offer tomorrow. People are impressed by perseverance. They recall you as a hard worker who will go all the way for them.
>
> Avoid negative persons. They rehash the deal that fell through or grouse that somebody else gets all the good prospects. Tell such people you'd like to talk, but have work to do. Don't become their wailing wall—lest you emerge with a negative feeling yourself. Think and work positively to be successful.

# Why Knowledge Is Power

To provide yourself with a solid base of confidence, you must

- Acquire knowledge, full knowledge, complete knowledge of your product or the service—what it is, how made, what it will do, what this means to your customer. Such knowledge you simply must possess.

- Arm yourself with knowledge of your customer, complete knowledge of her needs and desires. You must know almost as much about her as she knows about herself.

- Anticipate every objection that might possibly arise during the interview and be prepared to answer it.

- Know yourself. Know your strong points (we all have them) and your weak points (we all have them, too, alas). Heed the advice of Socrates: "Know thyself."

Check up on yourself regularly to see whether you are improving or retrogressing. Acquiring knowledge is your key to closing that vital sale to yourself.

# Protecting Customers from Themselves

Sometimes the knowledgeable closer must—diplomatically, you understand—keep a not-so-bright prospect from shooting herself in the foot. Lori Farmaghetti, New York City mortgage broker, knows how to protect the prospect from her worst enemy—herself. In the process, she closes the sale with finesse. She's a champion in a tough competitive business.

Farmaghetti, a look-alike, sound-alike to the Brooklyn movie character played by Marisa Tomei in *My Cousin Vinny*, knows residential mortgages inside out and outside in. She sells from knowledge.

"So you can imagine my surprise when Mrs. Sadie Cohen told me she and Dr. Cohen had decided not to take the 8¼% five-year adjustable rate I'd arranged with Independence Savings. I hit the ceiling and asked why."

The intrepid broker found that Mrs. Cohen's accountant had killed the sale because "you're always better off with a fixed rate."

Farmaghetti kept her temper in check (barely) and asked for paper and pen: "Now you're retiring in four years, is that right?"

Both Cohens nodded.

"And you know your fixed rate alternative now is 9¼%?"

"Yes."

"All right. Here's what that will cost you in four years—$48,000 and change. Right?"

Another nod.

"Now you pay the beginning adjustable rate for at least two years. After that, the bank can only raise it a maximum of one percentage point per year. Taking the worst case, the maximum raise, here are the figures. You pay $38,000 and change. That's the worst case. To me, that's a $10,000 savings."

But Sadie Cohen said: "It's fixed, they can't raise it."

"No, but what's that to you? You're leaving the house in four years and moving to Newfoundland. So what do you care how much they raise it? You'll be out of it."

Then Sadie got hot under the collar. "I'll go get my own mortgage," she shouted.

Farmaghetti, who knew what Sadie would and would not find in the market, encouraged her to go ahead. Two days later, Farmaghetti's telephone rang. An apologetic voice said: "We want the adjustable."

"You're driving me crazy," Farmaghetti said, playing the role. "But I think I can hold it for you."

She then took the papers out of her desk drawer.

"Thought she'd be back—if common sense could win over ego," Farmaghetti said. "It did. Accountants are deal-killers. Naturally, I didn't lord it over her. But without my help, she would've driven off the cliff."

Moral: Save their necks, close the sale, but don't gloat. In-depth product knowledge puts you light-years ahead in problem solving.

It's a practical way of closing the sale in your own mind *before* you meet your prospect.

In fact, this knowledge inventory is also the secret attitude of the well-trained doctor, lawyer, or nurse, an attitude that says: "I know I'm right, but I don't have to go around proving it."

But a one-sided sale is a contradiction in terms. You are one-half. The customer is the other half. His or her role is equally important, naturally enough. Start with a solid sale to yourself and you're halfway there.

## *M*ARY KAY'S POSITIVE THINKING

Mary Kay Ash is chairman of Mary Kay Cosmetics, Inc., the Dallas-based direct-to-customer selling company. Mary Kay's entire career is a tribute to her positive thinking, her knowledge of herself, and her sense of humor about herself.

She hates to see human potential undeveloped. "In every group, there are (1) people who make things happen, (2) those who watch things happen, (3) people who wonder what happened, and (4) those who don't know anything happened," Mary Kay says. "Many of us die with our music unplayed. My mother, who worked from 6 A.M. to 8 P.M. to support us, always said: 'Honey, you can do *anything* in this world you want to do! 'That adage became part of my life.' "

Many years ago, Mary Kay needed a job that allowed her to support three children and still be home part of the time. She started selling Stanley Products on the home party plan.

"At the end of my third week, I was averaging $7.00 in sales per home party," she relates. "At that time we gave away a complimentary $4.99 mop and duster when we entered the hostess's home. So you can see I was operating dreadfully in the red."

Mary Kay heard about a Stanley sales convention in Dallas. She borrowed the money to attend. "I converted my sample case to a suitcase," she recalls. "I took along a box of crackers and a pound of cheese, I had no extra money for food. I also put on a hat people had laughed at for 10 years."

On the train to Dallas, the women sang Stanley songs. Mary Kay was embarrassed. She pretended she wasn't part of the group. At the hotel when the other women decided to go out for dinner, she'd say: "Excuse me, there's something I need to do in my room." She'd go and eat cheese and crackers.

At that convention, she watched them crown a saleswoman queen and give her an alligator bag. She decided on the spot that's where she wanted to be next year.

She marched up to Stanley Beveridge, the company president, and said: "Mr. Beveridge, next year I am going to be queen."

He looked her straight in the eye and said: "Somehow I think you will."

The next year she *was* queen.

"You need the right mental attitude," Mary Kay says. "If you think you can, you can. If you think you can't, you're right. I know it's an old idea, but it's great.

"If you act enthusiastic, you will become enthusiastic. At first maybe you fake it—but then, it happens."

The bumble bee's body, according to aerodynamics, is too heavy to fly, she relates. The wings are too weak. But the bumble bee doesn't know it and goes right on flying. "What a wonderful symbol for salespeople who don't know they can't fly and who do," she says.

"Everyone must develop a goal. Each of us possesses infinitely more talent than we ever use," she believes. "Whatever you vividly imagine, ardently desire, sincerely believe, and enthusiastically act on must inevitably come to pass," she says. "When you want to do something, and you don't know how, start anyhow—and the pieces will fall into place."

Mary Kay believes good closers are activists. She reminds you: "On the plains of hesitation bleach the bones of countless thousands who, on the threshold of victory, hesitated and, while hesitating, died."

# *H*OW TO CHECK UP ON YOURSELF

Andrea Stone, top saleswoman for a national finance service, recently said: "I didn't begin to make much headway until I started checking up on myself. By that I mean a systematic method of finding out whether I was going ahead or backward in my closing."

How did she do this? "I used John D. Rockefeller's system," she responded. "Every night before he dropped off to sleep, Rockefeller spent 10 minutes reviewing the day. He tried to find reasons for successes. He was even more analytical about his failures."

Stone converted this system to sales calls. "The last 10 minutes of every day I go over everything that has happened," she said. "I am mercilessly truthful. If I have made an ass of myself in an interview, I don't try to find an excuse for it. I call myself an ass—and decide to be a higher-type animal in the future.

"With sales contacts that have been successful, I ask: Why? I look for the answer. When I've been unsuccessful, I ask: Why? In 90 days, after I began getting better acquainted with myself, I had lifted myself from lackluster to success in selling."

What do you look for in these personal checkups? Balance. *Self-confidence*, for example, is a valuable—even necessary—trait in selling. But too much confidence is a detriment, not a help, for it brings *arrogance* or *conceit*—sure death to the closer.

Too much confidence could also make you argumentative, so positive you're right that you win arguments and lose sales—win battles and lose wars.

That's why you need regular self-analysis. Keep on a moderate course of positiveness that rests on factual confidence. Aristotle had a name for this closing attitude. He called it *the golden mean*. Successful closers call it *the professional attitude*.

There's a one-on-one communications system that tells the prospect you *know* you can sell him. It's built on your personal appearance, your manner, and your feeling toward the prospect. A brilliant young salesperson of business properties in Chicago describes it this way:

"Your appearance says things about you before you even open your mouth. In my continual survey of real estate people, I find a direct correlation between the salesperson's success and appearance.

"Appearance not only has an effect upon the client or prospect, but also upon the salesperson. You cannot make a strong close while wearing a dirty shirt or wrinkled blouse!"

## *B*ERT'S NO-WORRY FORMULA FOR SUCCESS

Bert Schlain believes that *lack of worry* is a great contributor to closing in your own mind. Bert's been practicing this for 60 years as a salesman, sales manager, and consultant:

"Put each day into a capsule and use that day to the fullest. Yesterday is a canceled check. Tomorrow is a promissory note. Today is cash—the only life we have to live."

"Tension, anger, hatred, and hair-triggered temper bring on high blood pressure and lead to indigestion, ulcers, heart attack, stroke. Avoid such debilitating emotions." Eat, drink, and be merry—sensibly and moderately, Bert believes. If you must drink, set a sensible limit and stick to it.

About beer: "A little is a tonic; too much is teutonic," he says. "Get to bed in a serene frame of mind. If you read in bed, eschew action-filled books or suspenseful mysteries. Stick to travel, philosophy, history—restful and calming subjects.

"Don't borrow trouble. Many anticipated troubles never happen. Do today's tasks today—starting with the most urgent and working down. Sufficient unto the day is the evil thereof."

You can be old at 30 and young at 80, Bert Schlain says. "If you look forward to learning and doing new things, visiting new places, meeting new people, enjoying new experiences, testing new amusements, you're young!

"Pointless, aimless worrying accomplishes nothing. It can only worsen your mental and emotional state. Enjoy making others happy. Enjoy living every moment of every day. Relegate sad events to the pages of your memory book. Continue doing, planning, achieving, enjoying!"

Another sage counselor, Leroy (Satchel) Paige, said it this way: "Take it easy on the vices. The social ramble ain't restful. Don't eat fried foods. They angrify the blood. Don't look back. Something may be gaining on you."

CHAPTER FIVE

# Capitalize on Buyer Weakness to Nail the Sale

The more precisely you spot the buyer's weakness and apply your closing pressure there, the surer you are of closing.

A wise sales manager once said: "There is no hope for the satisfied person." There is no chance to sell him or her either. Unless you find a customer dissatisfied (which will be easy) or create dissatisfaction (which is easier still), you can't close sales.

Problems are the weakness of most prospects, problems that nag them, problems that need solutions. Guess who's just volunteered to help? You. Solve buyer problems, you close the sale. His or her weakness—need—is your strength.

Joe Bowlin, an erudite business executive in Fort Worth, recalls a salesperson who *didn't* tackle the prospect's problem: "He came to see me, a likable young fellow," said Joe. "He wanted to sell me a machine I needed in my business. He told me about his company's new model. I looked at the prospectus and told him I didn't like it.

"He did not know my problems and he didn't try to find out. Instead, he just said he was sure the machine would perform. Did he try to pin me down and find out why I didn't agree? Did he try to dig out my problem? No. He merely said it was a swell machine and he was sure it would solve my problems (which he didn't know and didn't try to discover).

"He didn't make a sale," concluded Joe. "No salesman ever makes a sale until he learns the buyer's problems—that is to say, where he's vulnerable."

57

# THREE GREAT COMPLEXES THAT GIVE YOU CLOSING STRENGTH

A complex is a subject or condition that causes us deep emotional feelings. Your knowledge of the prospect's complex gives you closing strength.

- *The ego complex* is the instinct of self-preservation. You see it in the way you assert yourself, in vanity, in pride, in fears.
- *The sex complex* includes mating instinct—love, jealousy, the parental drive.
- *The herd complex* causes us to want to fraternize—to feel loneliness and isolation in the absence of others. It builds friendships, gives us sympathy for and confidence in others. It governs our relationships with other human beings.

You must recognize and isolate these buyer complexes to understand shifting buyer attitudes at closing.

# CAPITALIZING ON CROWD PSYCHOLOGY

For many years salespeople went along blindly, sometimes making sales, often not, wondering why the buyer was so changeable. One moment she was rational and genial. The next moment she was narrow, unreasonable, impossible.

You are in the process of closing a sale. You are sure he is going to buy—all signs point to it. The buyer agrees with everything you say.

Then suddenly he veers completely around to become insulting and insolent. The change mystifies you. Why the rapid shift? Science has the answer. At the moment of buying, the buyer is not normal. He becomes abnormal.

When you're closing, buyers don't think as they usually think, don't act as they usually act, aren't the person they were a few moments before. They're entirely different.

In fact, buyer reactions at closing are more like a crowd than an individual, according to Dr. Donald Laird, formerly of Colgate

University. Crowds do not reason but are emotional, easily led, easily influenced, easily controlled by a person who understands the difference between a crowd and the individual.

At the moment of closing, you are not dealing with a normal, well-poised, serene, self-confident, individual—but with the touchy, critical, emotional crowd mind.

This knowledge will help you close sales. It will enable you to understand perfectly why the buyer is so critical, so unreasonable, why he says such strange and unseemly things.

Remember the buyer's mind at closing is more a crowd than an individual. Crowds are fearful. Crowds capable of great heroism, equally capable of great cowardice. Ten minutes after heroically hitting an invasion beach, an infantry company can suddenly become stricken with terror, cast down its weapons, and run. Often there's no logical reason for it. It's just that the crowd is unpredictable.

One of the world's great authorities on crowds, Gustave Le Bon, says to handle crowds—and this applies to handling crowd-minded individuals at the point of buying—you must:

- Assure by affirmation
- Make the crowd understand by repetition
- Inspire by setting the example

To close the sale, quote reassurance phrases and testimonials to allay and overcome fears. Repeat the same ideas in different words to drive away nagging doubts and insecurities. Inspire by example with self-confidence, by enthusiasm for your product, by your obvious knowledge of what it will do.

## UNDERSTANDING NINE BUYER TYPES

To understand why your buyer acts like a crowd at closing time, get on his side of the desk or on her side of the coffee table.

Here are nine different ways your customer thinks as a crowd from Dr. Vincent S. Flowers of North Texas State University and Dr.

Charles C. Hughes, a management consultant. Understanding types will improve your closing average.

1. *Tribalistic* customers have no personal buying values and blindly accept beliefs and preferences of authority figures. Beliefs originate from a chieftain, parent, husband, wife, or boss.

   To purchase, they must know your product does not violate tribal tradition. To sell this customer, you must be reassuring—not freewheeling, rational, or objective. Help her keep her good standing in her peer group, thus reinforcing continued respect of the tribal chieftain. Testimonials from public figures are effective here.

2. *The egocentric* buyer rejects tribal values and becomes overly assertive. This rugged individual *becomes* his own tribal chief and says: "To hell with the rest of the world. I think for myself."

   Sometimes this egocentric customer, believing salespeople are rip-offs, counters by attempting to rip you off *first*. Anything goes in The Egocentric's effort to dominate and win.

   Play the game by The Egocentric's values. If he plays con man, be a better con. If he plays tough guy, be tougher. The Egocentric is generally not concerned about product dependability, durability, cost savings, or guarantees. He is more concerned about product appearance, delivery, status, and the product's ability to symbolize his rugged individualism and power.

   Once The Egocentric decides to buy, he wants delivery right now—not in 60 days. Long-term involvement is not The Egocentric's style. Make complete financial arrangements each time. Don't expect repeat business to come easy.

3. *Conformist* buyers have difficulty accepting people with other values. They try to get others to accept *their* values, often subordinate to a philosophy, cause, religion. They tend toward disciplined vocations with clearly defined rules.

   Conformists seek product dependability, durability, cost savings, guarantees, brand names from reliable stable companies. They aren't trend-setters. They reluctantly make changes.

Your best strategy: be businesslike and straightforward with well-structured presentations. Point out "everybody is buying." Dress conservatively. Avoid comments on religion, politics, or sex. Set up an exact time for the presentation and be there. Be precise in every detail.

4. *Manipulative* buyers thrive on gamesmanship, politics, competition, entrepreneurial antics. They measure success in possessions, status, money.

They respond to fast-paced presentations. They don't need all the details. Simply present the highlights and wait for questions. Make sure you have more benefits in reserve when you present.

Manipulative customers will often play Stump the Salesperson. If you get stumped, you lose the game.

They try to negotiate price. They demand a written contract with escape clauses. The strategy: let them believe they've won the game—while you make the sale.

5. *Sociocentrics* value getting along over getting ahead. Approval of respected social leaders is valued more than individual achievement.

In dealing with a Sociocentric, relate your product or service to society. Play down status symbols, power, or materialistic gains. Present preservation of the environment, good taste, respectability, social responsibility, and benefits to people.

Sociocentrics prefer you as friend not as supplier. Be flexible. Don't threaten their sense of propriety. When you make the sale, they may take *you* to lunch.

6. *Existentials* must participate in the sale; they cannot be merely observers. Present the problem, give them access to information, let them make their own decisions. Build a participating rule for them in your demo. Emphasize problem-solving. The price has only secondary importance.

Be flexible and spontaneous. Stress simplicity and sense-making ethics. Avoid conventionality, status symbols, conformity, profitability, power, short-range benefits. Slant the benefits toward acceptance of yourself, your company, your product, and its effect on the customer and The Now. Let conversation be free flowing. Don't try to force structure.

7. *The Dedicated Delayer* fears being pressured or tricked into buying a product. He wants the last word, his self-respect and integrity intact. This prospect has been telling himself (and family or associates) he will not make a buying decision the same day the product is presented. This attitude reassures him he cannot be trapped into buying. Thus he builds a shield around himself. The prospect has every intention of keeping that not-today commitment. He can (and does) come up with fantastic excuses for not buying, real Academy Award material.

The master closer combats the Dedicated Delayer with logic and charm, sprinkled with enthusiasm, and surprise bargain offers that Delayers cannot refuse.

8. *The White Hat* customer sees himself as the good guy all the way. *He* is going to make a decision—*he* has the money and power to grant the closer his commission (or deny it). He's pulling all the strings. He sees the closer as The Black Hat, ready to pull some sneaky trick. Thus if The White Hat stretches the truth or misleads The Black Hat, it's all fair.

The astute closer plays the game until he can say: "Please put your initials right here, Mr. White Hat."

9. *Her creed: greed.* Not dishonesty exactly, but she wants to use her money to its fullest advantage. She wants the best deal possible and will use every trick to get it, including "I can get a better deal some other place."

The master closer thrives on greed in a prospect. He can always come up with a bottom-line-oriented close to feed the greed.

# *H*OW TO COPE WITH ATTITUDE SHIFTS

You're explaining your proposal to a buyer. You're making good progress. He listens courteously; he asks intelligent questions. But as you come nearer to close, his attitude changes. He seems dazed and turns critical, is easily offended—uncertain, takes offense at trifles. He hops on your harmless remark to throw off the sale.

Another buyer may affect a cantankerous attitude. Another may follow the time-honored practice of kissing you out the door. A third may clam up. A fourth try to put you on the defensive with cross questions. A fifth may ignore you.

Sometimes the customer will develop an inflated sense of her own importance. Yet before becoming a buyer, she probably was a modest personality. Her overimportance has changed her entirely. Recognize this and make your sale in spite of it.

All are defenses against being sold.

To close, your mission is to see through defenses and penetrate the guard. Remember the classic military rule: attack where defense is the weakest.

Two ways to verbalize this:

- "You'll pay a premium if you buy our product today, of course. But you'll pay a much greater premium if you don't buy today."
- "You must be smart to make money, but be smarter to keep it."

All buyer defenses trace back to one condition: fear. The buyer is thinking

- "Am I making a mistake in buying what you sell?"
- "Will my boss hate this decision?"
- "Will I get my money's worth?"
- "Shall I wait before buying to get a better deal later?"
- "Am I acting without sufficient thought?"
- "How do I know the seller is honest?"
- "Would it be better to save my money, not buy anything, get along as I am?"
- "Will I lose my hard-earned money?"
- "Should I talk it over with somebody?"

Fears. Fears. Fears. Crowding the mind, making the buyer unsure, complicating your closing. You must overcome fears. Buyer fears have one antidote and only one: reassurance.

# Applying Reassurance Power

Reassure your buyers they are acting wisely with forethought, getting good value for money. What you're giving them an opportunity to buy is exactly what good judgment tells them to buy—in value, satisfaction, profit, gratification.

Exactly what is reassurance? A restoration of confidence. At the moment of buying, prospect's confidence wavers. It's called *buyer's remorse*. It occurs regularly. Courage in their own opinions and judgment becomes shaken. They need an injection of confidence and courage. They must have reassurance.

Reassure your customer by what you *do* (your actions and attitude) and by what you *say*. Your attitude builds reassurance—the simple, well-poised attitude of the professional—the quiet self-confidence of a person who knows. You must *know* you know. Make sure your buyer *knows* that you know. *Attitude* is your most important asset in reassuring the customer.

This attitude must be followed by the spoken word, of course. Recently I considered buying an unfamiliar office product. I was uncertain and doubtful. The astute salesperson recognized that. He gauged my last-minute buying panic.

"I know just how you feel," he said. "You're not sure this machine will do what we claim it will do. Isn't that true?"

I admitted it.

"In that case, test the machine out, and see for yourself. Let us put it in your office. Test it against your present equipment. Let actual results make your decision. That's the way to handle the matter, don't you think?"

This masterful closing at a crucial time completely reassured me. I became imbued with his confidence. "Forget about test," I said. "Install the machine."

That effective salesperson recognized that unless he swept away fears and doubts he wouldn't make the sale. Far better than talk, he took bold action; to let me be the judge. It worked. He made an immediate sale. (My inner thoughts: "If he's offering a test, who needs to test?")

When you perceive serious performance doubt, offer a test. Usually the prospect won't accept it. Your offer to test will be reassurance enough.

Evidence (facts, figures, letter from authorities or satisfied users, reports, photographs) reassures prospects at closing time. They crave evidence—evidence you must give to build or reestablish conviction.

Often doubt takes the form of questions. Don't blow your chances by not knowing how to give advice. The prospect who asks advice is in doubt. If you fail to produce advice, the buyer will get it from someone else. You lose the sale.

I was trying on suits in a clothing store. We (the salesperson and I) narrowed the choice down to two. I didn't know which I wanted. Buyer's doubts began to fill my mind. I needed advice and reassurance.

"Which one do you think?" I asked the salesperson.

"Well, that's up to you", he replied. "You'll be wearing it."

This was the most inept closing line I ever heard. I nominate it for the *Guiness Book of Records*. He dashed my confidence. I walked out. A *soupçon* of advice could have made the sale.

When the prospect asks for advice, give it. Make it easy to buy. P.S. Good advice doesn't spring full blown from the forehead of Zeus The Closer. It requires *preparation* and homework. 'Nuff said?

## *T*APPING INTO MAIL-ORDER APPEAL

Good mail-order advertising—reassurance in print—tells you how to overcome fear. Customers are seeking to avoid loss of popularity, lack of prestige, lack of security, lack of love.

Frank Brumbaugh, selling-by-mail expert, reminds us that the American consumer

- Has money to spend
- Will buy if you appeal to basic needs and desires
- Tolerates short delays
- Is basically honest
- Is acquisitive but not genuinely ambitious
- Is somewhat lazy and wants knowledge served in easy doses
- Wants everything made easy
- Dislikes having to think
- Dislikes high-pressure or too-clever selling
- Responds to friendly approaches
- Does not like to write letters
- Is often a poor manager of time and money
- Is always looking for bargains
- Dislikes taking risks, but will gamble small amounts
- Desires security without effort or risk
- Is frustrated by the changing patterns of modern life
- Longs for the "good old days" or thinks he does
- Is unsophisticated and superstitious but unwilling to admit either
- Is afraid of anything he or she does not understand
- Is often suspicious
- Often acts illogically
- Likes to be the first to own something new
- Has a sense of humor
- Is receptive to sex as an appeal if handled tastefully
- Has a secret Walter Mitty complex
- Wants to comfort and beautify personal/business surroundings
- Wants to save time

"Basic instincts and emotions of the customer do not change," Brumbaugh says. "These are reliable and as constant as the sun and the moon. Products or services directed to these instincts and emotions will get results as long as man inhabits the earth."

How valuable to The Thoughtful Closer in appealing to basic needs and overcoming end-game fears!

## *U*NCOVERING YOUR PROSPECT'S HIDDEN NEEDS

Expert closers zero in on a customer's real needs, often not the same as *expressed* needs.

George Higpen, an outdoor advertising salesman in Nebraska, called on Samuel Geist, a department store owner. The prospect put up quite a struggle. Several times he told Higpen: "Listen, I don't want any personal promotion. So just forget about that."

Actually, Higpen hadn't planned a campaign based on personality. But after Geist repeated "No personal promotion" several times, Higpen got a glimmer of the *real* need. He came back with a campaign built on Geist speaking out for his store on vital local issues. He closed the sale.

"Most people hate to admit they're seeking personal recognition," Higpen said. "They think it makes them look ego-involved. So they articulate the opposite of what they actually want. This is particularly true if the prospect repeats the same phrase several times. That's dead giveaway."

To discover your prospect's *real needs,* learn to recognize these *human* motivations. Convert them to closed sales:

- *Security* (monetary gain, freedom from financial worry)
- *Self-preservation* (safety and health for self and family)
- *Convenience* (comfort, more desirable use of time)
- *Avoidance of worry* (ease of mind, confidence)
- *Recognition* (social status, respectability, wish to be admired)
- *Self-improvement* (spiritual development, hunger for knowledge, intellectual stimulation)

These combined *wants* are present in many buying situations:

*Food, Clothing, and Shelter.* Every civilized person is a consumer of these.

*Luxury as Necessities.* In modern society, certain products have become "necessities," even though survival does not strictly require them. Examples: two automobiles, color TV with remote control, VCR, fax machine at home/office, video tape recorders.

*Profit.* Convince the retailer he can sell more of your brand X than brand Y or that he can make money selling your X.

The alert real estate closer points out the high return on small down payment. The mutual fund salesperson outlines growth patterns of the stock market, projects similar patterns into future years. The stockbroker demonstrates tax advantages of buying municipal bonds. Desire for profit and lack-of-security fear are mirror images of one another.

*Business Efficiency.* An office machine salesperson shows the buyer his or her product saves time, eliminates errors, improves efficiency, and thus increases profits. He or she is appealing to security, convenience, and profit.

*Peace of Mind.* Products or services that bring inner peace range from safety baby-strollers to old-age pensions to life insurance. The American public spends millions of dollars on preventative medicine each year. If your product produces serenity, you're mining a rich vein.

*Recognition.* How many people buy homes, diamond rings, chic clothes, and backyard swimming pools to impress others?

# $O$VERCOMING 3 BASIC BUYER FEARS

What are the fundamental fears that must be overcome in closing?

To start with, buyers are afraid they'll lose money or not get their money's worth; that they are going to be cheated, that what you are trying to get them to buy costs more than they can afford.

Second, buyers are afraid the product or service might not be as represented; not worth the price. They're particularly doubtful when buying something new. (Yet at the same time, they love to be first in their circle to get an impressive new product. "It's simple enough," says publicist Elaine Siegel. "They want a dynamic new product that's been thoroughly tested in the marketplace.")

Third, buyers have large fears about what others might think. Perhaps her significant other will ridicule her. Or the neighborhood will poke fun at him. Or someone the buyer respects will scoff at an unwise choice.

Money is the one subject most of us think about most of the time. We dread loss of money more than anything. The antidote for money fears: professional reassurance.

To overcome fears about money, reassurance must consist of facts and figures. Show in black and white that the buyer is getting good and true value. Testimonials help overcome money fears. Nothing beats the testimonial for establishing confidence and inspiring action. Testimonials reassure the wavering and faint of heart.

Prospect fears about the product itself? Usually traces back to poor salesmanship prior to closing. Build absolute and distinct understanding with the buyer at each stage of the conversation. Once your buyer really understands the benefits, there is little room for fear.

If, in spite of your earnest attempt, the buyer is still doubtful, reintroduce evidence that proves the value all over again.

Another cause of fear: what others will think. Sweep away these fears. Reassure the buyer she is doing the right thing in the eyes of someone you know she respects and fears. Show how this action brings credit to the buyer, how others will think it's a wise decision.

Buyers are human enough to want approval. Show the buyer a list of respected companies or executives who have bought.

## $C$*LOSING WITH RIDICULE*

Daniel Brewer, an office equipment salesperson, used ridicule—usually a hazardous option—in selling laser printers to an airline's regional office.

"The office manager wanted to buy," the closer said. "But he was afraid his superiors would criticize him. So the sale bogged down. I called repeatedly. I argued myself blue in the face about the folly of obsolete dot matrix printers. No good.

"I figured if I could appeal to his pride, I could banish fears. So on my next visit, I slapped his dot matrix and said (loud for everybody in the office to hear): 'Model T Ford! Model T!'"

"What do you mean Model T?" the office manager said.

"Why, the Model T. Ford. The Tin Lizzy. Great car in its day. Just like the dot matrix printer. But a curiosity today!" Brewer said.

That impressed the prospect. He sat there thinking hard. Two days later he called and asked Brewer to replace his existing printers with laser printers.

"The buyer's fears of spending money were more than offset by the blow to his pride at running an office with Tin Lizzies," Brewer said. "Of course, I wouldn't do this to all my prospects. It is dangerous. But I knew my man and anticipated his reaction."


## $O$N SELLING THE EMPIRE

Joseph P. Day, the great New York auctioneer, sold the Empire Building to Judge Elbert Gary, founder of U.S. Steel, by overcoming fear.

Judge Gary wanted to buy a building, but nothing Day showed pleased the judge. Day sensed that, deep in his heart, Judge Gary wanted to buy the building where U.S. Steel had always rented offices. He also sensed the obstacle was Gary's fear of what other officers would think—officers who wanted "something modern." But Gary never said this in words.

Instead he found objections to the Empire Building—old-fashioned woodwork, poor location, and so on. Day knew these arguments did not originate with Judge Gary. Day also knew he must help his prospect overcome those objections. So he said quietly: "Judge, where was your office when you first came to New York?"

Judge Gary paused: "In this very building."

"Where was U.S. Steel formed?"

"Right here, in this very office," he replied.

Both remained silent. At last, Judge Gary spoke. "Nearly all my junior officers want to leave this building. But it's our home. We were born here. We've grown up here. And here is where we are going to stay."

Day had helped Judge Gary articulate his defense. Inside half an hour the deal was closed. The shrewd Day let the Judge sell himself. He helped the prospect overcome fears of others' opinions so he could decide to buy.

Buyers on the verge of spending money must be reassured they're acting wisely and in their own best interest. Buyers express fears differently. They may become sullen, suspicious, cantankerous. They may be quiet—even poker-faced.

Whatever their demeanor, buyers need your reassurance, your confirmation that the transaction is the wisest thing they could do under the circumstances. Every buyer has fears, and you must overcome fear, so you can move on to close.

## *S*COTCHING ORDER-BLANK FEAR

A customer who's been listening and nodding suddenly runs like a bandit when you flash the order blank. Many orders are spoiled when the salesperson introduces contract papers in the wrong way or at the wrong time. The sight can drive buying clear out of the customer's mind.

The order form triggers abnormal emotions. Buyers don't reason at all. They just respond to fear of putting names down in black and white. They're scared witless.

Take a tip from horse trainers. The first time the trainer puts the bridle on a new horse, he first lets the horse sniff the bridle. He puts it down so the horse can get the feel of it. This makes the bridle a familiar object and makes closing—that is, training—much easier. Buyers spook at the unfamiliar just like horses.

Handle the order blank so it will not frighten the buyer. Introduce it *early* in the conversation. Let the buyer get gradually accustomed to it. Bring it out, handle it casually, quote from it, point to it, read from it, keep it in plain sight during the interview. When the time comes to "put your initials right here," the buyer won't run. There's no reason to fear the common and familiar.

One savvy sales manager put together a book combining order blank and price sheet (in his field, prices change daily). The first thing the customer must know is the price. The salesperson starts by putting the book on the counter, opens it, and quotes the price.

The customer is face to face with the order blank without knowing it. The next logical step is to write in the order. It's all so simple, so natural, so logical. It eliminates an artificial barrier at closing time.

# $D$IRECT ANSWERS THAT REASSURE

At times, the buyer's weakness appears to be focused on one problem—fear of risk taking. When this occurs, try answering it head on. Here's how:

- Well, it may just come down to the fact that you're not comfortable with this right now. Let me ask you a question. When you first learned to drive a car, did you feel comfortable? When you got your first job, did you feel comfortable? Did you ever start anything that you felt comfortable with the first day? No. Well, this is no different. I know that in a couple of weeks, you will feel very comfortable and proud of this decision.

- We realize that this seems like a risky decision to you. For that reason, we are prepared to work twice as hard to keep you satisfied.

- Have you ever, ever in your life taken a risk that worked well? You are in the same position today. Take advantage of this opportunity!

- That's exactly why I suggest that you make the investment now. There is risk in all investments. Even a 5 percent passbook isn't guaranteed. We know that banks do fail. This is the safest time to invest. All the economic factors say the opportunity for reward is greatest now and the possibility of loss is very, very low.

You now possess the groundwork for closing more sales—by turning buyer weakness into closing strength.

# CHAPTER SIX

# How Prospects Tell You When It's Time to Close

A few years back, in personal selling theory, you waited for the right psychological moment to close the sale—that quintessential instant when everything was just right. The prospect's mind was attuned. His resistances were flattened. His purse was open. He was yours.

Today, of course, in this age of client-centered counseling of all sorts, the psychological moment has been displaced by another belief: close when the prospect tells you to close.

This means there is not one time to close. There are many. Get in on the first signal as often as possible and close twice as much in a day.

By using the trial close (merely an innocuous closing question that sounds like conversation), you determine if the buyer is ready. If so, you've got yourself a sign-up. If not, go on into the sale, build it, and try again. As a movie cameraman told legendary film director Cecil B. DeMille: "Ready when you are, C.B." Always be ready to close.

"A decent boldness," advised Lord Chesterfield, "always wins respect." Get in on the buying signal before the sale cools off. Boldness wins respect and orders. There are times in every sale when you have nothing to lose/everything to win by taking a chance.

One saleswoman, a seasoned pro, ran into unexpected resistance. The department store buyer trotted out all the objections, including a few neat little insults. The pro stopped prospect in midsentence. "Wait just a minute, will you, while I write this up."

"Write what up?" asked the buyer.

"Your order."

"But I am not going to buy, I just told you that."

"I know, I know. I heard you. But what you said convinces me you need my line."

Boldness won. The prospect signed!

When you think the buyer is ready for the close, push forward. Say nothing and do nothing unless it emphasizes the belief your customer is going to buy. Assume the only real question is *when*.

# *H*OW TRIAL CLOSES BRING BUYING SIGNALS

In implementing the closing procedure, you'll have a great deal more confidence after you learn how to tell when the buyer's ready. Keep your eyes open for buying signals—they are learnable.

Oh, sure, you may run into a few poker faces. But most buyers tip you off by little things. When these signals emerge, march in and try for the close. You're the activist. Although a buyer may express great interest and be able to afford it, you must take the initiative. Buyers, by definition, are hesitant about decisions.

When in doubt, go for the close. Some salespeople—fond of hearing their own voices—talk *past* the time when the prospects are ready. Close sooner rather than later—if it really is too soon, they'll tell you that too. Try again and again. Your motto: ABC—always be closing.

How to tell? By interpreting *buying signals* and using *trial closes*.

**Buying Signals.** In housing sales a prospect is ready to buy when he or she comments about the large size of a room or how well the furniture coordinates with the carpets or asks to go back to see a favored room again.

Other clear buying signals:

- "Does the refrigerator go with the house?"
- "Are the drapes included?"
- "How much is the monthly payment?"

Buying signals are often nonverbal. A buyer, once on chair edge, begins to relax. A sudden increase in friendliness, addressing you by your first name, offering—or requesting—a cup of coffee.

*Trial Closes.* The trial close is a thermometer to determine whether the prospect is cold, warm, or hot toward buying. When the buyer does not produce buying signals, or when the semaphore is confusing, trial closes help clear the air.

A trial close asks for an opinion—much easier for a prospect to give than a decision. If you get a no to your trial close, you haven't lost a sale. You've gained insight into prospect feelings. Valuable data!

Start your trial closes with *lead-ins:* "In your opinion, do you feel...?" or "If you were to own this home, do you feel...?" The buyer is not being pressured into a decision but is merely being asked for an opinion. Prospects like to express feelings.

And that opinion often supplies you with a buying signal. If so, try this close: "There appear to be strong reasons in favor of this product, wouldn't you say?"

## *R*EADING UNSPOKEN SIGNALS

Closing signals are often unspoken. Most buyers are not accommodating enough to tell you in so many words. Dr. Albert Mehrabian, UCLA professor of psychology, reports people express 55 percent of feelings and attitudes *nonverbally*, 38 percent through tone of voice. Pure words convey a mere 7 percent of meanings.

Nonverbal communication is vital in sales presentations. First, successful salespeople don't merely present a message—they *are* the message. Second, prospects show they're thinking seriously of buying by (1) adjusting seat distance in car, (2) polishing a table, and (3) rearranging a retail display.

Good closers study facial expressions as carefully as TV's Lt. Columbo quizzes a suspect (not as *leisurely* in most cases!). Certain expressions—particularly in the eyes—reveal conviction and desire. You learn from experience. Be on the alert to act quickly when they emerge.

In body language, the buyer steps back for a better look at the merchandise. She takes it over to the light to examine it more closely. The prospect scratches his chin. Or he examines the sample, reads the label carefully, lifts the product, pushes the keys, or pulls the lever. She picks up the literature once more and becomes absorbed by it. He picks up the contract blank and carefully reads a clause or two.

Body actions say in effect: closing is the next logical step. Prospects are much too cagey to tell you right out they're ready to buy. Play their game and laugh all the way to the bank.

You enter a prospect's office. She greets you in a friendly way, sits near you, nods during the presentation. At one point, she leans forward and touches your arm. You're getting all *green* lights. Time to close the sale!

Another buyer cradles his hands and touches one finger to his lips: *yellow* signals, signifying doubt. Step up your own *green* semaphore. Lean forward in your chair, smile, keep your hands unclasped. Use open-ended questions:

- "What are you looking for in this type of product?"
- "How do you see this type of product helping your company?"

If your prospect is aggressive from the outset ("Your product is grossly overpriced") avoid defense body signals (such as leaning back in your chair or crossing your arms). Instead radiate confidence and helpfulness in word and deed. When people say "I'm getting good vibes," this usually means powerful nonverbal signs.

## SELLING THE UNPROVED SERVICE

A most unusual prospect-centered close worked for Hubert Bermont, who sells a management consulting service in Washington, DC. Bermont had just formed his own consulting company via office, letterhead, telephone—but no clients. To stay alive he had to sell.

"I made three telephone calls to former colleagues," Bermont relates. "In each case, when asked why I wanted an appointment, I said I was seeking consulting work."

Next came the fatal question: "Who are you consulting for now?" Bermont had to say: "No one."

After batting 0 for 3, Bermont stole a page from Mark Twain. Twain, after unsuccessfully trying to mine silver in Nevada, arrived penniless in San Francisco. He went to the most famous newspaper and applied for a job as a reporter.

No jobs, he was told, no editorial budget. Twain told the editor he required no salary—he wanted to report and write for free.

Under those terms, Twain immediately got a job. His stories won wide readership. He then resigned, reminding his employers, "I'm not getting paid." The newspaper put him on salary and made him a foreign correspondent.

Bermont had the pattern. He visited the most prestigious company in his field, laid out an entire work load, and told the officer he wanted to do this free of charge. He told him honestly why. The client gladly accepted.

"I worked like hell for that firm, setting up meetings, solving problems, making projections, and filing daily progress reports," Bermont says.

Within two weeks, the boss visited Bermont. Not only was he impressed with Bermont's work, he was overwhelmed by his approach. He asked what fee Bermont wanted. Bermont named a price. They shook on it.

Bermont waited for buying signals. Granted, this is an unusual case. Not every salesperson can offer his product free. But you can offer free service, free help, free assistance. Offer something free and wait for buying signals. It pays.

P.S. On his next prospecting call, when asked about clients, Bermont dropped the biggest name in the field.

# CLOSING THE CAPTIVE PROSPECT

Getting your buyer all alone—no interference—is a closer's dream. However, don't appear to take unfair advantage. Even with a captive audience, wait until the customer tells you when to close.

Glenn O. Benz, sales director for Northland Aluminum Products, invited Jimmy Peterson, Pillsbury's grocery products division vice president, on a weekend cruise. Benz's mission: to get Pillsbury to name a new cake mix after the Bundt aluminum pan Northland had just produced.

"Autumn weather was perfect—clear, cool," Benz recalls. "Leaves at their height of brilliance. No TV, no telephone, no commercial radio, no noise."

They boarded the yacht with Peterson, a former naval officer, at the helm. Can you imagine a more captive audience? Further, Peterson asked Benz: "How can you help our business grow?"

As the yacht maneuvered between islands, Benz presented the plan: name the cake mix after the Bundt pan. Then he dropped the subject.

After two days of sailing, they headed home late Sunday night by car—but soon ran into an early fall blizzard. Visibility was limited. The only sounds were the purr of the engine and the swishing of windshield wipers. Benz was listening.

About 2 A.M., Peterson broke the silence, saying: —"It's a great idea. Come over to the office about 8 A.M. I'll get our staff involved and work out details with the marketing manager."

The rest is history. Bundt Cake Mix captured a large share of the market for several years. Pillsbury's one-minute TV commercial telecast coast to coast implied that every cook needed a pan to help produce this revolutionary cake.

Sales of Bundt pans soared to several months back order. Benz sold to department stores, discounters, drugstores, grocery stores, mail-order catalog showrooms, distributors, wholesalers, and the military.

Waiting for the customer to tell him when to close was an important factor to Benz. Another: selling the total marketing concept, not just a cake pan.

"Details were personally executed," recalls Benz, who later became director of marketing/sales for Shamrock Industries' Housewares division. "This comprehensive sale required countless personal calls, personal participation in store demonstrations, personal presentations to military/catalog/showroom buying committees, and personal calls to premium warehouses and distributors. Personal closing will always be with us. There's no substitute for personal selling."

## COLUMBO'S APPROACH TO CLOSING

Probably the nation's greatest enthusiast for listening for closing signals is David H. Sandler, a sales trainer in Stevenson, Maryland, and himself a first-rate closer.

Sandler believes 95 percent of salespeople close sales all wrong. "People buy in spite of hard sell, not because of it," he says.

Normally in an interview, the salesperson urges the customer to buy and the customer urges the salesman to get lost. "It's too expensive," or "I'll have to think it over" or "I'll discuss it with my partner" are standard objections. Many sales managers issue 27 different answers for handling these put-offs. Not Sandler. Here's how Sandler refutes popular wisdom:

- *Assumption one:* Salespeople should be outgoing personalities.

  *Sandler:* All wrong. The more experienced the salesperson, the more he or she knows to keep a low profile.

- *Assumption two:* The salesperson must learn everything about his or her product.

  *Sandler:* This usually translates into the salesperson trying to impress the prospect with how much he or she knows. Most salespeople describe product features before the prospect is interested. Seeds don't sprout on concrete.

- *Assumption three:* Always ask for the order and be prepared for objections.

  *Sandler:* Never ask for the order and always bring up objections before the customer thinks of them.

- *Assumption four:* The supersalesperson is a great talker.

  *Sandler:* The supersalesperson is a great *listener.*

Most people erroneously think of the supersalesperson as a James Bond or Angie Dickenson character—attractive, smooth, debonair. But the model Sandler recommends is Columbo, the television detective who appears rumpled, absent-minded, awkward. Suspects think he's bumbling and stupid—all the way to the slammer!

"Columbo makes no assumptions," Sandler says. "He doesn't try to read other people's minds. He gets what he wants by asking questions and more questions, and then a few more questions. That's what selling is all about. Asking, not telling. Listening, not talking.

"Selling isn't a dog and a pony show. The best sales are the ones you never see, where the customer does the work and the salesperson simply asks questions and writes up the order at the customer's instructions.

"Remember the law of inertia: a body in motion tends to stay in motion. If your prospect is swinging against you, don't try to block him or you'll both collide. Gently lead him to a neutral position. Then start the swing in your favor. Do this by disarming him. Say precisely what he doesn't expect."

If a prospect says she's not interested, she expects the salesperson to tell her why she should be. The tug-of-war begins. Prospects say no, salesperson says yes—back and forth—until one side gives up.

Here's how Sandler handles an unfriendly prospect.

*Prospect:* I'm not interested.

*Salesperson:* Maybe you shouldn't be. But let me ask you a question, what is it that you're really interested in?

*Prospect:* I really don't want to spend the money. . .

*Salesperson:* Well maybe you shouldn't. Let me ask you this— how much were you hoping to spend?

"At this point," Sandler said, "We've gone from no to neutral, and it's just a matter of time before the customer swings to yes. We accomplish this by saying maybe she shouldn't be interested, which surprises her, and then by asking her questions."

A prospect expects a gung-ho salesperson. If the salesperson, instead, refuses to sell, and tries to discourage buying, the prospect will almost always ask the salesperson to start selling. Instead of resisting the sale, the prospect is pulling for it.

"When Supersalesperson meets a Superresister, it usually means a gladiatorial battle," Sandler says. "The customer winds up on the floor scarred and bruised. The salesperson, huffing and puffing, is lying on top of him thinking he's done a good job.

"In good selling, behave just the opposite," says Sandler. "Let the customer do all the work. He talks. You listen."

Sandler's approach may not work for everyone. But isn't he just saying—one more time—listen for clues to close? And if you don't hear any, trial closes will bring them out.

Your grandfather said it this way: "You can lead a horse to water but you can't make him drink." No, indeed.

## $S$ANDLER'S REVERSE SELLING STRATEGY

Sandler also believes reverse questions keep the closer out of trouble. Watch the nonquestioning closer dig his own pit:

*Prospect:* Do you have more than one of these?

*Salesperson:* Why, yes! (excited and expecting to close)

*Prospect:* I wonder how many they make.

*Salesperson:* Lots of people buy this model.

*Prospect:* I'm sorry to hear that, I like to buy exclusives.

Look the unnecessary pressure the salesperson caused! Instead he or she could have employed bounce-back questions like this:

*Prospect:* Do you have more than one of these?

*Salesperson:* That's an interesting question. Why do you ask?

*Prospect:* I was wondering just how many they make?

*Salesperson:* That makes sense. May I ask you why that's important to you?

*Prospect:* I like buying exclusives.

The salesperson now possesses flexibility to deal with the real issue, to think it out without undue pressure. Here are more bounce-back examples:

*Prospect:* The price is too high.

*Salesperson:* (quietly and with assurance). Which means . . . the price is high, but with other benefits I can understand it.

Quite a contrast to "The price is too high" alone!
Or suppose it goes this way:

*Prospect:* The price is too high.

*Salesperson:* Which means . . .

*Prospect:* Which means we're going to have to do some talking internally to get support for this deal.

Sometimes it pays to ask the prospect her own ideal solution:

"Linda, if you had a magic wand that could produce the ideal solution to this problem, what would it be?"

The prospect now feels free to speak candidly. You may be surprised at the contempt!
When things get tense, Sandler suggests:

"Off the record, Homer, what price were you thinking of?"

Finally, you may hear:

*Prospect:* We really like you, Rich. We are giving you top consideration.

*Salesperson:* Thank you, Dan, let me ask you a question. What does "top consideration" mean?

Guess who has the ball back? The prospect!

## WHAT YOU CAN LEARN FROM ASTUTE RETAILERS

It's fashionable among business-to-business salesfolk to scoff at retailers as "order-takers not in *real* selling." But not so with Don K. Covington, president of Harbor Sales Company, Baltimore. He advises closers to look at astute retailers for inspiration. Covington cites this retail ace for watching buying signals.

My wife frequently asks me to pick up items from the bakery "on the way home." Actually, it's miles out of the way and parking is difficult.

So, under pressure of time and fuel economy, I stop at a more convenient store with parking, self-service, speedy electronic check-out, and quality goods.

Mission accomplished. Well, almost.

Under domestic third degree, I admit the product did not come from ABC but from the more convenient XYZ store. At that point, the product immediately becomes inferior, by my wife's standard. How come? I found out why when I accompanied her grocery shopping.

I watched her careful searching for special sale items, rebate offers, matching of discount coupons, unit pricing comparisons.

"Why skip the baked goods section?" I asked.

"We are going to the ABC bakery to get a pie," she said.

When we got there, happy customers were standing three deep at the counter. Each had a take-a-number rotation slip. Our number—84—and they were serving 56.

When our number was finally called, my wife announced: "We'll wait for Mary." Ah ha, so Mary's the secret ingredient, I thought.

Mary said a gracious goodbye to her departing customer. She turned to us and opened: "Hello, Mrs. Covington (personal recognition). How may I help you today?"

"I'm interested in a pie," Mary said. "Hope you have cherry. Our son and his family are coming to dinner. That's his favorite."

"Well," Mary said, "I'm certainly glad you came to ABC (brand identification) today, Mrs. Covington. This very morning our baker made some of his finest cherry pies."

She went to a rack of a dozen cherry pies, picked up one, but hesitated. She returned and took another pie. She looked directly into her customer's eyes and proudly said:

"This is the *very* pie for you, Mrs. Covington!"

Now all the cherry pies on that rack were undoubtedly made at the same time. However, a satisfied ABC customer reveled in the knowledge that her pie was especially selected and was thereby outstanding.

Good closing is a joy to behold.

The chances of you selling pies: statistically unlikely. But do you listen that *closely*—and relate that *well*—to your customers? If you do, you're closing a lot of sales already. (If not, a word to the wise.)

# *E*IGHT POWERFUL QUERY CLOSERS

To the customer, your questions are part of an amiable conversation. To you, these questions—when handled correctly—close sales. Here are examples of powerful query/closers at work:

- "Strictly off the record, is there any budget in your department we could draw on to cover the extra expenses—so you can get this training before the end of the year?"

- "You seem comfortable with the features. Do you feel as comfortable with the delivery date?"

- "I like helping you with this plan, and I promise to continue to do so long after the project is completed. Let me ask you a question. On a scale of 1 to 10, how do you rank our chances for getting this contract?"

- "You look happy with what the product can do. Do you feel as pleased with your ability to meet the modest payments?"

- "It sounds as if you and I are in agreement: It *is* indeed superior to the products you have looked at. *Am I reading you correctly?*"

- "Sounds like we have covered all the bases. Let me ask you a question. What do we need to do to get your business?"

- "Isn't the advanced design likely to turn your competitors green with envy?"

# $S$PEAKING NEGATIVELY TO GET POSITIVE RESULTS

Positive thinking plus positive speaking is sound counsel, in most cases. But at times in encouraging buying signals, you're better off knowing when to speak *negatively*, when *not* to say.

Bruce Alexander, a Tennessee real estate expert, believes that assertive nay-saying often wins the day:

> In real estate, always take house viewers to see property in your car. Don't be chintzy and think you're going to save gas by going in their car. You have no control in their car. *They* can decide when they've seen enough. Keep control.

> En route to the property, don't drive by vacant lots and eyesores. Choose the most scenic route. Don't spend valuable drive-out time in idle chatter. Spend that time talking negatively: "It's an excellent value but needs painting inside and outside."

> If you *don't* mention that en route, the viewers are going to mention it to *you* when they get there. Take that ammunition away from them.

> If the property's a mess, make it a bigger mess. Say: "The walls have got this and the carpet needs this and the lawn is this high. Oh wow, it really needs an awful lot of work. It's in terrible condition. But I'll tell you this. It's about $12,000 under the normal market price.

> When they get there, they're all excited about the terrific price. When they see the property, they'll say:

> "You know, it not *that* bad."

> If you don't tell them in advance, they're going to spend the next 15 minutes bending your ear about the fortune it's going to cost to fix it up.

> When you're showing property, get the viewers to tell you *then* and *there* anything they don't like. Sense what turns them on the most—that fabulous den, the lovely kitchen, the patio. After they see it all, wander back to that high-appeal spot. Make their last memory the best memory.

You know there's a built-in dishwasher, but you *don't* point that out. Say: "Gee, Tom and Mary, this property has all the features you wanted—lovely den, complete modern kitchen, just about everything. Wait a minute. I don't remember if it comes with a microwave. Did you notice that, Mary?"

If she didn't notice, let her go back into the kitchen and say to you: "Hey, it comes with a microwave. It even has that!"

And you reach the desired destination by assertive nay-saying. As David warned, in the book of Samuel: "Tell it not in Gath. Publish it not in the streets of Askelon."

## *B*E FOREVER ON THE ALERT

When you begin looking for buying signals you will find it comparatively easy to decide when to close. The more experience you have in watching for signals, the easier you'll recognize them. They soon become second nature.

He says, "When can you deliver?" You say, "When do you want delivery?" He says, "As soon as possible," He's sold.

Take out the purchase order and say, "What's today's date?" Ask for a date to get involvement. When she gives you a date, she is saying, "I want to go ahead."

Never talk after you've decided the buyer is ready for the close. If you do, you'll often lose.

Close as soon as you can. Don't permit any sale to drag on one second longer than necessary—even if you've delivered only half your major points. To any hint that indicates close, drop everything, stop talking, step in—and try to close.

Experienced salespeople can tell whether the prospect is favorable, unfavorable, or indifferent. We all dread the *indifferent* prospect who doesn't respond no matter what. Here's the person who needs the most work. The minute you feel it's time, try it. You'll be surprised how often it works.

Watch! In the fine art of closing sales, remember this guiding rule: "Nothing is more important that being forever on the alert"— advice from Henry David Thoreau. No one before or since counseled better on closing: be forever on the alert.

# CHAPTER SEVEN

# Fine-tuning Your Closing Climate

As you prepare to experience *fine-tuning the closing climate,* be aware: you're getting to the end of the section on psychological preparation. First, you put *closing* on a light-table to see what it is (and isn't). Then you learned to *think* about closing—getting your mind right before Part II, where you move into the buyer's mind.

Salespeople once thought you could read character by a prospect's nose length or the shape of the cranium. Today we know better. We evaluate prospects by listening to their problems and dreams—not by studying specimens in the zoo.

Appearances alone often deceive. A seedy character walked into a Miami real estate office. He looked like a farmer spending the winter in Florida. In fact, he *was* a farmer from Iowa, retired and "looking for a place to put a little money."

Fortunately, the customer relations lady refused to prejudge. She looked beyond the misshapen hat and clumsy shoes. She "cultivated" the farmer courteously, taking pains to explain the different property listings.

He was a quiet, slow talker. So she didn't rush him. She noticed he was conservative. No get-rich quick promotions for him. Her diligence paid off. The retired man bought an expensive parcel of land. He kept on buying. Each time they met, she made progress: she kept watching, watching, watching for clues. In the end she sold him $2 million worth of real estate.

Each prospect gives clues. Each tells you how to keep fine-tuning the closing climate.

# $V$ERSATILITY: YOUR CLOSING ACE

Did I hear you say you aren't cut out to sell certain types of buyers? Horseradish! A good closer is versatile. Adjust yourself to the buyer's mood and mentality. Take buyers as they come—the hard-boiled, the easy, the suspicious, the pleasant, the fast, the slow. All are mother's milk to the ace fine-tuner.

Sure, there are different types of buyers. Plan ways to handle each. Establish the right psychological climate for each encounter.

Rate of thinking varies. One buyer thinks ahead. The next needs to be dragged along. Another seems to keep up with you and sees things pretty much as you explain them. (Don't be shocked—it happens!)

If you talk too fast to the slow thinker, your closing can't reach optimum efficiency. Talking too slowly to the fast thinker is as bad—because you irritate the buyer. Early in every sale gauge your presentation to your buyer's speed.

You like the buyer who makes up her mind in reasonable time, or decides things quickly. You don't like the indecisive buyer who can't make up her mind at all.

Yet the raw material you make sales from—day in and day out—consists of buyers of this kind. Adjust your closings to your listeners. Style-flex can help.

# $H$OW FOUR BASIC BUYER TYPES THINK

Dr. Paul Mok, a Dallas consultant, divides customers into four basic types: intuitors, thinkers, feelers, and sensors. Further (surprise!), each salesperson is also predominantly one of those four types.

"First find out what type you are—*then* what type your customer is," Dr. Mok says. "Then alter your behavior to harmonize with the buyer's. It's called Style-flex. It works."

Here are the four types:

1. *The Intuitor* speculates, imagines, envisions. To succeed, she must perceive your product as an instrument for accomplishing her long-range master plan.

2. *The Thinker* rationalizes, deduces, analyzes, weighs options. He must perceive your product as proved, tested, and reliable—reflective of his own analytical judgment.

3. *The Feeler* empathizes, remembers, reacts, relates. She must perceive you as a personal ally. She buys based on judgments of people.

4. *The Sensor* makes decisions on what his senses tell about your product *right now*. He's striving, driving, and competing to get that edge. He must perceive your product as providing him with a tool to win his game.

Remember, there are few pure styles. Most people draw on varying characteristics at different times. But generally you and your customer are more one dominant style than another.

No one style is good or bad. Each can be used effectively or ineffectively. Positive characteristics are associated with each and also negatives, usually resulting from overextending positives. (Any strength carried to extreme can become a weakness.)

"Think of your TV's volume-control knob," Dr. Mok says. "The more you turn it, the louder the sound. Turn it far enough and the sound gets distorted. Strengths work the same way."

An overextended Sensor becomes so competitive and bottom-line-oriented customers see him as cutthroat, power-hungry, money-hungry.

The overly cautious Thinker becomes so detailed and analytical he never makes a decision. He insists first on holding the proposition up to the light from every possible angle. He may be seen as rigid, nitpicky, inflexible.

The Intuitor's originality may be viewed as unrealistic. Her broad-gauged, big-picture visualizing may seem scattered or impractical.

The Feeler's spontaneous, emphatic, probing, and introspective behavior may seem overly impulsive, too personalized, sentimental, or subjective.

# Analyzing Your Prospect's Style

How to tell your prospect's style? Look at the condition of his desk, pictures on the wall, general office decor, attire. Listen to how she talks on the phone. Read her letters and memos. Look for

### Clues in Speech

| | |
|---|---|
| Intuitors: | wordy but aloof, impersonal |
| Thinkers: | ordered, measured, businesslike manner |
| Feelers: | warm and friendly |
| Sensors: | abrupt, to the point, controls the conversation |

### Clues in Writing

| | |
|---|---|
| Intuitors: | writes as he speaks in intellectual, often abstract, terms |
| Thinkers: | well organized, structured, specific, tight |
| Feelers: | short and highly personalized |
| Sensors: | curt, action oriented, urgent |

### Clues in Office Decor

| | |
|---|---|
| Intuitors: | futuristic, think-tank style |
| Thinkers: | correct, non-distracting, tasteful but conventional |
| Feelers: | informal, homey, warm, personalized |
| Sensors: | cluttered |

"Once you know your style and your prospect's style, do everything to make them cooperate, not conflict," Dr. Mok says. "Flex your style. Harmonize with your prospect. Suddenly you're both on the same wavelength. Nobody's computer is flashing *reject*."

# Closing with Style-Flex

Here, from Dr. Mok's style-flex archives, are ways nine successful salespeople have closed sales by analyzing the customer's style and adapting their own style to match.

1. A Thinker (soft drink syrup salesman) discovered his prospect was a Feeler and digested his one and a half-hour presentation into 4 minutes. He landed an order for 150,000 gallons of syrup.

2. A heavy equipment salesman resented his crude interrupting prospect. Then he realized his prospect was a bottom-line Sensor. He stopped bombarding facts the man didn't want and got a $100,000 order in 18 minutes.

3. A strong Thinker CPA, realizing his prospective client was a Feeler, modified his normal approach of presenting a detailed outline. Instead he invited the prospect to "meet the staff and get a feeling for the people who would be working on your account." The prospect signed a letter of agreement that day.

4. A Intuitor salesperson for a major financial magazine shifted from his usual conceptual approach to get on a Thinker's wavelength. He presented a 90-minute detailed presentation including advertising options and variations. He left a detailed proposal and asked the prospect to analyze and review it. Two days later the prospect signed a contract for $160,000.

5. A land development saleswoman, gauging prospect as a heavy Intuitor, shifted her normal bottom-line chance-of-a-lifetime price-is-going-up approach. She spent 15 minutes talking about esthetic value of the land. She encouraged the prospect to envision the property 10 years hence. She got a down payment 20 minutes later.

6. A life insurance agent found her prospect bored and restless as she systematically went through her 35-page presentation. Sensing the prospect as a strong Sensor, the salesperson abruptly closed her portfolio and said: "Let's look at the bottom line, what it's going to cost you, and what your spouse gets should something happen to you." Ten minutes later she wrote a $200,000 straight life policy.

7. A computer hardware salesperson made a presentation to three owners of a medium-sized commercial art studio. In his usual Thinker style, the salesman arrived in his three-piece suit with three different, detailed proposals in his attaché case.

To his surprise, the three owners were late and all wore jeans and running shoes. Quickly sensing these three owners as Intuitors not likely to sit still long, the salesperson made a brief opening statement of philosophy, took off his coat and unbuttoned his vest, and indicated he preferred to have his customers design their own system. He asked the owners to go to the blackboard (located in their office) and, using their own imagination, diagram a system that would handle their needs.

"Don't worry about hardware names. Just indicate what you want it to do." the closer said. When the owners finished, he went to their design, and using a red marker, put the name of his hardware component over the appropriate place in the design.

He then stepped back, looked at the design and said: "Gentlemen, that's a helluva system,"

Following a quick demonstration of his components, the owners placed an order. They never saw his detailed proposal.

8. An account representative for a major brokerage firm found that by sending Feeler notes to Feelers, one paragraph of "suggested action" notes to Sensors, and longer speculative letters to Intuitors (he saved the firm's detailed market analysis newsletter for the Thinkers), his closing level increased dramatically.

9. An industrial products salesman, a powerhouse on the telephone, trained his secretary to identify a caller's probable style based on greeting, tone of voice, and basic phone manner. This enabled him to begin style-flexing right away.

The salesman not only saved valuable time but started logging more repeat business than in the past.

Dr. Mok, a pioneering sales trainer, says you can become an expert in analyzing personality types—and close more sales: "Learn your predominant style," Dr. Mok says. "That's what you are most natural in. Discern the customer's style; then match your style to his or hers during this encounter. It closes sales."

It makes sense. After all, each person prefers to buy from the same kind of personality type. Don't you?

# *H*OW TO WORK PERSONALITY QUIRKS TO ADVANTAGE

In addition to broad personality styles, you'll frequently run into smaller quirks of human nature that at first appear to be closing barriers. Once you understand them, however, you can convert these quirks to your advantage.

- *The Close Dealer.* He's never expansive or magnanimous, but always backward and niggardly in seeking an advantage. He's always on the defensive, making you uncomfortable with picayunish attitudes. Don't try to push The Close Dealer too much. You can't high pressure him, but you can lead him.

- At the opposite pole, there's *The Egotist.* He's sure he knows more about what you're selling than you do. He irritates you by telling you about your services. He think's he's the quintessence of buying skill. But The Egotist carries with him seeds of his undoing. Play on his ego. Ask his advice. Consult him on details. Compliment him. Praise him. Play on his weakness—and close.

- *Facts Only.* Emotional appeals leave this buyer cold. She deludes herself that she lives in a world of reason. To sell her, ply her with facts, crowd her with statistics, appeal to her reason. Then she's not so tough.

- *The Money-Minded.* Bob Schiffman racked up a top record as a Cadillac salesman in New York—one of the world's toughest and richest car markets. He sold 100 cars a year and earned a place in famous Crest Club, an elite membership limited to 200 salesfolk at any given time.

Schiffman closed sales by always assuming his prospect was money-minded: "No matter what your product or service, work in a financial benefit and sell that," Schiffman advises. "This is particularly true if you sell business executives. To them, the world *is* money."

Schiffman always did his financial homework before facing his customer. One day, the president of a manufacturing company wasn't responding to Schiffman's approach on a new Cadillac.

Schiffman took figures out of his pocket: "Mr. Leiter," he said. "I've just done some arithmetic for you. If you take this $28,000 car by trading in last year's car for $24,000, you can make up the extra $4,000 in tax savings. Here's how the figures work."

The man signed up.

"I even had customers I could show how to *make* money by trading cars," Schiffman says. "How's that for a benefit?"

Bob Schiffman never sold cars. He sold financial benefits. Come to think of it, he was merely flexing his style to suit the customers—just as Dr. Paul Mok advises.

- *Mr. Indecision* is probably the buyer you like the least. He shakes his head, expresses doubts and fears, and says: "I just don't know." He won't make up his mind. What then? Make up your mind *first*, his mind *second*, and push him to a close. Apply a little more pressure than to any other type.

- *The Chiseler* is always seeking some advantage. He won't buy unless he is getting a better deal than anyone else. He's always looking for bargains, price, price, price, price. You soon learn how to handle him. Your product is always "made to order" for this buyer. He almost always responds favorably to it. For him, it is what doctors call a specific.

- Then there's *Mr. Irascible*: rude, rough, human. He rants, swears, bluffs, curses. If you are timid, you won't sell him. Stay with him until the storm blows over. Once you crack *Mr. Irascible*, he's usually soft at the core, not that hard to close.

- *The Complainer*. No matter what you do, nothing is right. He always has a pet grievance, from self-persecution, and thinks your organization works 24 hours a day to defraud him. You can't make light of his grievance.

  Listen to him with patience and sympathy. Let him talk himself out, and then he won't be very difficult. But watch—he'll try to get you to take *his* side against your firm. This a good salesperson never does.

- Probably you don't like *Ms. Moody* either—she's a buyer who's all smiles one time and barely speaks to you the next.

You can't tell which way she's going to jump. Use patience and understanding and be willing to follow her lead. Taking your clue from her goes a long way toward selling *Ms. Moody*.

- *Closing the Bargain-Minded*. In an unforgettable scene in *Oliver Twist*, Oliver astonished the workhouse manager by asking for *more* at breakfast.

More! Isn't that what buyers want above all? And isn't your job to provide *more* and close sales in the process? *More* is all in the way you present it.

Walter A. Lowen, a pioneering headhunter, once saw an astonishing sight in a candy store. One saleswoman served a waiting line of shoppers. Other saleswomen stood idle. Customers appeared quite happy waiting in the bus line.

When the crowd thinned, Lowen asked the successful server: "Why do they come to you in preference to the others?"

"It's easy. The other girls scoop up more than a pound of candy and then take some *away* to make exact weight. I scoop up *less* than a pound and *add* to it."

Each woman allocated customers one pound. But the ace server gave *more*. Think of ways to give your customers more, no matter what you sell. You can close sales with *more* when you create the right psychological climate.

## *A*BOVE-AND-BEYOND SERVICING

Two salespeople, both on their first selling job, appeared equally capable of succeeding. Yet Jack Farber always seemed to get the breaks. He closed sales right and left and brought in orders. Jared North brought in alibis.

Jack became the top salesperson for the firm, the big earner, while Jared barely got by. Eventually Jared drifted out of selling. Jack is now sales vice president.

What was his secret? He had *go-ahead*. Whenever he tackled a prospect he went all out. Some of his ideas were not sound, but good ideas offset the bad. At year-end, his sales were always growing.

Once I accused Jack of being a born salesman. "Not at all," said he. "I am always willing to go ahead—sometimes against the odds. The momentum puts me over." This was his candid explanation. I liked it. Even though conditions were not always right, Jack went ahead and tried for a close. He didn't wait for ideal conditions.

John Chapin sells bicycles in Durham, North Carolina. His sales rise 20 percent per year. Once he gets his teeth in a sale, Chapin will do anything that needs doing to make it work.

"One December, I had presold 22 bicycles as the largest part of Santa's gifts for 7-to-9-year-old girls," Chapin recalls. "Shipment was delayed by dock and warehouse strikes and then a winter blizzard. On December 21, rather than face 44 parents trying to explain why Santa Claus wasn't coming—and not wanting to lose the sale—I drove 2,000 miles round-trip in snow to pick them up."

This above-and-beyond service is a requirement of successful closing. Are you willing to go that far? Ace closers are—and do.

Frank Irving Fletcher, known for his close-to-call ratio, said: "A salesman should expect *twice* as much as he gets with the wistful reservation that it's only *half* of what he is worth."

Too many salespeople don't think this way. They want big money but in a timid way. They cannot actually see themselves closing the sales it takes to earn the big money.

One $100,000-a-year salesperson used this formula: "Never be satisfied. Always try to sell every buyer more than he wants. Try to sell more buyers. Be dissatisfied. I am—even now."

T. Coleman du Pont, of the famous family, gave this advice to salespeople: "Don't be satisfied merely with your share of the business. Want it all. Try to get it all."

## SELL BY GETTING UNDER YOUR PROSPECT'S SKIN

Art Harris, manager of retail sales development for WRGB, one of General Electric's TV stations in Schenectady, New York, believes you create the right climate when you get under the prospect's skin. Here are three ways Harris uses this technique to sell television time:

*Capitalize on interruptions.* Interruptions in sales presentations can provide clues about a prospect.

"My initial visit with Mr. R. was brief and not encouraging," Harris says. "Yet during my 10 minutes in his office, while he took several phone calls, I looked around the room.

"In a glassed-in bookcase, I saw three bound brown leather copies of Jeppesen's Airway Charts (I'm an aviation buff.)"

On his way out, Harris asked the receptionist if Mr. R. was interested in aviation. Was he ever! He had his own plane. He expected to get his instrument rating shortly.

Harris sent to Washington for an area aviation chart—fields, airways, omni stations.

The station artist superimposed TV's measured coverage area on this air chart. Harris sent it to Mr. R. The covering letter explained: the station's coverage extends from the Poughkeepsie VOR to the Glens Falls radio beacon—aviation talk, of course.

Harris asked when they could meet again.

"A week later I had a phone call from Mr. R.," Harris says. "Soon I was a passenger in his Piper Twin Comanche. He showed me, in VFR conditions, how his instruments worked."

How could Mr. R. refuse to visit the television station to see new videotape recorders? Soon Mr. R. was sitting in the control room watching his own TV commercials being taped. Harris had closed the sale.

*The letter route.* Mr. D. was tougher. He also listened in a perfunctory way. But there were no clues from his office.

Harris gave the parking lot a quick once-over. No clue.

He subscribed to the newspaper in Mr. D.'s city. He struck oil that time.

"One of the first issues carried a letter from Mr. D.," Harris says. "He protested the proposed razing of an 80-year-old hotel—a historic building that should be preserved."

Harris fired off a letter to Mr. D., agreeing emphatically with his protest. He enclosed a brochure about a historic walking tour of the area.

"Back came the friendliest letter I've ever seen from a prospect," Harris says. "Only three people had commented on his letter. He was astonished that someone so far away had seen it."

Harris closed. Mr. D. became a 52-week buyer for six years.

*The family: Yes and No.* Get close to the customer. But not ham-handedly. Don't say: "You have a ten-year-old. So do I. Is he in Little League?"

Harris sticks to the prospect himself. He doesn't involve his family *unless* the prospect takes the lead.

"Mr. S. had given me a signed purchase order for TV time," Harris relates. "But he relied on me to pick good spots. As we got better acquainted, we went to the Saratoga racetrack together.

"During business or social hours, Mr. S. never mentioned his family. When he described his forthcoming trip to Japan, I did not ask if his wife was going."

Good thing. Harris later learned Mr. S. had just become a widower. How awkward to come on cornball with: "How's the wife?"

Art Harris learned the value of getting under the customer's skin—with restraint. Closing the sale also means keeping it closed during an ongoing relationship.

# *H*OW TO LISTEN EARLY FOR SIGNALS

Warren Armstrong is an advertising agency principal in Lancaster, Pennsylvania. He considers a good ear—that is, listening for buying signals at the first meeting—a vital tool in clsoing new clients for the firm. Moreover, Armstrong says you must listen *early*.

"Get on base with the prospect in your initial sales call—before the presentation," Armstrong says.

"This means selling yourself and establishing the right climate and rapport. It means listening. If you don't come away from preliminary meetings with a clear and complete understanding of what the prospect's looking for, you haven't made first base."

Recently Armstrong met with a prestigious retailer and his son. Although founded nearly 200 years ago, this retailer had never had an advertising agency.

The first two meetings were devoted to listening. As frequently happens, the father and son had different ideas. Armstrong decided to continue meeting until they resolved what they really wanted to accomplish.

"We decided father and son's differing ideas could be settled by marketing research," Armstrong says. "I recommended this. They agreed. Our facts in hand, we presented—not what one or the other wanted—but what research indicated! We got the assignment.

"Listening is the most important tool of all. Talk strategy only after listening instructs you what to say. Closing will succeed only in relation to your ear-analysis power."

## Knowing when not to talk

Good closers are unerring judges of just how long they should talk. Salespeople who lack this judgment can talk themselves into sales and then talk themselves out of sales and often do.

Mark Twain told about a preacher who began exhorting his congregation to give money to send missionaries to China.

The preacher made a masterful presentation. Mark Twain in the back row, was moved. He resolved to give $25. The preacher went on with his talk. After 15 minutes, Twain cut his contribution down to $10.

The preacher didn't close his sale, but kept on talking. Twain decided to save $5 of his $10 and give only $5.

Still the pastor continued to talk. Twain, more bored, resolved to give only $1. At length, after about another half-hour, the preacher did close. The collection plate was passed. Instead of giving $25 as he had planned in the beginning, Twain took $1 out of the plate!

Good closers realize the fewer words said at the moment of closing, the better. One of the most effective closers, Harry Emsley, had a serious speech impediment. By ordinary standards, he shouldn't have been a salesman at all.

But Harry was a great salesman. He did little talking. Talking was hard on him and harder on the prospect. But he asked questions that led the buyer to conviction. He closed his sales with a minimum of words. More salespeople should take a leaf from that book.

Harry, as a beginner, was new to the firm and to the territory. The territory was tough. To send him into that killer territory was like throwing a Christian to the lions. His boss had qualms about ruining such a promising career.

He could have saved his sympathy. Harry Emsley didn't need it. He started making sales. He made larger sales than ever were made in the territory before. He confounded his boss.

He quickly became the number one salesman. Why? Harry was an idea man.

He bristled with ideas like a pincushion. He had ideas on how his customers could display products to their best advantage.

"Say, Ed, I was up north last week and picked up an idea I think you could use here. Let me tell you what it is."

The customers saw themselves cashing in on ideas other retailers had proved out elsewhere.

"If they can do it," they reasoned, "so can I." So they bought ideas from Harry Emsley—and his products.

Harry became a top man. He still goes about his territory with bright new ideas. He's still selling bigger orders

## *T*HE POWER OF ENTHUSIASM

Another quality present in practically all great closers is priceless *enthusiasm.* Turn them down, repel them, order them out of the office, tell them never to come back, and their enthusiasm is still undiminished. They believe in their company, in their products, in themselves, in their customers, and probably in their stars. They go on in spite of discouragements.

Take the electric fan salesman traveling through northern Alaska calling on Eskimos. As he visited each igloo, the residents would exclaim in amazement: "Fan? What do we want with a fan? It's 60 degrees below zero here now!"

"Sure, I know," soothed the salesman. "But you never can tell about the weather. Tomorrow it may jump up to zero."

## *K*NOWING WHEN TO COOL IT

There are times when the best salespeople change plans and try not for a sale but an exit. At times, it's good salesmanship *not* to try to close.

Inept salespeople sometimes stick and try to make a sale. Good salespeople leave and come back later when the wind is more favorable.

It takes judgment. It takes more than judgment. It takes *courage* to carry the sale up to a certain point, to cast aside all the advantage you have won, back out, and come back another day. But it's often the best kind of salesmanship. Just as it is often the best military tactic.

Robert E. Carl, senior vice president of Vantage Companies, Dallas learned to retreat today and close tomorrow in selling H.L. Hunt, at that time the richest man in the world.

"Long before this two sons became household names in the silver market, the cherubic-looking Hunt had formed a public affairs organization called Facts Forum," Carl recalls. "Its mission: public enlightenment about current political issues."

Carl represented a printing company and had sold Hunt several orders in the past.

The legendary Hunt, a quiet and modest man, shunned publicity. He brought his own lunch to work everyday in a plain paper bag. He drove a three-year-old standard-brand automobile. He wore off-the-rack suits.

"Yet that day the man with a reputed income of $1 million a week was visibly disturbed: not enough people really understood Facts Forum. I saw a selling opportunity."

Carl told H.L. Hunt he'd have a suggestion the next day. His idea: a newsletter.

Back to his own office, he did a layout for *Facts Forum News,* wrote a sample story, estimated printing costs.

"The next day, I presented the plan to Mr. Hunt: low cost versus the broad understanding communicated to thousands throughout the nation," Carl relates. "A falling unit cost as circulation increased."

Hunt listened attentively—and then scowled. He hustled Carl out of his office. Had Carl suggested an overly ambitious idea?

"I wondered through a long weekend where I had gone wrong," Carl said. He had

- Established personal rapport with a qualified buyer
- Demonstrated superiority of product
- Keyed it to the buyer's special problems
- Presented a visual concept of how to meet his needs
- Relegated price to its proper perspective in the decision buying
- Enumerated benefits

Carl decided not to push and let Hunt make the next move.

"Monday morning I got a call from Mr. Hunt," Carl says. "He wanted to get started right away! I'd done it right. He was just a slow reactor."

Eventually, *Facts Forum News* became a multipage national magazine—and a very profitable piece of new business.

"That experience convinced me that despite cable television, wondrous computers, and other sophisticated devices—personal selling will always be a vital and nonreplaceable link in closing sales," Carl says. "Here was a man who could literally buy anything he wanted, but bought only after I personally demonstrated what he really needed."

Bob Carl knew when to effect a strategic retreat. He had to go away and chew nails for a weekend without pressing a good—but easily upset—customer. He closed the sale by knowing *when* to wait.

# GUARANTEED CLOSER-KILLERS

Good salespeople also avoid other activities absolutely guaranteed to create an unfavorable closing climate:

- Overtalking
- Appearing too eager
- Going off half-cocked or making a half-baked presentation
- Trying to crowd the buyer too much by clumsy high-pressure methods

Wandering away from the subject is another effective killer, and so is negativism. The right closing climate is positive.

# CHAPTER EIGHT

# Using Empathy to Close More Sales

O. C. Halyard, a crack real estate salesman and sales trainer based in Maitland, Florida, is an expert on empathy. His entire presentation is designed to build empathy with the prospect. In many cases, he uses prospect questions to build toward an empathic close. Says Halyard:

> The *Sincere Buyer* will have questions that are often buying signals. Remember, people criticize what they like. Use these questions to build empathy.
>
> The prospect asks: "Is the seller leaving the drapes?" This is a buying signal. Ask: "Would you like to have the drapes?"
>
> Prospect: "When will the seller give possession?" Answer: "When would you like possession?"
>
> Objection: "The rooms are too small." Answer: "You think the room is too small?" Your buyer may answer: "Yes, but I guess it isn't that bad." The fact you don't have the same feeling helps convince him it's really not an objection.
>
> If the objection is illogical, don't disagree, Say: "I understand how you feel, Mr. Jones, but have you considered this?" Above all, don't argue with the prospect. Even if you win, you lose.
>
> Convert objections to benefits. For example,
>
> - "The small property will be a lot easier to maintain, the taxes will not be as great, resulting in more leisure time and money saved."

- "I know you would have preferred larger bedrooms. However, this home is typical of this price range. Most families require maximum space in the family room and kitchen as we find here. This is where most of our day is spent. To be in a location as desirable as this, we must consider the benefits of the size of the other rooms."

A price objection to $4,500 will not seem as large once you convert it to a per day or per week investment.

After a showing, sit with the prospects in the most comfortable room in the house and discuss the home. Then give the prospects an opportunity to talk privately.

Many salespeople talk themselves out of sales. Instead, listen to the prospect, ask good questions to guide his decision. Let them help sell themselves.

When she is agreeing with you, give her the opportunity of confirming her own decision. Don't interrupt. Show interest with an occasional nod. If she pauses, sit quietly, allow her to organize her thoughts. Answer questions briefly without bringing up new items. When she indicates she is sold, get her signature.

Your trial-close asks for an opinion. Take the prospect's buying temperature before you ask for the decision. Ask questions on minor points when you expect a positive response.

- "In your opinion, Mrs. Jones, do you feel the kitchen has adequate table space?"
- "In your opinion, do you feel this yard offers the privacy you want?"

Use the word *feel* rather than *think*. We do not want them to go into deep thought. We simply want their emotional reaction. Then when the buying temperature is warm, close.

Note how each step in Halyard's presentation is designed to prove his understanding of—and regard for—the prospect's needs and opinions. When you build this much empathy as you go along, closing is a logical final step.

No salesperson ever became great without using empathy. It is the secret of human relations. Its meaning is simple: "The complete visible understanding of another's feelings and motives."

When you are empathic, you understand the prospect's feelings and motives, so you can address yourself in his or her terms.

# EMPATHIC WORDS THAT CLOSE SALES

The effective closer doesn't traffic in what prospects *think*—but draws on "feel" words in asking questions and in reassuring prospects.

Here are empathic words to put on inventory:

| | |
|---|---|
| angry | mistrustful |
| annoyed | |
| anxious | optimistic |
| apprehensive | overwhelmed |
| | |
| bothered | patient |
| burned up | perplexed |
| | pleased |
| cautious | pressured |
| comfortable | puzzled |
| concerned | |
| confident | relieved |
| confused | reluctant |
| curious | resigned |
| | risking |
| delighted | |
| disappointed | satisfied |
| disconsolate | shocked |
| discouraged | skeptical |
| dissatisfied | surprised |
| distressed | suspicious |
| doubtful | sympathetic |
| | |
| elated | tempted |
| exasperated | threatened |
| excited | troubled |

|                | turned off          |
| glad           | turned on           |
|                |                     |
| happy          | uncertain           |
| hesitant       | uncomfortable       |
| hostile        | unconvinced         |
| hurt           | undecided           |
|                | uneasy              |
| indifferent    | upset               |
| indignant      | uptight             |
| inquisitive    | unsure              |
| insecure       |                     |
|                | wonder              |
| let down       | worried             |
| loyal          |                     |
|                | you want to be sure |

## *O*NE EXTREME EMPATHY PLOY

A man got up to give a presentation before a group. His fine reputation as a public speaker and salesperson had preceded him. We were in for a treat.

What a letdown! The man couldn't talk at all. He hemmed and hawed, he groped for words, he stammered. But a strange thing happened. The audience, instead of criticizing him, tried to help the poor fellow discover the words. We found ourselves helping him to make his presentation.

He wanted each listener to invest $250 in a home study course. Inside of half an hour each did!

It was masterful. After the meeting, in private conversation, the master—Paul J. Meyer, of Waco, Texas—revealed his secret. It is the secret every salesperson must learn and use! *Empathy.*

According to Meyer, "When I grope for words and you try to help me, we are doing something together. This is what empathy means. I do not want to shine, sparkle, be smarter than the folks in my audience."

"I want them to think they are brighter, smarter than I am. That they will want to help me. That is what I want."

The essential point: you are employing the proved weapon of asking (even though unspoken) the other person to do you a favor—rather than doing her one. It works in nearly every human situation.

Look at the popularity of sing-alongs at concerts. The audience is *helping* professionals perform! Key to effect: the audience always applauds itself the most.

Try and you'll find out.

# WORK TO GET THE PERSON RIGHT FIRST

Jack B. Perkins walked into my office, exuding a master-closer personality. He radiated such self-confidence, I got the feeling he'd always been that way—a lucky natural-born salesperson destined for success from boyhood. He fascinated me with his engaging manner, the easy way he presented his wares. We all envy magnetic personalities.

"Most of us struggle for years to gain what's natural with you," I told him. "I envy you—being born with such gifts."

"You'd hardly say that if you knew what I was up to until two years ago," he said. "A dismal failure. I tried a dozen different things and I bombed out on each. I flopped at everything I touched."

What brought about the change?

"It sounds so silly I don't often tell it," he said.

Two years before, eking out a living, Jack Perkins stopped in a cheap motel in Kansas. After a scanty dinner, he watched baseball on TV. After the game came a sitcom showing a father trying to develop his gifted son into a mental wizard.

Kevin was too young to read so the father bought jigsaw puzzles—each puzzle more difficult—to develop the lad's mind.

Dad had just unwrapped the most difficult puzzle yet—intricate cuttings, a saragosa sea of pieces. When complete it would be a map of the world. He told Kevin: "Do this puzzle in a day and I'll give you ten dollars. If it takes you two days you get five dollars."

"Okay, Dad," the boy said and went to work.

Fade out. Fade in 15 minutes later. Dad was astonished. Kevin had done the puzzle. Each piece fit perfectly. The father asked: "Kevin, how did you get the complicated world map done so soon?"

"That's easy, Dad," the boy said. "The front side is a map. I looked on the back. It's a picture of a person. So I worked on *getting the person right*. Once I did that, I knew I'd get the world right."

And that, Jack Perkins said, was the most important lesson of his life.

"It struck me like a ray of white light," Perkins said. "Get the person right, and you get the world right. If I got my customer right, I'd have my world right. So I resolved to make more sales by getting the person right.

"The next day I paid more attention than ever to my customers and prospects. I studied them. I tried to really communicate with them. From that day on, the antagonisms I thought were built into selling (bickering, disappointments, misunderstandings) all disappeared. It was a new world. A world I'd dreamed about but never expected to see. Get the person right! Then you'll get the world right!"

The closing techniques in this book work best when you get the person right first. Harmonize closing techniques with your prospect's desires, in keeping with his or her ideas.

Before it's anything else, closing is the great art of pleasing people, particularly one person—your prospect. Few of us buy from a salesperson we dislike. We turn down a bargain if it means buying from an irritating salesperson.

Think about the last person who slighted you, rubbed you the wrong way, or violated your precious ego. Ego from the Latin means *I* or *self*. Most people are naturally afflicted with what one salesperson appropriately calls "I trouble." Bear this human frailty in mind. Build on it in closing.

## *P*LAYING TO EGO YIELDS EMPATHY

Denise Claridge had special knowledge of only one thing—antiques she had collected as a hobby. Taking a few pieces from home as stock, she rented an old house on a highway near Boyertown, Pennsylvania, and opened shop. Her friends gave her six months to go broke.

Six years later, she had expanded 100 times. Her reputation spanned three states. How did she succeed? She learned to harness ego.

"I soon discovered not to talk about myself, but to get people to tell me about themselves," she related. "Nine out of 10 customers, with just a little persuasion, sold themselves—if I let them talk. They were pleased to show off their knowledge. They liked what *they* told me about my antiques so much they bought them!

"Eventually I worked out a closing technique called Feeding the Ego. When a customer comes in, I show her a piece, make a few comments, and then sit back and ask her what she thinks about it. She usually rises to the occasion grandly, proud to show off her knowledge. I'm glad to listen. In the process of telling me about my wares, the prospect gets a much better estimation of herself, of the merchandise, of me. My business is marked by pleasant friendships and good profit. I feed the ego."

To make your closing more effective: tie into your prospect's ego. Follow the sage advice of Abraham Lincoln: "Whenever I am getting ready for an argument with a man, I spend two-thirds of my time thinking of him and of what he is going to say, and one-third of my time thinking of myself and what I'm going to say."

Keep your prospect's ego out in front as a perpetual guiding light.

In the final analysis, closing will always be the art and science of understanding and controlling human nature. If you get the human side of any job right, the closing techniques in this book will be twice as effective.

What about the so-called science of character analysis? The misinformation about this "science" has done salesmanship a great disservice.

Don't try to be a judge of character. Do not try to prejudge anyone or like or dislike anyone on that basis. Try to sell everyone you talk to. As you come to know each prospect better, you naturally will learn what manner of person he or she is—that is the person's character.

# $S$IX EMPATHY QUESTIONS THAT CLOSE SALES

Prospects love to share their experiences with you—when you ask right. Try these Q's when you seek A's:

- What is your experience in dealing with your boss? Is she likely to go for this design? Why or why not?

- I value your opinion. Does your company see this service as a necessity or as a luxury? How can we get them to see it as a necessity?

- I respect your judgment. How much time should I take in explaining to your supervisor? Does he like brief meetings or more detailed explanations?

- You are an expert on the inner workings of your company. I realize that you don't have a budget for an expenditure of this type now. *Is there any other budget we can tap into?* I value your help.

- What has been your experience in terms of quantities? Should you order _____ boxes per month? What do you think?

- Your company has stopped doing business with some suppliers in this field. What went wrong in these relationships?

# $H$OW TO PRY OPEN THE CLAM

You can talk to The Clam, but he doesn't talk back. He just looks at you. This is disturbing. You lose your poise. But The Clam can be opened easily and successfully if you play on that powerful force— the ego.

Appeal to The Clam's vanity by drawing a picture where he plays a main part. He'll respond by becoming a great talker. Georgina Thompson met one of the most difficult tight-lippers. He was as immobile as The Sphinx. It was demoralizing. One day she said to him: "If there's anything I admire in a man it's not overtalking. When I am with you, I am with a thinker. You don't talk, talk, talk all the time—I like that. Would you tell me how you developed such a magnificent gift?"

That is pretty strong language. Thompson didn't know if he'd throw her out. But she didn't much care—she wasn't getting anywhere the other way.

For the first time, The Clam opened up. He talked well once he got started. He explained why it was foolish for people to talk all the time.

"I'd rather keep my mouth closed and be thought a fool than to open it and remove all doubt," he said.

He talked on and on.

Three years later he was still talking every time Thompson saw him. She brought out his *speech* by complementing him on his *silence*.

What worked here may not work on others. Still the principle is the same. If you can make The Clam the central figure, he will no longer be a clam. Talk about his hopes, his aspirations, his business, his problems. Compliment him judiciously. Ask his advice. Encourage him to drop the mask to reveal the human underneath.

## *H*OW TO APPEAL TO A CHATTERBOX

Other prospects talk all the time and so fast that you can't get a word in edgewise. Subject: everything under the sun. You find yourself talked out of the office before you even get near the closing point.

The handling principle is exactly the same—appeal to ego. Direct the conversation onto creative uses of your product, giving her a chance to sell herself. Interrupt only long enough to compliment her upon being an interesting conversationalist. Then direct her thoughts to the purchase this way:

"You said something a minute ago that appealed to me, Ms. Mason."

Pause for an instant, then say: "You said you believed everyone ought to make some provision for perpetuation of her business."

She: "Yes."

You: "I don't need to tell you Ms. Mason that I agree, as every sensible person must. Now that is just where our proposition fits in with your picture." Then go into your service.

Appealing strongly to the prospect's ego will banish other thoughts and give you a clear field to close.


# *T*HE VITAL HUMAN FACTOR

With today's emphasis on high-tech and instant communications, you can easily forget that closing is based on the low-tech art of treating people as people.

The closer has perfect command of the inner workings of the word processor with laser printer. But that knowledge is not going to sell a single unit unless seller convinces buyer that she *needs* and *wants* the product.

Ever had the terrible experience of shopping for a car and being barraged by a million technical terms you never wanted to know? Your brain throbs while you try to put benefits of the five-year payment plan against the three-year lease-buy option. You flee from the showroom. Gone is your initial excitement about that bright red Optima.

It's been said for decades: people don't buy features, they buy personal or business *benefits*. It's truer in this high-tech era than ever before. Any closer who forgets this is in deep do-do, as the playground kids explain it.

Consider this paradox: people are all the same. Yet each person is unique. Trying to learn one set of tricks for dealing with every individual is a hopeless quest—you'd need a million different techniques. But when you realize that everyone needs recognition as a special individual, you're on the right track.

You can build empathy without a single spoken word: just smile. The closer who does not smile, does not please. Great closers use this important technique often. It unquestionably increases chances of closing sales.

Take a worst case scenario—your prospect tells you he isn't going to buy. At this point, smiling is the last thing you feel like doing.

You feel let down, whipped, irritated. But you can't show it. Smile. That tells more eloquently than words that you appreciate his point of view and understand his decision. It also covers up real emotions until you can decide just how to reply.

One sales manager engaged Jay B. Iden, leading Broadway director, to teach his salesfolk how to smile! Iden took the crew one by one, rehearsed their best smiles, criticized them, pointed out errors, and embarrassed them. Many thought they already knew how to smile, since they did it each day on the firing line. But this specialist in communicating human emotions pointed out, "Often what you think is a smile is a self-satisfied *smirk.*"

A smile wins goodwill. A smirk destroys it. The eyes make the difference. In a true smile, the eyes also smile. In a smirk, only the mouth does. The eyes may continue to be hard, harsh, unfriendly, self-indulgent.

After two weeks in a smile clinic, the Iden-trained salespeople went out and increased closings 15 percent. The right kind of smile will do it.

# *T*HE PAUSE THAT REFRESHES THE CLOSE

One of the most dramatic elements in a stage play is the strategically placed pause. Sometimes the white space in an ad is more eloquent than the large headlines. In closing, the pause—the block of silence—often nails the deal.

The pause enables you to control the interview as nothing else can. It gives you one up on the buyer. It helps you recover your own poise if the buyer catches you off guard. Silence is a powerful tool in influencing others.

You've been trying to close a buyer and she's turned you down. Her objection is specious and you know how to answer it. Instead of answering, you pause. Say nothing. Look at her, smile, and remain silent. The pause gives you an advantage. Few can stand silence. She'll be wondering what you're going to say. This gives you one up when you start to talk.

Your silence also compliments her—you take your time to think before you start to answer. It shows her you consider her objection valid enough to be thought out carefully.

When the buyer asks your advice, use the pause. Silence, as an aged and wise philosopher said, is a tremendous weapon—if you have the courage to use it. Practice until you can use the pause without difficulty, until it becomes second nature. Remember, you can influence the buyer with silences quite as effectively as with words. Sometimes more so.

## *W*HY SHORTER CALLS NET MORE CLOSES

Want to increase your closing percentages? Make more short calls, fewer long calls. It's that simple. Don't dismiss it. Great ideas always get down to simple terms.

A sales trainer, spending a week in the field, found more than *half* the calls reviewed were *unduly* prolonged by salespeople. They lingered. They told stories. They visited. They didn't want to leave.

Take a look at this problem differently. Your objective: to get through with a presentation promptly, eliminate small talk, try to close, and then pleasantly and calmly get out.

The buyer for one large chain won't talk to salespeople if they don't have anything new to say or show. But when there's something new in packaging, cost changes, new products, he's glad to listen. He discourages lunch with salespeople as a waste of time.

"Ninety percent of buyers aren't influenced by lunch anyway," says he. "Most buyers can afford to buy their own lunches and prefer to."

During interview, he wants the salesperson to eliminate small talk entirely.

One great salesperson makes it a point to be the first to rise in every interview. He gets in, says what he has to say, gets on his feet, and moves out. He is an outstanding closer. Now he's ready to go somewhere else and close there!

## CLOSING LAB

(Following each of this book's three parts you'll find a Closing Lab, a dialogue between veteran sales manager Crayton Simons and bright trainee Katrina Bellmore. Here are dialogues that amplify Getting Intimate with Closing.)

*KAT:* Questions, we learn, uncover clues to fitting your product to prospect's needs. *How* do we ask questions?

*CRAY:* Begin on a general basis and gradually narrow to the specifics that will zero in on the answers you need.

*KAT:* Does this mean: establish rapport first?

*CRAY:* Yes. When what she tells you appears leading to a useful point simply say: "Tell me a little more about that."

*KAT:* Good advice. I once worked with a saleswoman who sounded like a prosecuting attorney.

*CRAY:* The witness trapped in the witness box must answer. Your prospect may just terminate the interview. Maintain the consultative sound.

*KAT:* From her viewpoint, my prospect's holding a pleasant meeting with a trusted confidant. Then I'd say: "What features would you like to see on a machine that solves your problem?

*CRAY:* Good. Then you can say: "You said earlier that service is an important issue. What kind of service will you require with the instrument?

*KAT:* So we keep working, questioning up to closing.

*CRAY:* Right. You're approaching end game. Soon you're ready for the final assumptive probe: "When would you find it convenient to schedule delivery?"

*KAT:* Then we've closed the sale!

### CLOSING LAB

In this session, the energetic Kat has corraled real estate negotiator O. C. Halyard to sit in for out-of-town Cray.)

> *O.C.:* In real estate, you've got the buyer on one side, seller on the other, and the broker in the middle. Who's the smartest?

> *KAT:* The broker. Without her, nothing can happen!

> *O.C.:* Well, the broker's the pivotal character, as they say in the theater. But the buyer is the smartest! The buyer is not just looking for this one specific house. She's looking at perhaps a dozen—to find the one best house at the best price. The seller has tunnel vision. He has one home in mind: he's been living in it for the last five years. But his view is narrow. He cannot compare it to his competitors.

> *KAT:* So the broker must fill in this gap.

> *O.C.:* Yes. I'm the broker. I help my seller price the property, say, between $170,000 and $225,000. (Later, after buyer and seller get into serious discussions, we'll get another estimate from mortgager's appraiser.)

> *KAT:* So the seller usually accepts your range?

> *O.C.:* Yes. If not we hold our own little negotiation on *that* until we get agreement. I then list the house for sale. Say I list for $225,000. The buyer gives me a firm offer for $180,000. Now we have to negotiate. What I never do is quote the price right away. Otherwise, the seller'll say: "Oh, no way. I told you $225,000. I won't accept a penny less." If I call them and say: "I've got an offer on your home. I'd like to come out this evening—right away, they want to know the price. So I have a colleague place the call. She says "I'm calling for Mr. Halyard." They again ask about price. She says: "I don't know. Mr. Halyard didn't tell me." They ask to speak to Mr. Halyard. "He's out of the office, but he wanted to make sure he could see you this evening."

> *KAT:* So you go out.

*O.C.:* Yes. Five minutes early is okay. One minute late is bad. Usually I see the couple. Both greet me at the door. He says: "Tell me about the offer!" She says: "Hey, how much is it?" But, telling them in the door is no better than on the telephone. Otherwise, they'll say "don't bother to come in. Don't waste your time. Don't waste my time." But if the seller hears the price too early, it makes the broker do his motorboat imitation: "But-but-but-but . . . ." When you do that, you're in trouble.

*KAT:* How do you handle delay at the door?

*O.C.:* Take charge. Start walking toward the family room where they have favorite spots. But don't let them settle there. This is important business. Go to a table. They'll follow you. Get them seated.

*KAT:* Where is the offer?

*O.C.:* In my briefcase. But I've memorized everything in the offer—including the price. There could be a dozen points.

*KAT:* Are kids in the room a problem?

*O.C.:* First, don't call them kids. Always children. Parents can call them brats. But not you: children. No, you do not want children in the room.

*KAT:* So what do you do next, coach?

*O.C.:* I start personalizing the buyers in conversation. Just names on the paper isn't enough. I name the children and they say they're four and six. Mrs. Wilson used to teach school, plans to go back to teaching someday. He's an aircraft plant foreman. Then I tell sellers about the offer's fine points.

*KAT:* Suppose they object to a point?

*O.C.:* No matter what, I don't take issue. I concentrate on getting them nodding and agreeing. Soon they know me better—know the buyers better. This is obviously a serious venture. Then I take out the offer, and as a final point, I quote the offering price—typically 10–20 percent lower than buyer's asking price.

*KAT:*  What happens next?

*O.C.:*  Usually he blows off steam. "You've got to be kidding me!" He'll get up and walk around the chair and maybe kick the dog. Sometimes he swells up like a toad—right up to the breaking point. I let him go. I keep sitting—quiet.

*KAT:*  When the storm passes, then what?

*O.C.:*  After he quits barking, I tell the couple about our competitive market analysis. I quote prices of recent sales and describe the situation in each. I say: "We don't make prices. *You* don't make prices. The *market* makes prices." Take these factors into account when you make your counteroffer." They say: "Well, uh, okay, uh." I remind them the house is not sold yet. So we hammer out a counteroffer. But by that time they've agreed to a new price. We just need to decide *what* that price is. I go back to my market analysis. I say: "These recent prices indicate your home should sell for somewhere between X and Y. Based on this information where would *you* recommend we counteroffer?"

*KAT:*  You don't *tell* them. You let *them* tell you.

*O.C.:*  When they name a price, I obediently write it down. I tell them I'll be in touch with the buyer. I start back at the beginning. My colleague calls the buyer to make an appointment. "No, I'm sorry, I do not know what the counteroffer is. No, Mr. Halyard is out of the office. Will 7 P.M. be good?" Each meeting gets us closer to goal.

*KAT:*  That's why you call it closing through negotiation!

*O.C.:*  It works with customer objections, too. I have another tape. Listen to a sales class:

*O.C.:*  Wayne, you just volunteered to be the customer—we're selling you a house. (to class) We'll use Wayne's questions as buying signals. We'll answer to build empathy. Wayne: your questions:

*WAYNE:*  (Falsetto: playing to grandstand) Is the seller going to include the drapes?

*O.C.:*  Well, would you *like* the drapes?

*WAYNE:* (Own voice) When will the seller give possession?

*O.C.:* When do *you* want possession?

*WAYNE:* Well, I need to get in the house before school starts.

*O.C.:* Stop the action! Now class, Wayne wants to get into the house before school starts. That's a buy signal. We ask a question to answer a question. Great way to build empathy!

*VOICE FROM CLASS:* Hey, Wayne's got no school-age kids. Why does he care about school? (laughter of group)

*O.C.:* We all know that. But do we argue to win the battle and lose the war! No. Instead we say: "I understand, but have you thought about this?" Then we go into whatever *this* is. Now another question, Mr. Customer?

*WAYNE:* I don't like this little bitty shotgun house. Too small.

*O.C.:* I understand your feeling, Wayne. But this property will be a lot easier to maintain, your taxes will not be as high. So you'll get more leisure time and save money on the purchase.

*WAYNE:* The bedrooms are too small.

*O.C.:* I know you'd have preferred larger bedrooms. However, this home is typical of this price range. Most families want maximum space in the great room and kitchen, which is what you have here—where most of our day is spent. To be in a location as desirable as this, we must consider the benefits of the other rooms. What else, Wayne? (fade)

*O.C.:* Kat, notice when the buyer is agreeing, you give him the opportunity of confirming his own decision. Don't interrupt. Show interest with an occasional nod.

*KAT:* If he pauses, I sit quietly, allowing him to organize his thoughts and answering questions briefly without bringing up new items?

*O.C.:* Right. When he indicates he is sold, get his signature.

*KAT:* I see you use the word *feel* rather than *think*.

*O.C.:*  Yes. We don't want prospects to go into deep thought. We simply want their emotional reaction. Then when the buying temperature warms up, close the sale.

*KAT:*  I just wish my last IRS examiner could take an empathy tip from O. C. Halyard.

*O.C.:*  An ex-IRS agent is the hardest to train in closing sales. He assumes the other person is *wrong!* The empathetic closer assumes the other person is *right.*

## PART TWO

# CAPITALIZING ON YOUR KNOWLEDGE OF SELF AND BUYER

Now that you know who you are and who your buyer is, it's time to start bringing buyer-seller encounters to that third act curtain—the close. Here you draw on closing keys documented and applauded by professionals.

Major keys that you'll use most often become second nature. You augment with specials keys that empower you to respond to unusual situations—often simple-sounding keys that pack a wallop. Both major and special closing keys apply to products or services/consumer or business buyers.

You'll soon own these closing keys for systematic draw-down throughout your selling career.

# CHAPTER NINE

# *Y*our Master Formula: Seven Closing Keys

By now you've probably reached this conclusion: closing sales is not hit or miss. Good closers follow a formula. They know the value of everything they do. These men and women are precisionists.

Their precision shows up in the way they adhere to a tested closing formula. Learn it now and use it all your selling life.

The master closing formula, venerated by every good closer, is composed of four simple parts. Yet by following these rules, great closers achieve selling miracles and make fortunes. So can you.

The classic four-part formula is

1. Make every call a selling call.
2. Try early in every sale for a close.
3. Close on every resistance.
4. Keep trying time after time.

Do I hear scoffs about "too simplistic" and "not adult" out there? I thought so! The biggest problem with great ideas is getting them down to simple. Your fellow pros have been simplifying for decades. Now's the time for you to capitalize on their sweat equity. Sure, nothing new or complicated about it—if you use it time and time again.

Let's dissect the formula step by step.

## 1. Make Every Call a Selling Call

Why make a call if you don't try to make a sale? You aren't a visitor or an office loafer. (Yet some "salespeople" qualify for both these titles.) You are a closer. Your one purpose: to bring in orders.

Adopting your first rule—make every call a selling call—gets you forever over the notion of being a *goodwill ambassador or a missionary.* It will tag you with the only honored title you'll ever need: *salesperson* who specializes in *closing,* salesmanship's moment of truth.

Every so often (even the best closers miss one now and then) you'll end up a goodwill missionary. Let it be accidental, never scheduled, when it happens.

If you make every call a selling call, you'll obviously try to close on every call, won't you? That leads you to the second rule.

### 2. Try to Close Early at Every Presentation

You know Hugh Bell's feeling about closing early. Most good closers feel that way: try early, sometimes with your first words!

Tom Cook, a strong and urgent closer, started every sale with an appeal for an order—often his very first words. Buyers cannot deny that strong an urgency very long.

Cook's method is as guileless as a child asking for candy.

"Mr. Phillips, I am calling on you today to get your order for my service, provided I can prove its value to you."

That's it! No backing and filling. No skulking in the bushes. No double-talk. Just a clear-cut statement: "I want an order and I'm here to get one."

Usually he did. This ex-preacher carried home $100,000 a year.

Great closers aren't all that speedy about their closes. But all try early in the conversation to get the order. Mark your second rule well and use it consistently. It will send you to the bank regularly.

### 3. Close on Every Resistance

Close on each objection. Strange advice? Wait, it works. That's all that counts, isn't it, techniques that produce more sales and dollars?

The buyer has just thrown a resistance at you. He isn't going to buy. Doesn't like your product. Doesn't like your firm. He's already loaded up. To hear him tell it, he's so poor his old aunt in Keokuk has taken a part-time supermarket checker job to keep him going. You don't expect him to buy, do you?

Buying is just *exactly* what you expect. When he says no, rush in with a closing action.

Jack Nickerson, who sells a management service, is calling on Caleb Busch, a buyer twice his age (always a challenge for a youngster.) The veteran Busch is a closer-baiter. He prides himself on never having been sold. He buys, yes. But buying must always be his idea, never the seller's.

This day, to confound the problem, Busch isn't feeling well. Further, his mutual fund is down. He's in a hurry to get rid of Jack.

"No sale, son," he says. "I am not interested. I've forgotten more about management than your outfit will ever know. Good-day."

He turns to papers on his desk. What does this dismissed young salesperson do? Tries for a close, of course. He starts filling out the agreement.

"Who said I wanted the service started?" bellows Busch.

"I heard you," says Jack. "I didn't believe it. I don't believe *you* believe it. What do you say we get going on this at once?"

Caleb Busch, who wanted the service but as his idea, signed.

"Do you do that with all your prospects, get orders when they have just told you they aren't going to buy?" Busch asked Nickerson.

"How else? I'll never have the prospect in a more vulnerable position than when he is turning me down. When a boxer throws a punch hard, he's off balance. Same with a prospect. He's unpoised and his mind temporarily is closed. What better time to go after an order?"

That won't work everytime. It may not work three times out of five. But if you try to close on a resistance and lose, what's the risk? The buyer has already said no. Learn, memorize, practice, and live by the third rule: close on each resistance.

### 4. *Keep Trying No Matter What*

Keep trying to close, even after the buyer has turned you down, no matter how many times. Keep trying to close.

Go back into the sale a bit. Build it back up again. Then try for another close. Try all the closing actions you can think of until she buys—which she is likely to do—or finally gets rid of you for good.

I baited an old pro salesperson once to see how often he'd try to close. I put him off purposely, consciously, unreasonably, but he kept right on doggedly trying to close.

I needed his product for my office. I wanted it anyway, but wanted to see how many times he would come back. He tried 16 times.

When all was over, the order signed, I asked him how many more times he would have kept trying for a close.

"As long as you would have let me—a week if necessary," he said.

That was an old pro talking, recommending the fourth rule of the formula—keep right on trying.

# *T*HE SEVEN SECRET CLOSING KEYS

True selling professionals follow this four-point formula, linked up with time-tested closing keys.

Now you're going to preview the closing keys—secret and special. But always remember the *formula* and activate it through the *techniques*. Many salespeople have closed volume sales with the crudest of techniques. But no salesperson who strayed from the four-point formula ever made it big.

Rudyard Kipling described the five senses as "five serving men that taught me all I know." Closers use *seven*—seven secret keys that unlock sales.

Actually, you'll be equipped with an arsenal of closing keys as powerful as the bandoleers of a helicopter machine gunner. Master and use these seven keys. Once you learn the basics, the variations come later.

Closing sales is like playing poker. The rules of the game are simple. Almost everyone can learn how after a few hands. But no serious player so completely masters poker that he stops trying to learn more. Amarillo Slim, who frequently wins the World Series of Poker in Las Vegas, wins one year fully aware that someone can knock him off next year, as sometimes they do.

The rules for closing sales are simple, but no one has ever mastered the technique enough to stop trying to get better. In the chapters ahead, you'll get details on seven tested keys for closing sales, with examples from the world's most effective salespeople.

Adapt and adopt these techniques in your closing. Each key depends largely upon circumstances and upon two personalities: yours *and* your prospect's. Some techniques won't ever seem natural to you. Some will. Some you may never be able to use effectively. Others you will. You don't have to use them all to upgrade your closing considerably.

Keep as many arrows in your selling quiver as possible. When time and place are right, you own the inventory to close a difficult sale—any kind of sale. Start by knowing all. If you may find one or two foreign to your temperament and personality, don't use them. But start with knowledge. You'll be surprised at the uses that crop up.

Temperament—yours and your prospect's—has a great deal to do with your choice of closing technique. If you master all the closing techniques via diligent practice, you'll have seven times as much opportunity to close. Don't fall into the rut of using one closing technique over and over. Adjust the seven keys to your personality, your products, and your prospects. More sales will certainly follow.

Here are your seven secrets of closing sales:

1. *Beyond Any Doubt.* You close by assuming the prospect is going to buy. You take it for granted the buyer is going to say *yes.*

2. *The Little Question.* By getting the buyer to decide upon something of secondary importance, such as upholstery color in the automobile or master bedroom shape in a $300,000 house, you make the buyer tell you he or she is ready to buy.

3. *Do Something.* Good salesmen and saleswomen follow this rule: physical action is the easiest, surest, quickest way to make the buyer buy. Nine sales in 10 should be closed by physical action in some form.

4. *The Coming Event.* This is based upon an impending event that hastens the prospect along in buying. Although it can suggest high pressure, it has a legitimate place in the closing canon of an effective salesperson, as you'll see.

5. *The Third-Party Endorsement.* Here's narrative closing. You tell stories about other users to illustrate points and bring action.

This technique—one of the most effective—helps you make difficult sales otherwise not possible.

6. *Something for Nothing.* You rest your case by introducing a special inducement to buy. This technique is almost perfect if properly used. It appeals to the something-for-nothing weakness in each human being.

7. *Ask and Get.* At certain times, the best closing strategy is asking boldly for the order. This technique, like the other six, must be used carefully, at the right time, and under the right conditions.

Mastering these seven closing techniques will make the difference between $30,000 and $300,000 income.


# *H*OW TO FIT THE TOOL TO THE NEED

The obvious question is: *Which* of the seven should you use *when* in a given closing situation? Some prospects will not respond to certain techniques. Some are harder to sell than others. Some react favorable to one technique. Others wouldn't respond to that technique under any circumstances.

Take the Coming Event key: a proved way to close, if properly employed on the right prospects. But some suspicious characters are offended if you push them by mentioning an event that might affect their ability to buy later. On the other hand, the technique has often worked with 7 out of 10 buyers.

How can you tell which buyers not to try it on? You know because you make a continuing study of prospects and customers. As you go through a sale, make mental database notes on the type of prospect you're talking to. Select the closing techniques most likely to cause this prospect to buy. Consulting, and adding to, your mental inventory pays great dividends.

You can't treat all prospects alike. Scrutinize each's characteristics (bound to surface if you talk long enough) and attach those characteristics with the closing technique most suitable to that temperament.

# $T$AILORING THE KEYS TO YOUR PERSONALITY

Not surprisingly, some salespeople do better with one technique than with others. Not all closers are constituted to employ all seven techniques with equal skill and effectiveness.

Practice, first in your mind, then on actual prospects, each of these seven techniques a number of times. Soon you'll be able to tell which are most natural and effective for your temperament.

Then develop your favorites as much as you can. But don't neglect the others. When a buyer doesn't respond to your pet technique, put different-colored chips in the pot.

When the closing moment arrives, judgment takes over—judgment based on filed-away experience. If you should misjudge your prospect, don't give the sale up as a lost cause. Go back. Rebuild. Try to close again, using a different technique.

Often a prospect impervious to your best attempts one way will respond to another technique. The more techniques you master, the more opportunities there are for closing. Actually, you'll tend to pick the right key on reflex—once you know them all well. Again, use depends on your belief in a certain key, personality, and yes, your *size.*

The approach of a 250-pound former football tackle selling steel to industry will probably be marketed differently from a 97-pound cosmetics saleswoman. He may prefer a more "physical" approach—she more finesse and charm. (Surprise: it might be just the reverse!) Yet both can be effective closers.

Sure, you'll have favorites. Red Motley usually selected the Third-Party Endorsement: telling stories came naturally to him. He told what someone had done, how well it worked. He closed sales that way.

W. N. Blayney, a rough-finished fellow who moved a lot of wholesale meat, laid on Ask and Get. It was natural to him. He couldn't tell stories like Red Motley. He was a terrierlike digger, and he capitalized on his talents that way. Now it's time for you to dig into each chapter and cash in on methods perfected by champions.

# CHAPTER TEN

# Closing with the Beyond Any Doubt Key

The marquee on the one-man show said "Banjo Dancing." A critic was quoted: "Fascinating Americana." Yet as people filed into the theater, they wondered. After all, in a one-man show, everything depends on the lone performer's abilities and sustained appeal. But when Stephen Wad ambled up from the back of the auditorium, the audience was his.

After a rousing opening, singing and playing the five-string banjo, Wade pulled out a ballpoint pen and pointed to a man in the front row:

"Now, you're ready to buy this pen. Only 25 cents." The audience member paid his quarter and took the pen.

"Never lose a chance to sell customers with money in their hands,"

He ran to the stage and grabbed two handfuls of pens.

"These pens write on both sides of the paper," he said and collected for 10 more.

He ran up and down the aisles.

"These pens write in any language," he said and sold 20 more.

The audience was rabid. People stood up, money in hand, yelling:

"Here! Take mine! I'm next!"

After selling 40 pens for a quarter each, Wade ran out of product—and went on with the show.

"The act—patterned on the performance of an actual salesperson—is also part of Americana," said Wade. "In this country, if you assume people are going to buy, ask them right, they *do* buy."

# No DOUBT ABOUT IT, YOU WILL CLOSE

You've just attended an outstanding demonstration of the Beyond-Any-Doubt key. Wade never had any doubt that his audience would buy. (Afterward, each purchaser found he'd bought an advertising specialty pen promoting Banjo Dancing—the kind of premium promoters often provide free.) But because the audience sensed Wade knew they'd buy, they bought en masse a promotion piece for the show they'd already paid to see.

Now watch a full-time professional closer use the same technique. Bill Decker sells furnishings to hotels, motels, universities, and other institutions.

Bill Decker is a master. In his field, you cannot rush a prospect off his feet, you must use slow sell, soft sell, then you must close hard.

In selling a $250,000 order for furnishing and equipping a new motel, Decker has to make closes to

- The architect or backer (specifying buyer)
- The motel operator (actual buyer)

The specifying buyer is always involved. "Usually it's the architect," Decker says, "sometimes the interior decorator. It may be the financier (almost always a shrewd buyer as well)."

Decker goes to the specifying buyer first. He uses the Beyond-Any-Doubt key. He assumes his furnishings and equipment are what the buyer wants. No doubt about it. He paints word pictures of how enhanced the motel will be with these installations.

"It will be wonderful to have quality furnishings like this from the start!" he says enthusiastically. "You do want that appearance and long wearing, don't you?"

"Sounds good," the specifying buyer says.

Sale number one is thus made. Then Bill approaches the motel operator or owner, armed with the approval of the designer or financier. Of course he tells the operator that "these features are precisely what Ms. Specifier wants."

He plays each against the other. Tinker to Evers to—not to Chance—but to Sign-up. It is the simplest of all closing keys: he assumes he'll get the order and gets it. An interesting and successful closing technique: Beyond Any Doubt.

You've already learned about the buyer's emotional mental condition at closing—it's not normal. This means you must be absolute in everything you say and do—never doubtful. Doubt, waver, question, wander, quibble, and so will the buyer. Be positive, dogmatic, absolute, and confident, and you'll build like qualities in her mind—and close.

To use Beyond Any Doubt, you sweep the buyer forward by holding that assumption strongly in your mind and in front of the buyer's eyes.

You're sitting in the prospect's office. You sense it's time to close. The Beyond-Any-Doubt key fits in naturally. You say: "May I use this phone for a minute? I want to call the office and tell them how you want this handled." The buyer says: "Certainly." That's your answer: you've got it!

Wasn't it that simple, natural, and easy? You merely assumed she was going to buy, and pushed forward. She bought. But perhaps she wouldn't have if an unskilled salesperson had asked for the order with less assurance.

The great secret of this technique is the undoubting assumption in your mind that the buyer is going to buy. You *know* she's going to buy. Of that you are positive. You assume it's merely a question of getting together on a few details such as terms and delivery. The only question is *when*. As William S. Gilbert wrote in *The Gondoliers:*

> Of that there is no possible doubt
> No possible doubt whatever.

## *H*OW TO LEAD YOUR PROSPECT

The word *when* is magic in nailing down the close. Even unspoken *when* is useful. If your customer wants what you are selling, there's almost certainly a peak time when her receptivity is at its height. Get her to center on the question of time, and you nail the decision.

Suppose you're showing clothes to a retail customer. She likes the coat but is indecisive. You say: "Let me see. You want this garment by next Sunday at the latest. This is Friday. We can manage that nicely. We can get delivery Saturday."

You do not need to ask *if* she'll buy. You assume she will. Unless there are definite obstacles to prevent it (such as inability to pay), you'll close the sale then and there. The Beyond-Any-Doubt key often makes buying easy.

To vary your closing, ask her: "How soon *must* you have this suit?"

The assumption that the prospect is going to buy must come from you. It must be in *your* mind *first*, inextricably bound up in your opinion of yourself as a professional closer.

If you hesitate, so will the customer. If you have doubts or qualms, doubts or qualms will fill his mind. You must be self-assured, positive, forceful. Say nothing or do nothing not predicated on absolute belief you will close.

A management consultant was shopping for expensive Manhattan office space. The rental agent knew her business. She showed one suite after another, never assuming for a moment her prospect wasn't going to lease. The only question: *Which* offices would suit the prospect best?

After explaining the different offices, the rental salesperson judged it was closing time. She deftly employed Beyond Any Doubt.

She led the prospect into one suite overlooking the East River: "Do you like the river view?"

The prospect said, yes, he did.

Then the poised closer took him to the other side of the building and asked if he liked the skyline view.

"Very much," the counselor responded.

"Which view do you like better?"

The prospect thought. Then he said: "You can't beat the river."

"That's right. That's the space you want, of course," said the closer.

The prospect never had a chance to escape.

You'll develop many ways to use Beyond Any Doubt. This technique is valuable because (1) it's useful in so many different situations, and (2) because it's so safe. You cause no offense by mildly assuming the prospect will buy. You apply no pressure. Quietly and gently you lead him to a decision, having arrived at that decision in your own mind first.

When contractor Samuel Horowitz, one of the greatest salesmen of his generation, started talking to Frank W. Woolworth about building what became the Woolworth Building in New York, he ran full tilt into opposition.

But superpersuasion was mother's milk for Sam. After another fruitless call on Frank (the same evasiveness and indecision), Horowitz, with a slight show of resentment, rose, extended his hand, and said testily: "I am going to make a prediction, Mr. Woolworth. You are going to build the largest building in the world, and I am going to build it for you."

He walked out.

Several months later when work had started on the building, Woolworth said to this master salesman:

"Do you remember the morning you told me I was going to build the largest building in the world and you were going to build it for me?"

"Yes."

"Well, I never was able to get that out of my mind."

Of course, you don't sell million-dollar buildings. But the same closing technique works with your product or service.

The same quality assumption, the same self-confidence, the same serenity and belief that sold the Woolworth Building will close sales for you. What are you waiting for? You know the prospect's going to buy!

# *W*E'VE GOT TO GO

Old Amos Hawkins, an inactive British army sergeant-major, was too valuable to leave on retirement when war started again. But the recruiters couldn't get him to go back into the service. The local magistrate talked to him, told him it was his duty to enlist. Nothing doing. His wife and sons worked on him. He was adamant.

Other influentials appealed to patriotism, pride, obligation to country. They were all whipped. This was one war, Old Amos said, they'd have to handle without him.

At length, his former company commander said: "I believe I can get Amos to enlist. Let me try."

"You'll fail," the recruiter said. "We all tried."

"Just the same, I'll go to talk to him."

He went to Amos's retirement cottage. They talked old times. The captain didn't appeal to patriotism, duty, self-sacrifice.

"Do you remember the time we bogged down at Vimy Ridge, and how hot they made it for us?" he asked Amos.

"Very well, I do."

"And do you remember the mud and the rats?"

"No man can forget that!" responded old Amos.

They talked like this for maybe 10 minutes. Then the captain, after a long silence, rose and said:

"Well, Amos, we're in it again and I guess we've got to go."

Amos rose at ramrod attention and said: "Yes, sir. We're in it again. We've got to go!" He went down the recruiting office and reactivated. Beyond Any Doubt

E. F. Gregory, prominent in health and accident insurance, uses this key almost to exclusion of any other. Gregory doesn't ask his prospect for name, address, age, and so forth. He asks: "Did you ever have an operation?"

"Yes. Ten years ago."

Gregory writes that information on the application blank. He puts it on the desk in front of him. Seeing Gregory write the prospect came to life in a hurry:

"Hey, I didn't say I was going to take the policy."

Gregory's calm reply: "I know you didn't. Right now, as I look at you and talk to you, I see no reason why you couldn't get it. But our underwriting department is pretty fussy. After we have run through this health chart, I can probably tell you whether you can get it or not."

Now the prospect starts proving he *can* qualify. By the end game the prospect has come to see he *does* want the insurance.

See how safely you can close with Beyond Any Doubt?

# $A$SKING FOR MORE VIA SIDEDOOR

A variation on Gregory's technique is to ask for more than you expect. A man who wants to borrow $25 asks for $50. In self-defense, the friend says he can't possibly let him have $50, but would $25 help?

Former Vice President Tom Marshall of Indiana (famed for "What this country needs is a good five-cent cigar") concluded the best way to get an appropriation approved in Congress was to ask for twice as much as required. Congress, thinking itself shrewd and economical, cut the budget in half—to exactly the amount Marshall wanted. This technique has since become standard practice in Washington, DC.

In your closing, outline a recommendation more ambitious than you think the prospect can approve. If he needs the larger amount, and takes it, wonderful. Chances are he'll suggest a compromise, a smaller amount.

James Morris, an office equipment salesman, racked up an extraordinary record in a hard field by suggesting that the customer put a number of machines on trial—a far greater number than the prospect can use. Cutting down the order distracts the prospect's mind. No longer is he concerned about whether to try the machines in the first place—only about the correct number to try. This try-a-larger-number works!

# $A$SKING FOR MORE AND GETTING IT

Charles Mandel, top-flight magazine space salesman, takes the ask-for-more plan one step farther: he asks for more and expects to get it *all*. In many cases, he does.

"If a guy wants to buy a page, then my job is to sell him two," Mandel says. "A salesman's job is to maximize the buy. When I call on an advertiser who wants to buy a page, I know my job is to convince him to take four."

Mandel, whose selling expertise pushed him up the ladder to publisher of *Science Digest,* tells his sales force to turn a maybe to a yes, a 2-page buyer to 4 pages, a 4-page buyer to 12 pages.

"Recently, one of my salesmen walked in with a 12-page schedule," Mandel said. "He told me how wonderful the advertiser is and how much he loved the magazine. I said, 'Terrific, let's go back and see him.' My salesman thought I'd blow the whole deal. I asked the buyer why he bought 12 pages. He had co-op money he had to spend before Christmas. I said: 'Why don't you buy 36 pages?' The order went from 12 to 36 pages.

"Actually, when the advertiser says he wants 12 pages, the salesman's job is just beginning. His problem: to get the advertiser from 12 to 13 pages. After all, the buyer bought 12 *on his own!*

Mandel believes *why* is the key question.

Charles Mandel asks for more, expects to get it, and almost always does. This is Beyond Any Doubt—up one power.

Suggestion is perhaps the most powerful force in human relationships. But many salespeople use the indirect method to vast profit. Psychologists tell us 7 out of 10 people are responsive to a suggestion that is proposed properly.

"You will want this suit to wear to the Friday meeting, won't you?" you ask. "Yes," says the prospect.

"Will this color go better with your drapes than the other?"

"I think it will."

"Do you think three dozen will do as a starter?"

"Yes."

So it goes, you making suggestions, your prospect agreeing.

The happiest thing about the indirect question is that you are very seldom turned down. Ask a person directly to buy, and she can say no. But it won't happen when you use the indirect question.

# *N*INE NAIL-DOWN CLOSERS

At times, the closer does it all right with Beyond All Doubt. The prospect is at the edge. But, not quite over. You need a nail-down statement. Try the following:

- Aren't you excited about getting this new _____?
- Can we get your OK here on this agreement?

- Can't you just see the smiles on the people in your office when you tell them you're putting in this new machine?
- Please initial these shipping instructions.
- Can we start celebrating your purchase?
- Aren't you glad you decided to take the bull by the horns and make a decision today? *May I have your autograph?*
- Are you happy you've made this productive decision?
- Isn't it a great relief to put an end to your search?
- Isn't it wonderful that you have found what you've been looking for?

## *T*HE MEHDI SUCCESS STORY

Mehdi Fakharzadeh[1] one of closing's major success stories, is a prime user of Beyond Any Doubt. Yet he is probably the most unlikely salesman extant. In 1948, Mehdi came to the United States from the Middle East. He had to learn English. He started as sales trainee for Metropolitan Life. He also had to learn insurance. All the odds were against him.

Today he's the top producer on MetLife's 25,000-plus sales force. Sales commissions have made him a millionaire.

Mehdi always assumes each prospect will buy. Most do. He never doubts his ability to sell—or the prospect's ability to buy. Mehdi sold nine Key Person insurance plans to a prominent New Jersey utility consulting firm.

"He was very businesslike," one partner said. "He didn't come on strong. Direct opposite of high-pressure salesman. He spoke factually. He quoted figures, after he presented his case, the only sensible thing to do was to buy."

Mehdi's Beyond-Any-Doubt presentations to business owners appeal primarily to reason. Listen as Mehdi discusses Key Person insurance with Tony and Tom.

---

[1]Reprinted with permission from *Mehdi: Nothing is Impossible,* published by Farnsworth Publishing Company, Inc., Rockville Center, Long Island.

*Tom, what would happen to this business if* (Mehdi never suggests the person he's talking to will die) *your partner Tony dies? The loss of a key person can hurt a company more than almost any other tragedy. It's one of the major reasons companies fail. I have a plan that can protect your company.*

*I don't know if we can afford it.*

*I recommend insuring you and Tony at $300,000 each. If your partner dies, my company will pay the money tax free.*

*That sounds like too much insurance coverage.*

*Is it? You and Tony together account for $6 million in sales each year.*

*What do you earn on each dollar of sales?*

*Last year about five cents on every dollar.*

*So there you are. Five percent of 46 million is $300,000. A business policy will insure your profits. But, Tom, that's not all. It will make it easier for your company to borrow money.*

*How's that?*

*Consider. What is a bank's concern in loaning money?*

*Getting the money back, of course.*

*Well, if Tony dies, your business might fail, since both of you together account for $6 million in sales. You could go bankrupt. Buying my plan insures your company's capability of paying back a major loan.*

*And it will cost how much?*

*Practically nothing. It's like transferring money from one pocket to another. The money you transfer to my plan will always be available to you. Through the first 12 to 13 years of the plan, the difference between your annual outlays and the amount available to you is about 2 years' worth of outlays. After that, more money becomes available to you.*

*So how much do I give you each year?*

*Depending on your age, about 2½ to 3 percent of your gross income.*

*That's about $12,000! Do you know how much return on investment I can get on $12,000 in my business? Fifty percent!*

> *I know you're a very good businessman and can earn this rate of return. If your company faces an emergency, the insurance company will loan you back all the money you pay in minus 2 years during the last 12 to 13 years. They will charge you only 5 percent.*

> *But as I borrow money, I have less coverage, right?*

> *That's certainly true—which is why it is important to pay back policy loans as soon as you can. But at least until the loan is repaid I can add a clause that the cash value of the plan is guaranteed. We request that part of your dividends purchase one-year term insurance equal to the amount of cash value. So you see, my plan helps protect your company's profits in case something happens to you or Tony.*

> *Your company gets tax-free money equal to your profit contribution. This profit protection, in turn, helps bolster your credit rating. Further, the money you pay into the plan is still available if your company should need it for emergencies or any other reason. You win all the way around.*

Did you ever see the slightest doubt in Mehdi's mind that Tom was going to buy? You didn't? Neither did Tom or Tony.

No wonder Mehdi's clients say: After Mehdi's finished, there's only one thing you can do—buy.

Beyond Any Doubt is useful and effective, the simplest to apply, the safest to use. Often you'll surprise yourself by getting business you had decided was impossible. Assume the prospect will buy, can't help buying, and you are going to make the sale. Then proceed as if settling a few details.

# CHAPTER ELEVEN

# *The Little Question Key*

Closing is hardly ever a simple either-or situation. If you force the buyer to give you a *yes* or *no*, it'll often be a *no*. But if you lead the buyer gently, by giving her easy safe questions to answer, the buyer will often tell you, in effect, that she will buy.

Don't force the buyer into a corner and demand an answer to a major question. Give her a simple little question confirming what you are selling. In answering, she is buying.

This is the basis for the Little Question key to closing.

## *D*ON'T ASK "IF," ASK "WHICH"

On Long Island, Bryce Harrow broke all records selling a $35,000 luxury car. Once he talked to a customer and built the customer's interest, it was all over but the check signing. Harrow landed three out of five deals, the talk of the industry.

A corporate expert from Japan came to learn how Harrow did it. The expert trailed Harrow for a week, watched him sell, and kept tabs on everything. The corporate expert concluded Harrow was strongest where many others are weakest—in the close.

Harrow had worked out a very effective closing technique, and like all great techniques it was simple, natural, and apparently indomitable. It worked on the old, it worked on the young. It worked on men or women. It worked on the arrogant as well as on the meek.

Harrow knew his car, so of course, he'd explain its plus points, intrigue his customer, appeal to the ego—all good tactics. Then when closing time came, he was extremely nonchalant—nonchalant but not indifferent. He brought out a little book of gold monograms, the kind you see on doors of swanky cars. He placed them in front of the customer.

"Now let us decide which style monogram is most appropriate to your persona," he would say.

Mind you, the customer hadn't said anything about buying the car, hadn't even indicated he was more than interested in it, hadn't said he was convinced. No matter. Harrow talked engagingly about the monograms. He discussed his choice and asked the customer if he would like the same typographical design. No? The customer leaned toward Old English type in a car monogram.

"Pretty hard to read, isn't it?" Harrow suggested. Yes, harder to read than Roman type. True enough. But class—it had class, didn't he think? This Harrow admitted. The discussion of monograms went on, and finally the customer decided upon the very best monogram.

And in deciding upon the monograms, he had agreed to buy, and pay for, a $35,000 automobile!

Harrow was using the Little Question Closing—merely about some secondary or subordinate phase of the product or sale. Yet, in answering that question, the buyer gives you permission to enter his or her order.

Buyers are sometimes gun-shy about a high-risk decision they'd may prefer not to make. The Minor Points Close asks the prospect to make a low-risk decision on delivery dates, optimal features, color, size, payment terms, or order quantity. The video system salesperson says: "Would you prefer the single or the multiple changer to accompany your video system?"

You don't ask 'em if they want it, you ask 'em *which*. Like this:

- "Which would you prefer: the red one or the blue one?"
- "When would you like delivery: on Friday or will next week be okay?"
- "Will that be cash or charge?"

Now, some closers claim this technique works all the time. With this question, the prospect *has* to buy. Ridiculous! He *doesn't* have to buy! But the Little Question gives you a decided edge, because it leads the prospect in the direction you want. It works many times!

## $N$AIL-DOWN-DETAIL/WRITE UP THE SALE

The Little Question assumes that your sale is already made and that you are simply tying up a few loose ends.

The handbag saleswoman approaches the prospect examining a purse and says: "What a lovely purse! It matches your shoes so perfectly. Would you like to take it with you or shall we send it to your home?" If the prospect has not yet decided to buy, no harm done. The saleswoman simply helps her find a purse more to her liking.

A real estate salesperson, after showing a prospect a $290,000 house, says: "Mr. and Mrs. Rockland, I know you'll be delighted with this fine home. How would your name appear on the mailbox? Would it be Jim and Esmeralda Rockland?"

Again, the prospects' decision to buy is assumed. Instead of asking them, "Do you want to buy this $290,000 home?" the salesperson suggests a very small decision. If the prospects respond by saying, "Oh, The Rocklands will be fine," they've agreed to buy.

The subordinate question skips over the primary question—which always is: "Are you going to buy this from me?" It ignores that question entirely; it assumes that the buyer is going to buy; it poses a question on an unimportant detail.

Yet when the customer answers that unimportant question, he has given, without setting up a conflict, his consent to buy.

The Little Question is the smoothest way to close. It can't possibly cause offense. If the customer isn't ready to buy, she thinks you *really are* asking her about details. She doesn't see it as turning on the heat. If she *is* ready to buy, she accepts the question as a matter of course and buys, believing she made up her mind and that you didn't have anything to do with it!

Earlier you learned how to launch trial closes as soon as possible. Questions are the ideal way to express your experimental close.

You: "Do you prefer the tan or the blue suit?"

Buyer: "I like the blue best." It's the same as saying: "I will take the blue suit." But much easier for the buyer to say!

Bill Tobin says: "Give the customer a choice of two yeses! 'Do you like the blue or white color?' (Sell one or the other—or both!) 'Would $10,000 be too much?' (See a $5,000 article instead!) Any answer is a buying commitment."

If he isn't ready to answer, he will tell you there are certain points he'd like to clear up. Or he may ask to see other choices. Whichever way, you haven't lost a thing—but you have gained a great deal—by asking the question.

If unleashing a force this powerful, be aware of certain dangers. If you fail to handle the question deftly, the prospect will get the idea you're giving her the rush act. Then, of course, she'll tell you: "I'll do my own deciding, thank you!" But if you're gentle enough and shrewd enough in presenting the right question, she won't know *you're* doing the deciding.

The Little Question, employed often and in the right way, will close prospects who cannot be influenced by any other technique.

# $Y$OUR ASSUMPTIVE CLOSING TECHNIQUE

Robert Connolly tacks the Little Question on his assumptive close. It works.

In using the assumptive technique, you assume your prospect has made the purchase decision. You proceed by explaining the next action needed.

When the prospect has not yet reached a positive decision, the assumptive close will draw him closer, or at least cause him to declare himself. With the assumptive close, you at least find out where you stand and you often get the order.

Your prospect seems to feel one piece of property is what he wants. But he appears inert, unable to make a decision. Perhaps he is stalling. Try the assumptive close.

"Mr. Jones, I can see that you feel strongly toward the (blank) residence and that it fills your needs very well. Tell you what: let's submit an offer at $10,000 below the asking price and see how much we can save for you. Would it be more comfortable to do the paperwork at my office or here?"

Never be afraid to tack the Little Question onto the assumptive close. If you speak with sincerity and concern for your prospect's interests, assumptive closing can only help.

"At worst, your prospect will let you know how you can help him toward his purchase," Connolly says. "Always remember, he wants to buy, to say yes, to solve his problem. Any assistance you can offer, properly rendered in terms of your prospect's interest, will be of value to you both."

## *U*SING THE WIN-WIN CHOICE

Lola Peterson, a Chicago millinery saleswoman, led her department three years running. Her secret: she sold The Lookers. A Looker says frankly he or she is "just looking" and most retail salespeople dislike her intensely.

But to a capable and skilled salesperson, The Looker is uranium ore waiting to be mined. Lola Peterson viewed it that way. She said to herself: "It's Little Question time." It worked many times.

When she gets The Looker at a closing point, Peterson merely asks: "Would you like to wear this hat, or shall I send it to your home?" Nothing original about this. But using it consistently builds a distinguished closing record.

A real estate subdivider sold $3,000,000 worth of lots in a single year. His closing question: "Do you want this lot registered in your own or your wife's name?"

One of the best salesmen introduced his question so gently and adroitly the prospect couldn't possibly resent it. He was demonstrating a very intricate and expensive computer installation. His presentation had lasted two hours. He appeared to have no eagerness whatever to close. He remained leisurely and friendly.

When he judged the time had come, he merely said, very quietly and matter-of-factly: "Shall I ship by UPS or FedEx?" See how easy to order, merely by making a secondary choice about transportation? The prospect made the choice and the sale was closed without fuss or uncertainty.

# *H*OW *TO MOTIVATE THE HESITATER*

Hubert Bermont tells about using the Little Question in a different way—by asking why the customer is hesitating:

> At one point, I was losing sales I couldn't afford to lose. I reached excellent rapport with prospects. They seemed to trust me and like my merchandise and prices. But I faced indecision I couldn't overcome.
>
> "I have to talk it over with my wife."
>
> "Let me go home and think about it."
>
> "I'll definitely call you tomorrow."
>
> I just couldn't close those sales. So I set up a meeting with a veteran salesperson earning $125,000 a year in commissions. I explained my plight. He said something I never forgot:
>
> "As long as you are going to strike out anyhow, why don't you strike out swinging?"
>
> "I thought I *was* swinging!"
>
> "Why don't you simply ask the customers why you're not closing the sale?" he suggested.
>
> "Since they like you, since they like the merchandise, and since they like the prices . . . instead of asking *me* why they are walking out without buying, why not ask *them*? You're forgetting the most crucial final step. Asking for the order!"
>
> I tried that. I asked the very next customer who faltered why he was hesitating. He looked puzzled and then said: "I really don't know why. I have no reason. Write it up."
>
> This simple question closed 8 out of 10 such prospective sales. By simply swinging, I didn't strike out half as often.

# *G*IVE *YOUR CUSTOMERS A MINOR CHOICE*

Always give customers a minor (never a major) choice. Be happy with a *small* question. Remember the advice of theater pioneer

Stanislavsky: "There are no small parts, only small actors." There's no end to possibilities. It's versatile, fascinating, strong, safe, and simple.

No matter what or who you're selling, whether you're big ticket or discount, the Little Question is a closing workhorse.

When closing time comes, merely ask about something secondary—and thus leave the buyer (not the choice of buying or not buying) with a minor subordinate decision.

The buyer usually won't hesitate about making a minor choice. Yet if you ask for a major choice, your buyer could shy off.

The Little Question brings big closings—via tiny questions—over and over again.

# CHAPTER TWELVE

# The Do Something Key

The four-color mailing piece suggests that you buy a "wonderful nature magazine." On the tasteful page is a blank space. In the envelope are two gummed stamps. "Paste down your stamp indicating your choice of terms and rush it back to us," the copy explains.

Why the stamp? Why not merely send back the order? For a very good reason: people are more positively inclined to buy when they *do something.* You sell more subscriptions when you give the prospect the option of pasting down the stamp, experts say.

The *why* of it may mystify mail-order gurus. But the seasoned salesperson understands it very well from daily practice. People respond to the Do Something key. It closes thousands of sales every day.

Right in the middle of his presentation Court French had Toni Beacham's attention. Things were going well. Then French stood up, crossed over to Beacham's desk, and asked: "May I use your phone?"

"Of course."

"I just want to make sure that we have enough of this product to take care of your needs," he explained. "I'd hate to see you disappointed after we have gone this far."

The prospect didn't stop him from calling, so French assumed the sale was closed. And it was!

French was using the Do Something key. You start to do something that implies consent. Unless the buyer stops you, you've closed the sale. It is a whopper of a closing key. Master and use it.

One manufacturer hit upon a closing plan using the Do Something key that increased sales 28 percent in one year. He sent each retailer a huge blue pencil. In a personal letter, he asked retailers to follow a simple routine in talking to a prospect about his product.

His product was a CD player. After the retail salesperson demonstrated the musical appliance, he stepped toward the prospect and offered the large blue pencil, saying: "Suppose you take this and initial the inside of the cabinet?"

"What for?" the prospect asked, puzzled.

"It's your personal selection. The one you pick is the one you get."

"But I was just looking," objected the customer.

"Certainly. I understand. But there is only one question to decide: Does this wonderful instrument give you all that ear could want in music? If it does, you want it. Now if you will take the pencil and initial the instrument, I'll have it out to your house so you can play it before dinner."

Pretty strong salesmanship! A powerful force working in favor of getting the customer's initials inside the cabinet. In the majority of cases, when the salesman got as far as offering the blue pencil to the customer, he got the order.

The blue pencil, the physical basis for closing sales, proved matchless. Wherever used, in large cities or in hamlets, in large stores or in crossroads, it worked.

# *T*HE SECRET: DO AS WELL AS SAY

Actually, of course, the plan was something more than a blue pencil. The pencil was merely a symbol. The force is putting physical action into closing.

A secret of all great closers: they *do* something as well as *say* something. In selling, as in life, actions speak the loudest. By using action as well as words in your close, you bring sales to a fruition—where mere words sometimes aren't enough.

Use this sound and workable principle: start something the customer will have to stop to avoid giving tacit consent to buy.

A saleswoman, talking to a prospect, senses it's time to close—time for physical action. She had placed the order blank on the counter earlier in the interview, so she doesn't shock the prospect by flashing it now. She begins to write her order, as if talking to herself.

"So many dozen of such and such," she says, writing that down. "And so much of this." She writes that down also. She keeps eyes glued to the pad, not looking at the buyer. To avoid placing that order, the buyer must do something right away. Interrupt. Tell the saleswoman she's premature. Not all buyers have the courage to stop the action, even if not fully determined to buy when you start writing. Most buyers let you go ahead and write the order—and sign it. Physical action exerts a peculiar fascination on the human mind.

Remember the insurance salesman who started a fountain pen rolling toward his prospect? Theatrical directors know the power of actions in influencing audiences. If you spend much time around the theater, you soon know action is often more important than dialog. It's also true in selling, where actions bringing about the close are frequently more persuasive and more powerful than words.

At a murder trial, the defense attorney picked up Exhibit A, a hand gun, and pointed it to his head. As jurors and spectators gasped he pulled the trigger. Click! Because of a faulty firing pin, the gun did not fire. The lawyer knew it would not fire. He had tried it many times before the trial. The defendant was acquitted.

That lawyer could have dragged dozens of gunsmiths and weapon experts to the witness stand. But their testimony would have been paltry compared to that demonstration.

Drama! Showmanship! The same techniques that turn prospects into buyers. A well-timed dramatic touch gets attention and *holds* it. The buyer's attention span is short. But take out a yo-yo and twirl it and she'll take notice in a hurry. Every product or service has demo potential. Closers jab pens into the floor, paint buyers' walls, demolish articles apart piece by piece. Car-wax sellers set cars on fire.

# $S$ELLING SAFETY SWITCHES

Harold Jordan drew on the Do Something key to build a multimillion-dollar enterprise in Detroit. He sells safety switches, widely accepted these days. But when he started, few knew what a safety switch was, and the rest didn't care. Serious pioneering was required.

Jordan was the entire salesforce, and there were no sales. He tried talking to prospects about the necessity for switches. Nothing. So he built entirely around Do Something. It made sales. As he added salespeople, he taught them how to use it. In a few months, the business had grown beyond his projections for the first five years. Eventually, it became worldwide.

How did it work? The salesperson entered the prospect's office, put a sample on the desk, and said: "Pull the handle." That physical action started the sale. Nine in 10 by count pulled the handle.

"You see," said the salesman, "no flash, no danger of fire, no chance for a man to be electrocuted when he pulls the switch." Then he added:

"What kind of safety switches are you now using in your plant?"

"Not any," the prospect said.

The salesman registered shock. "What? Not using any safety switches in your plant?"

"No. We've been operating for 10 years and haven't had an accident."

Meanwhile the salesman was pulling the lever of the switch. He pushed the sample over where the prospect could touch it. The majority of prospects pulled it once or twice. It was the natural thing to do. The salesman continued: "Carrying any fire insurance?"

"Certainly."

"How long?"

"Ten years."

"Ever had a fire?"

"No."

"Why don't you quit carrying insurance?"

"Why, we may have a fire any time, and we want to be protected!"

"That's just it. You also could have a switch accident today. One accident will cost more than equipping your entire plant with safety switches."

Closing time. The salesman, his order book already nonchalantly on the desk beside the product sample, picked it up and inquired: "How many 3-amp open-knife switches do you have in the plant?"

If the prospect knew, he would say. If he didn't know (usually the case), the salesman said: "Call in your electrician, will you, Mr. Sutton? I'll go through the plant with him and make a count of the switches."

After returning from the inspection, the closer had the order written. He casually handed the pencil to the prospect. "Just your name at the bottom, please."

By actual count, 9 prospects out of 10 signed. If they did not sign, the closer came back in 30 days and repeated the routine, using the already-filled-out order blank as his presentation. Of those remaining only 1 out of 10 failed to sign.

Eventually Harold Jordan made the safety switch standard in industry. Chalk a big one up to Do Something key.

## $M$AKE IT EASY TO BUY

Do Something can vary from (1) sliding the fountain pen toward the buyer's lap to (2) asking a prospect to initial the inside of a cabinet to (3) putting the buyer's name on an order blank. But the principle remains the same: start an action that results in a sale *unless* the buyer puts an actual stop to it.

The famous Book of the Month Club was founded on that principle: (1) you get a notice that BOMC will send you this month's selection *unless* you call it off; (2) when you do get the selection, you've bought it *unless* you send it back. P.S.: The shipping box must be *destroyed* to get the book out. No easy way to reship. No wonder BOMC has been thriving for decades—using a physical action that's hard to stop!

You don't need glamour tools to harness this power. Every morning Ned Sterling sits with a list of calls in front of him. He writes the name and address of each prospect on an order blank.

"You're wasting order blanks," his boss reminds him, pleasantly.

"Aren't they cheap?"

"We'll print as many as you need, Ned," says the boss.

When Sterling makes a call, he puts the order blank, the prospect's name on it, right under his nose. ("I want him to get used to seeing it.")

Sterling makes his presentation, then he fills in quantity/price on the order blank, sometimes over the prospect's protest. He pushes the order blank to the prospect: "Just initial here, please."

There is something mighty fundamental about this—make it easy to buy, hard not to buy.

The only thing you could lose in writing beforehand are order blanks (which, as Ned Sterling points out, are cheap).

Another firm, experimenting with advance fill-outs, found four out of five prospects confronted with their names on an order blank, signed.

Always put your prospect's name and address on the order or draw up a simple letter of agreement in advance. What do you have to lose?


# *T*HE COTTAGE CHEESE CLOSING

Sometimes the Do Something key takes strange forms. Gary Fink, a champion insurance agent, once sent this letter to a prospect:

> Dear Dale:
>
> As per your request, I'm using this means of summarizing our luncheon meeting of the first of July at the Athletic Club. To the best of my recollection, you had an egg salad sandwich on pumpernickel with a side of cottage cheese and skim milk, and I ordered a diet burger with cole slaw and two Tabs with lime.
>
> If you have any questions or want any further information, please feel free to contact me at your convenience.
>
> Gary

Gary Fink makes more than $150,000 a year selling insurance in Minneapolis. He believes in the Do Something key.

# DRAMATIC PAUSE WITH WATER

Bruce Alexander, ace Tennessee real estate salesperson (in a state full of formidable competitors), applies the Do Something key with a finesse of a seasoned character actor.

After a negotiation session with a house seller, he arrives at the prospective buyer's house, his tie askew, his hair awry. The buyers, of course, are eagerly awaiting word of seller's reaction to their latest offer.

When Mrs. Prospective Buyer opens the door, Alexander rushes in, rolls his eyes, holds his head and says: "Quick, gotta have a glass of water!"

The couple rush to the kitchen, fearing some health calamity. He gulps the water, sits, closes his eyes. The pause is dramatic. Slowly he looks up.

"In the last 10 years, I've never had a negotiating session like that," he says. "I'm really off the wall. But I held out for you. And, believe me, this is the final offer he's going to make. I just hope I'll recover."

The final offer, of course, is still more than prospectives wanted to pay. But by now, they're convinced that the superachiever has already gone all out. In many cases, they buy then and there. Do Something wins again.

# OVERCOMING BUYER'S FEAR WITH DETAIL

The reason some salespeople are afraid of order blanks: they're afraid the customer will be afraid.

Get that order blank out in front as early in the sale as possible. The buyer gets used to it. When the closing time comes, it won't shock. Be nonchalant about the blank, never make an issue out of it. Treat it as merely one more detail.

When you present the blank, make it difficult for the buyer to catch your eye. Look down at the form. Be busy writing. This is that rare selling moment when you *don't* want eye contact. If you look up, the buyer may tell you she isn't quite ready to buy, she wants to think it over. But if you keep looking at the blank and writing, the buyer must stop you from doing both to prevent you from getting the order.

After the order is filled in, pass it along "to check, Ms. Buyer." At the same time, pass the pen, quietly suggesting that she put her name "right on that line, please." Do it all in the same quiet, non-chalant manner. Because of that highly sensitized abnormal way the buyer *thinks* at closing time, your confident quiet manner often gets a sign-up.

## *T*HE GIVE-BACK ORDER FORM

Penn Glade, a successful office supplies salesman, always makes it a point (after he's pushed order blank to customer) to ask for the blank back.

"I'm wondering if the price on item three is the price you ought to have," Glade explains. "A buyer as important to us as you are must have the best offer we can make. Yes, that's right, our rock-bottom price for quantity customers."

Just as casually he pushes the blank toward the buyer to sign.

"Taking it away makes her more eager to get it back. Seldom does a customer fail to sign when she gets the blank back the second time. Besides, my scanning the blank to see if there's any mistake develops confidence."

Use the Do Something key, that useful closing workhorse. It's the action step you need when your customer is undecided, when *doing* something rather than *saying* something will win the day.

## *W*HY SHOWMANSHIP SELLS

Psychologists tell us people remember one-fifth of everything they hear, two-fifths of everything they see, but four-fifths of everything they *see and hear*. No wonder it's vital to *show* 'em as well as tell 'em.

The fast pickup of an automobile, the strong suction of a vacuum cleaner, the rigid strength of a piece of plastic, or the soft texture of a carpet—all become powerful when *seen* and *felt*.

But showmanship is equally important in selling intangibles. When the product itself can't be seen—insurance, securities, advertising promotions—all the more reason to find out a way to show the benefits.

Any product or service can be demonstrated. Your prospect has five senses: sight, sound, feel, taste, and smell. Appeal to as many as possible each time you demonstrate.

Moreover, in your demonstration: *get the customer into the act.* The buyer must get into the act to get sold. Putting on a dazzling performance is an important first step. But when the buyer's the star, that's clincher time.

Showmanship sets you apart from your competition. Today, whatever you sell, somebody else is out there with a similar product or service, calling on *your* customers. When you put on a better show, you rise above the thundering herd. Do Something wins again.

# CHAPTER THIRTEEN

# Sign 'em Up with the Coming Event

In this era of inflation, what better argument than telling your prospect the price will be higher tomorrow? The buyer, sure it will be, signs now to avoid paying more later. That prices will rise is unchallenged today.

Using soon-to-rise prices in closing sales is part of the Coming Event key. Behind the key is a philosophy as powerful as any in human affairs—the threat of loss.

Remember what you learned earlier about capitalizing on buyer fears? The avoid-loss opportunity comes to you every day of the year. Dramatize the possibility of loss, and the buyer is putty in your hands.

People are often unmoved by future promise or current satisfaction. But if they fear losing what they already have, they'll break through a wall to act promptly.

Chauncey Depew, raconteur and successful businessman, described avoid-loss this way:

"If a man came in my house at three o'clock in the morning, awakened me, and told me that by going downstairs I could make $100, I'd kick him downstairs and go back to bed. So would you.

"But if the same man woke me and told me by getting up, dressing, and going with him I could avoid the loss of $100, I'd say: Be right with you!

"The fear of loss is one of the strongest fears in life," Depew concluded.

# Avoid Losing What You Don't Yet Have

The Avoid Loss motivates the buyer even if she's about to lose what she doesn't have yet—but *they* are trying to take away.

What happens if someone tells you that you cannot have something? You instantly want it! When you face an indecisive prospect, start shaking your head and choose the comment best suited:

- "I'm not sure I have your size. Would you want them if I can special order?"
- "My customers have been buying all we can produce. I'm not sure if I have any left."
- "Well, I know you are thinking of ordering X amount but we really need to order [a larger amount] because we now have it in stock and I don't think we will be able to keep up with demand and fill your summer order."

For the right product, person, and situation, avoid less is an excellent close. You get the prospect so excited he cannot wait to buy. Do him a favor by encouraging him to buy now—using this standing-room-only close.

# The Compelling Need: Stop That Loss

The Coming Event key trades on this desire to avoid loss—no matter what it costs. You point out: if the buyer fails to take advantage of your offer, he or she will suffer irremediable loss because of some impending event or action.

Note this subtle difference between this appeal and stressing how much the customer will profit if he or she buys. The avoid-loss appeal is infinitely stronger and more moving. Rooted so deeply in human nature, it practically never fails.

To use this technique, you describe an impending event that requires action at the moment of closing. The event itself is of little consequence. Retail stores use it in advertising: "On May 25, prices will be advanced 10 percent." The message: buy now to avoid the loss.

This appeal works even when the loss is implied. Witness the gasoline station in New Jersey that stood just outside the Holland Tunnel. As motorists approached the tunnel entrance leading to Manhattan, they read a large sign: *Last chance to buy gas in Jersey.* The station did booming business for years. After all, if this is the last chance, better get it. (What the station doesn't say, of course: when you get through the tunnel, you'll get your *first* chance to buy gasoline in New York.)

Another example: the con-man who ran the classified ad, *This is your last chance to send me a dollar*—followed by his address. Thousands sent in dollar bills.

"Last chance," they thought. "Better get in on it before we lose."

The principle works equally well on the ethical firing line. The saleswoman reminds you the business lot you want will be optioned at three o'clock. She suggests if you don't act quickly, you won't have a chance to get it at all. After three o'clock you'll suffer loss.

You do not want to suffer loss, so you decide to buy now, even though you might have wanted to think it over longer. If what the saleswoman told you about the impending event is true, there is nothing wrong with this technique. (Of course, the unscrupulous falsify impending events. This may work for a short time. But once buyers get onto a four-flusher, as they do, it doesn't work any more.)

The clothing salesman tells you the suit you're undecided about is the only one of its kind left. Furthermore, another customer, who looked at it yesterday, will be in again at noon.

"But, of course, you're here now," he tells you, "and if you decide, I'll have to tell Doctor Elliot he's too late." You buy. The Coming Event moved you along.

The life insurance salesperson comes in the day before your age changes: you'll be out $20 per $2,000 if you wait until tomorrow. That's $10 per $1,000 lost *overnight!* You never want a loss like that. You may not be quite ready for more insurance. But the prospect of losing if you don't buy is more than you can stand. You buy to avoid the loss.

The coming event can be a condition. The prospect wants to postpone decision. You tell him of the small quantity left of a certain item. Retail stores use this in limited quantity sales. One mail-order enterprise sold 100,000 sets of books by pointing out that only a few more sets were available.

The possibility of being left out, of losing something, is too much for the average prospect and he or she buys—when this technique is properly presented.

## *H*OW TO OVERCOME A BUYER'S DELAY

Although Do It Now is the great American maxim, many buyers—as every salesperson knows—are terribly inclined to wait until *mañana*. "I'll be glad to do that, Mr. Waterson," you tell him, "but I am afraid that Wednesday, or next week, will be too late."

"Why?"

"Because—"and then you tell him the event or condition, a rise in price, or inability to get the merchandise you're talking about.

If this coming event is a certainty, you are not risking anything. If he really wants your product, you're only pushing him to buy now rather than later. If the coming event is not a certainty, but merely a probability, you can still make a good case for it.

"Now, I won't take an oath that the price of this paper will advance from 20 to 40 percent in the next 30 days," a paper salesman told me. "I don't know. But this I do know. If the past is any indication, I may be erring on the conservative side to predict price increases of a mere 40 percent. Let me show you what the market did two years ago, when conditions were almost identical with conditions today."

Using actual figures of two years earlier, he convinced me that if I did not buy now, that coming event (expected and not guaranteed) would cause me loss. Of course, I bought. My fear of losing was greater than my unwillingness to wait until I had thought the matter over.

## *S*IX TESTED COMING EVENT CLOSERS

Practice these tested closers that best suit you and your prospect situation:

- This offer is only good today. Wonderful buy, isn't it?

- I can't assume that you can get this price next month. Better start saving money today!

- Let me point out: this offer ends on the 20th. The new price list is on press. Curious about how much you'll save by ordering today?

- If I were in your shoes, I'd grab this right now. Did you know we're almost sold out?

- Hey! This is a very special opportunity—only two left? Last week we had 50 left. I've reserved one for you—until 5 P.M. today!

- Some may say our price is high, compared to what other companies charge. I'm sure they know what their product is worth. So do we. Ours isn't high enough for what it does. We're expecting an increase any day. Why not start now and get our quality at today's price?

## CLOSING WITH THE DRAMATIC GESTURE

You can *create* a Coming Event. Richard Considine is a master in closing with the dramatic gesture.

Considine is president of Lincoln Logs Ltd., Chestertown, New York. He was the company's first salesman, and he remains the driving force behind the company's sales success. One day at 5 P.M., right after he founded the innovative housing firm, the telephone rang. George Jones, from Rochester, was inquiring about a log home. Dick described the advantages and how easy it is to build on a do-it-yourself basis. Jones was interested but not decisive. After all, a home is a big-ticket item.

Dick wheeled in the *created* Coming Event.

"Mr. Jones," he said, mentally canceling his evening's plans, "I'm three hours away from you. I'm going out to get in my car and drive to Rochester. I'll be there before 8 P.M. tonight. I'm sure we can and work out this log home for you."

By 9 P.M. Considine had a $1,000 check as a binding deposit. The dramatic gesture had closed the sale.

"Anytime I get buying signals from a prospect, I drop what I'm doing and help them make a decision," Considine says. "Any salesperson who doesn't put closing ahead of *everything* isn't a real closer."

## *T*HE COMING EVENT THAT NEVER WAS

A local ad agency owner, W. C. Newton, knew his tourist state was looking for help in advertising. He created his entire sales presentation on being in the state, knowing its problems, and giving the client his undivided personal attention—which, he contended, New York agencies couldn't do.

It was a southern state; the time, winter. Basking in the warm sun on the morning of the presentations, he picked up the local newspaper. On page 2, a half-page ad said: "When a blizzard rages outside, light up a Blanko cigarette and enjoy yourself."

In the ad, a couple sat in front of a beautiful fireplace. A big picture window framed the blizzard outside.

Newton knew the ad had been placed by his strongest competitor. He abandoned his prepared presentation and bought a dozen copies of the paper, walked into the screening room, and passed out newspapers, opened to the ad.

"The competition for this account has narrowed down to the Bigshot Agency and my firm," he said. "I've told you all along I'm right here, know your problems, and can solve them better than an outsider. The ad you're looking at was prepared by Bigshot. It's a beautiful, well-executed ad. This space in this particular paper, in this city, cost the cigarette company $974.28. That's the client's money, just as it will be your money that either I or they spend on your advertising.

"Now, I have just one question—how many of you have ever seen a blizzard?"

Two of the 12 held up their hands.

He made the sale.

"I knew the big agency could outsell me on everything except one benefit," he admitted. "I was lucky to find out such a beautiful way to dramatize it."

If you have only one benefit to sell, use the coming event that never was—*that's* your closing summary.

## *A*NTICIPATE YOUR PROSPECT'S FUTURE NEEDS

Take an anticipatory look at your prospect's needs in the months ahead. Include your product or service into those needs.

Sid Bostic, a successful salesman of medical equipment, had been trying for some time to interest Dr. Colin Burns in replacing his sterilizing equipment. But the good doctor was an expert in delay.

"Some day I'll probably want to look further into that equipment. But now I simply can't afford it. Maybe next spring. By that time, we'll know more about this recession talk. The political picture is so uncertain. The stock market isn't too optimistic. My banker predicts another Black Monday before the winter is over."

Sid had been hearing the same story from Dr. Burns for a long time. Earlier it was: "Perhaps after Election Day. Maybe collections will be better by then."

So Sid decided on action. He created an event. He telephoned: "I have been wanting to talk to you, doctor, about a matter of great importance. It concerns you very seriously. Will you have lunch with me on Wednesday?"

Surprised, Burns agreed.

At the luncheon table Dr. Burns came right to the point. "What is this important thing?"

Sid took a card from his pocket and laid it face down.

"When does your lease expire, doctor?"

"Next fall, in October."

"Suppose you couldn't renew your lease because the building was being sold?"

The doctor looked worried. "Where did you hear that?"

"Well, it isn't official, but I understand the university is looking into the possibility of opening a new campus in this neighborhood. But assume it's true. You'd have to move, isn't that so?"

"Well, yes."

Sid continued: "You could relocate your office. And regardless of the political situation, or a possible recession, or any other temporary condition, people would still need your services. And so you'd decide to move."

The doctor nodded.

"Then why don't you decide right now? You've got more than 20 years of active practice ahead of you. You certainly aren't going to stay in that cramped office forever, are you?"

The doctor smiled. "You're right about the crowded space."

Sid passed the card across the table. Dr. Burns read the typewritten message, "He who must see everything clearly before he decides never decides."

"My father had that motto framed on his wall," Sid said. "Successful people don't wait until decisions are forced upon them. They anticipate them."

"Funny thing," Dr. Burns said, "Grace and I talked about this when we bought our first car and later when we bought our first home. She has always been the one to anticipate the future and insist it will all work out. And it always has, somehow."

The doctor slapped the table. "All right, many thanks for your advice. I'm going to be moving my office this summer."

Two weeks later Sid got a phone call from Grace Burns: her husband had signed up for a 10-year lease in the new professional building. She told Bostic the doctor would be soon talking with him about completely new equipment.

"But first," she said, "Thank you so very much for getting him out of that dreadful hole-in-the-wall office."

Hooray for the anticipated event!

## *D*IVERT YOUR PROSPECT WITH ARRANGEMENTS

Tom Tierney sells a business consulting service to management and draws on a similar technique. After describing his service and his top people, Tom moves in for the close.

"Mr. Smythe, you've heard us outline what we plan to do in solving your problems. This will require us to sit down with your top people and get quite a bit of data as our first step in doing the job. My plan is to have four people here tomorrow."

Immediately the prospect became involved in hosting the four visitors, who they should see, when this should be scheduled, and so on. Or he may say the day after tomorrow is better.

Obviously, the sale is closed—by a coming event.

# NERVOUS BREAKDOWN AS EVENT

Albert D. Lasker, in his day the nation's best and richest advertising agency character, worked himself into a nervous collapse. While in the hospital, he got word that a certain prospect meeting was set. It was the critical closing opportunity.

Lasker fought off nurses and doctors, jumped into his clothes, and arrived at the meeting where the corporate brass were talking in millions.

"Gentlemen, I came here to get your account for my firm," he said. "I have no business being here. I am in the hospital having a nervous breakdown. Now if you will sign this contract, I will return to the hospital and finish my job of getting well."

Lasker was master of the controlled coming event—even his own breakdown!

Many times in your own closing you'll find the Coming Event key is the strongest possible lever. Naturally, if you go around predicting impending events that cannot possibly happen, you destroy confidence. Use it honestly and with discretion. Stick to facts. Dig out new facts to make it work, if need be.

The Coming Event key frequently ushers in *another* Coming Event, the closing of your sale.

# CHAPTER FOURTEEN

# The Third-Party Endorsement

When you use the Third Party Endorsement key in closing sales, you recruit someone else—usually an expert or a respected colleague of the customer—to tell your story for you. As a salesperson, you're assumed to be less than objective about your product. The third party, with no axe to grind, has high credibility.

Morris I. Pickus, Los Angeles selling genius, calls the endorser the Friendly Third Party. Pickus will not make a sales call alone. He always takes the FTP along.

During the sale, Pickus will cite his FTP, knowing that the prospect, being imitative as all human beings are, is personally identifying with the success of the third party.

"If she can do it, I can do it," the prospect thinks.

Frank H. Davis, a master salesman, is talking to an important prospect. The sale has reached the experimental close stage. Davis recognizes the buying signal, so he launches an effective narrative wrap-up. As the introduction to closing, he tells his customer a story.

The customer is enthralled. He leans forward, not to miss a word. He imagines himself in place of the characters in the story. It's human nature: he sees point by point the parallel between what they lacked and what he now lacks.

Immediately he senses the wisdom of the solution the story characters found—buying what Frank Davis is selling. When Davis deftly places the order blank before him, the customer signs. He has been completely sold.

# *U*SING A BUSINESS STORY TO CREATE A BUYING CLIMATE

Often the Third-Party Endorsement key calls for a business story—not for entertainment (it may be entertaining as a bonus) but to make the customer see herself within another's experience. Each of us imitates, with childlike faith, when the proper example is placed before us.

Consider yourself in a buying mode (as we all are frequently). When a salesperson relates the experience of someone in business that you respect or admire, you immediately say: "If he could do it in such a manner, I can do it the same way."

Give the buyer half a chance and he'll imitate. The shrewd closer gives customers many opportunities to employ this very human tendency.

Breakstone Tally, a great salesman, could have become a novelist or screenwriter—he's an enormously effective storyteller. His stories grip you, put you into the picture, make you want to act.

"Tell your prospects stories," Tally advises, "to close more sales."

You're selling merchandise to retail stores. But the prospect is reluctant. "No demand for that product," he says. Time for a story.

"When I first called on Associated Stores, the buyer—I think you know Jonas Simplot—told me the same thing. But he tried the products anyway."

And what results! You cite figures. You talk profits. You point out new store traffic. And your prospect drools.

# *T*HE CONNOR AND TEDMON EXPERIMENT

Stone Wheaton tells endorsement stories better than most. Watch him work toward the close with Louisville retailer Joan P. Atter:

"Do you know Connor and Tedmon of Nashville?"

"Very well," Atter says.

"What do you think of them as businesspeople?"

"They've built a tremendous business in Nashville in face of great competition."

That's Wheaton's go signal. He launches into his story: what Connor and Tedmon have done in Nashville with the products he's suggesting to Atter. He tells the Connor and Tedmon story in a running narrative.

When he first called upon Connor and Tedmon, Wheaton relates, he found such and such a condition prevailed. (It "happens" to be almost exactly the same business condtion Atter faces.) Hite Connor wasn't exactly sure Wheaton's products could correct the condition and give him what he needed in profit. (Neither is Atter sure at this particular moment!)

As an experiment—but only as an experiment—Conner decided to put in Wheaton's line. (That gives Atter courage: maybe he also could try it. Here's a respected precedent.)

"But now Connor and Tedmon are thanking their lucky stars they experimented," Wheaton says. "Sales increased 30 percent in a year's time. Their turnover has speeded up. Profit is better than ever. They have attracted a new type of customer."

Thus does Stone Wheaton talk, confirming his statements, of course, with evidence. He's saying: "Don't take my word for it. Follow someone who's already proved the experiment works."

Meanwhile, Atter is telling herself if Connor and Tedmon can make profits with these lines, she can do as well, maybe better. Further, Connor and Tedmon's acceptance of the product line is a recommendation—evidence to overcome her own wavering.

In every case, when you use the Third-Party Endorsement, the prospect usually unconsciously (sometimes consciously!) compares his business with the narrative. Success of the story character is *his* success—if he does what you suggest (buy). The prospect sells himself. You don't need difficult, intricate, or high-pressure closing methods.

Stone Wheaton closed the sale. The Third Party did it.

The Third-Party Endorsement works for you in various forms. Telling stories is perhaps the most common. The testimonial letter is another. A customer or client list is a third.

We're all fascinated by the opinion of others. Don't you believe another user quicker than you believe the seller? Of course you do.

# $M$AKING TESTIMONIALS TESTIFY

Very early in business history, sellers found that testimonials—"I've tried it and I like it"—are powerful convincers.

Salespeople started using testimonials by word of mouth, quoting a user. Much better: testimonial letters on the user's letterhead in his or her own words.

Ace closers often carry a book of photocopied testimonial letters. The more you show, the better. Besides, the more varied your inventory, the easier to select just the *right* letter in each case.

Any letter from a *person* your prospect knows—or knows about—is worth its weight in plutonium. Next best: a *company* the prospect knows or knows about.

One successful mail-order merchant discovered sales letters that included testimonials from satisfied users pulled a healthy response. If the testimonial came from a townsman of the reader? Even more effective!

The clue for you: get letters from buyers your prospect knows, either in person or by reputation. Since you won't always have time to get the right letter for the specific buyer, collect them constantly. Then pick and choose.

One Chicago industrial sales manager calls it The Avalanche. Instead of testimonial letters in a sales kit, he tells his reps to carry loose letters. At closing time, the salesrep brings out one testimonial letter, hands it to the prospect, lets him glance at it, hands him another as soon as he puts it down, hands him a third. Soon the prospect's desk is literally covered with an avalanche of letters.

The more letters, the better. No prospect can see his desk covered with comments by satisfied users and not be impressed and ready to sign.

# $T$HE HARD-HITTING CUSTOMER LIST

The list of buyers is an effective third-party tool salespeople should use more often. Compile a list of prominent customers. Salesfolk who sell book or magazine subscriptions, two rather difficult sells, almost always use a customer list in closing.

Holland Steel, an expert salesman, carries a customer list of many pages. The names are in the customer's own handwriting (much more effective). He puts this list on the desk.

"We are mighty proud of our customers, you know," he says. "You know Judge Hollister of the Supreme Court, don't you?"

"Oh, yes."

"There is his name. I expect you know Andrew Read, president of the Nationwide Manufacturing Company."

He chats interestingly about the names and then says: "Here are the types of people who have taken advantage of this offer. People like . . . ," and he reads more prominent names. "You know what people of that caliber are, what their judgment is. I want to put your name down alongside that of Judge Hollister and Mayor Preston."

Without going into any other kind of sales argument, he closes the majority of his prospects. Only they really close themselves. The imitative faculty is strong in each prospect. All you do is steer it in the right channels—jump-start it with the third-party endorsement.

## *F*RANK'S STORYTELLING CLOSE

Frank Davis—there was a great salesman!—rose from a Missouri hill farmer to vice president of one of the world's largest life insurance companies. He did it through sheer *closing* ability. And at least half of Davis's great sales depended on the storytelling close.

Frank told closing stories to the high, to the low, to the old, to the young. His methods? So obvious you wonder why customers didn't see through them! But they never did. They were enthralled. They never knew (or didn't care) he was using a selling technique.

Davis closed sales by relating experiences of men and women with insurance. He told these stories logically, naturally, with ease, charm, and high interest. He told them so well that listeners saw themselves reaping the benefits. They couldn't help buying.

In his stories, Frank went to great lengths to make every single detail correct. He insisted on memorable names. His two main characters were Homer McGillicuddy and Helen Barley.

"You cannot forget Homer McGillicuddy and Helen Barley," said this great salesman. "They get into your bloodstream. No one can ever forget them."

Once Davis was talking with Conway Kremer, a crusty executive and the hardest of prospects to sell. Kremer didn't like Davis, didn't like anyone or anything. He was insolent, insulting, detestable.

The sale didn't appear to be progressing very well. Kremer, through his antagonism, had Davis stymied at every turn.

"An accident occurred in Chicago last week that made me think of you, Mr. Kremer," said Davis, and a closing story had been launched. Interested at once because he was the central figure, Kremer said: "Is that so?"

"I stopped in at the Marriott newsstand. At first I didn't pay any attention to the woman behind the counter. Then I heard her say: 'Frank!' I looked and I said: 'Why, Helen!' It took me so by surprise. 'Helen, what are you doing here?' I finally asked.

'Why Frank, haven't you heard?'

'Heard? Heard what?'

'About George?'

'No. Don't tell me he's . . .'

"She began to cry. 'Yes,' she said, 'George is gone. He passed away six weeks ago.'

'No!'

'He died very suddenly. One night he came home, the picture of health. Two days later he was dead.'

"She sobbed harder. I didn't want to be indelicate enough to ask her if he left her comfortably fixed. But she volunteered."

Davis continued telling it to Kremer:

"George didn't believe in college endowment insurance for his son, Biff. He always told me 'I can invest my own money better than any old insurance company can.' He was absolutely sincere. He believed it. But his investments didn't turn out. Then came the recent stock market crash. And his wife, Helen Barley, was back behind the newsstand counter. Biff, who'd been a freshman at Notre Dame, is a dropout.

"When I told you, Mr. Kremer, that it reminded me of you, what I meant was this: George Barley looked a great deal like you.

You always reminded me of him. Of course, what happened to him couldn't possibly happen to you. But no one could have suffered the sorrow and reproach in that poor widow's eyes without being moved by the deep responsibility we all bear to our families."

Silence. Frank, the old pro, knew when to clam up. Then Conway Kremer, that hard-boiled tyrant who'd been browbeating Davis five minutes before, said: "I've reconsidered. How soon can you have me examined for insurance?"

He saw himself in George's position. He saw his own wife in Helen's plight. He didn't want that. So he bought the insurance.

Frank Davis used this powerful technique in closing sales. Use it in closing yours. On hearing a related story, your prospect will immediately identify himself with characters. In putting himself in the character's shoes, the buyer sells himself.

In telling your stories, don't make heroes out of characters the buyer has no respect for. Remember Connor and Tedmon? First the salesperson asked if his prospect *knew* them. The prospect said she admired Connor and Tedmon. Only then did the salesperson tell his story. If the prospect said she didn't think much of the two men, the salesperson would have said: "I believe I can understand your feeling, Ms. Atter. But I think you'll agree that they're pretty good retailers, won't you?"

With a *yes* answer, he can use the example. Otherwise: quickly try another name.

Put your big toe in the water before plunging into the rapids. When your stories ring with conviction, they're powerful in closing sales easily and naturally. But test the character first.

## CLOSING AUTHORITY-ORIENTED PROSPECTS

The Authority Close differs from others in one important way: you do not ask the prospect to make a decision, you issue instructions for the prospect to buy immediately! Further: you, the seller, are the Third-Party Authority. Caution: This special close is designed expressly to wilt the authority-oriented buyer. Use it only on such prospects. But that's a large group. Thousands of prospects have been conditioned since childhood not to act unless told to do so by higher authorities:

Parents

Teachers

Spouses

Bosses

Doctors, lawyers, CPAs

When contacted by financial service closers, the authority-oriented prospect usually says:

- "That sounds good!"
- "I didn't know that!"
- "That yield is really high, better than I'm getting now."
- "I would love to double my money."
- "I do need safety and income."

They say everything except, "I'll buy." They don't feel right making a financial commitment until some higher authority tells them it's OK. *You*, as the authority, can be particularly effective with people who

- Had strict parents tell them what to do all their lives
- Had private schools tell what to wear and what to say
- Attended military schools
- Are strongly controlled by a spouse, child, lawyer, CPA, or teacher

In the full-authority close you're telling the prospect *you* are the authority—you say it's the right decision, so he or she *must* do it.

Of course, the full-authority close isn't for everyone. But consider it when calling from a who's who list where you can check for private schools and military academies, two good clues.

# CHAPTER FIFTEEN

# Closing with Something for Nothing

We spend our lives trying to get something for nothing. We never succeed, really. There's no free lunch. But that doesn't keep us from trying again and again.

The desire to get something for nothing works because human nature loves a bargain. This is universal. A man once got a call about an unusual bargain in elephant sandwiches. An entire carload was suddenly available. Quality was A-1—the best elephant sandwiches on earth.

"But I'm a vegetarian," the man told the caller. "I eat no meat. Even if I did, I don't believe in killing off endangered species. On top of that, I'm on a liquid diet. Doctor's orders. There's no way you could possibly sell me any elephant sandwiches."

"I forgot to tell you," the caller said, "These elephant sandwiches are only 25 cents apiece."

"*Now* you're talking *my language,*" the buyer said.

A fantastic bargain. Almost something for nothing. It's a powerful appeal.

Of course, the prospect knows he gets what he pays for and not a bit more. But he keeps on hoping to get something for nothing. This means you must keep this closing key brightly shined and in strong working order.

It overcomes one of your most powerful adversaries—procrastination.

The saleswoman promises the prospect something extra—it can be an add-on of no consequence whatsoever—and the prospect, hard-headed and crafty otherwise, falls like an axed steer.

Many times, you find your customer willing to listen, easy enough to interest. She believes what you say. She wants your product, no doubt about that. But when it comes to saying the final word, taking the final step, she puts you off. The sale bogs down. And there you are. Nothing you said or did brought the transaction to such a state.

Procrastination: that democratic force as inexorable as the law of gravity. The Something-for-Nothing key, as the name implies, recognizes procrastination and enables you to close in spite of it. It gives the buyer a special inducement to buy now. It also plays upon the dreaded sense of loss if the customer fails to act now.

## *T*HE FINAL INDUCER: FREEBIE IN RESERVE

Something for Nothing is best used as a final inducer. Hold it in reserve until the end. This sales inducer works because of the prospect's desire to get something special, not generally available, an exclusive. It offers something valuable or something trivial, something real or something fancied. It shows us we will lose if we don't act. So she buys to avoid the possibility of loss.

A woman went into a restaurant and asked the price for a bacon-and-egg sandwich.

"Two dollars and forty cents," the waiter said.

"How many eggs?"

"One egg."

"How many slices of bacon?"

"Two."

She thought a while, shook her head, and started to leave. Before she reached the door the waiter yelled: "But, Madam, the bread is absolutely free."

She bought the sandwich—couldn't resist the free bread.

Your success with Something for Nothing depends on *how* and *when* you use it. Sometimes SFN is the only strategy that will fetch the order. Sometimes you can close without it. Wise closers hold Something for Nothing as a last resort.

"Better to reserve and not need rather than need and find it's already squandered," Bob Arnold says. How true!

## $S$ANDBAGGING AT THE FINAL ROUND

In poker, the crafty player often portrays a strong hand as weak to sucker the other players. Then in the final round of betting, he puts all his money in the pot. Poker nuts call this *sandbagging* (you saw it handled by masters in *Big Hand for the Little Lady* on the screen with Henry Fonda and Joanne Woodward).

Sandbagging is also valuable in closing because, again, your prospect goes away thinking he's got something for nothing. You walk away with a signed OK.

The principle behind this is subtle. Your sandbag may be something added, like a special price, an extra piece of equipment, or special terms. Or it may be a benefit conferred by a new use for an established product. Often this extra has really been a part of your proposition from the start, but you hold it back. Ideally, the sandbag must not *look* tacked on. It must be perceived as benefit that *justifies* the purchase.

When the proposition is strong without the sandbag, the clincher makes it irresistible.

Ethan Streeter sells a marvelous piece of safety furniture. It's a beautifully designed high chair during infancy that converts to table/chair for the toddler. Streeter has worked out several strong closes. He's found some mothers are most concerned with the immediate utility. So he withholds the set of wheels that attach to the underside to convert to a stroller as well as a high chair and (later) a youth chair/table. Thus he has a sandbag to drop should closing become difficult.

Make sure your proposition is strong *without* the sandbag, then it will seem like another overwhelming benefit.

You'll see the other reasons why the ace closer is also a business actor. You've just seen why he or she is also a masterful poker player—sandbags at the ready.

# *U*SING THE VALUE-ADDED TECHNIQUE

A first cousin to your basic sandbag is value added, also powerful since the prospect perceives it as Something for Nothing.

To *add value* to your proposition, sometimes you educate your client to new uses. At other times you show extra features and benefits never discovered without your help.

At the critical closing moment, show how your proposition not only fills expected needs, but *unexpectedly* fills the need you've created or intensified.

In selling computers to financial managers, demonstrate how to do bookkeeping, filing, and spreadsheets. When the financial manager bites on word processing, build and intensify the interest in the feature you've been withholding.

# *G*IVE CLIENT REASON TO SIGN NOW

Pierre Vendome, a French Canadian mobile home dealer, is an adroit SFN user. He builds in the cost of $170 microwave oven before he quotes the price of a mobile home. When the customer wavers or talks about visiting other dealers, Vendome says:

"Wait! I will do *eenythin'* to get you to buy today. I'll *geef* you this microwave which costs $170. *Eenythin'* to get you to buy today."

The couple, seeing their chance to get a free microwave, often signs. Vendome throws in the oven only at the last minute. If he doesn't need it, he doesn't use it—he just makes $170 more on the sale. Something for Nothing. It works.

Don't launch all your Patriot missiles at once. Hold one in reserve. Try to close with one of the other major keys first. But when the buyer remains adamant and you need something special, trot out SFN.

Lloyd Allard, the champion sign seller to restaurants and motels, loves something for nothing. It provides of sense of urgency—the essential element in almost every close. Allard knows he must provide the prospect with a *reason* to do business now.

In countering "come back next week," Allard says: "Mr. Customer, I can't come back next Thursday. I'm going to be in Pittsburgh next week. I'd have to fly over here just to see you."

He follows with Something for Nothing:

"Mr. Customer, if you'll let me write this order today, I'll deduct the price of a round-trip airline ticket to Pittsburgh from the price."

It becomes win-win. Allard makes the sale. The customer gets the price of the ticket Allard doesn't have to pay for.

"You'll find you can build urgency into any closing situation, " Allard says. "Of course, the urgency you create must be logical to be effective."

# GREAT VALUE! EXTRA! EXTRA!

Auntie Mame said: "Life's a bowl of cherries and most poor bastards are starving to death." She could have added: "Yes, and on the hungry lookout for something free." Or, at least, the *illusion* of free.

The inducer can be a piece of trivia—a street guide, a road map, a desk calendar—an item not worth more than a couple of dollars. But it often pushes sales worth several thousands over the line.

Fred C. Kelly learned this selling houses. A fancier of collies, Kelly usually took a puppy along when showing a house. One day, Carson and Esmeralda Brown were considering a $248,000 home. They liked the house and the view. But the price—aye, there was the rub. The Browns hadn't intended to pay that much. Besides, certain things didn't entirely please them—the arrangement of rooms, closet space, and so on.

The sale headed for the white water. Kelly had given up all hope. Then the wife looked at the pup, and asked "Does he go with the house?" Kelly replied:

"He certainly does! What home would be complete without a dog?"

Mrs. Brown said they'd better buy. Mr. Brown agreed. The deal was closed. The special inducement in a $248,000 home was a collie puppy!

Kelly experimented with different inducers: cherry trees and lawn swings against competitors who held good cards in price and value. The inducers, worth little in actual money, outweighed the real advantages. But nothing worked as well as a warm tail-wagging puppy.

Back in vaudeville days, comedian Fred Allen recalled playing a town so far back in the woods the assistant manager of the hotel was a bear! Animals provide that extra benefit!

Think about the way clever promoters presented vaudeville acts—starting with the headliners. But they always held one back. At the bottom of the poster, in larger type, the theatergoer read: *Extra! Added! John Simplon and His Talking Dogs!* A Something for Nothing benefit.

If you run into a closing snag, introduce an inducement. It can be your choice of many things as long as it pushes the prospect's value button.

# $D$ON'T BE AFRAID TO GIVE TO GET

At first, Perry Walters had difficulty selling a $25 book—until he introduced Something for Nothing. He raised the price to $27.95 and put the buyer's name on the cover in gold—free. Sales went up 200 percent!

The floor salesman in the music department ran headlong into an obdurate prospect. He tried several closing techniques. Nothing happened. He decided to use SFN.

"I'll tell you what I'll do, Mr. Matson," the salesman said. "I'll give you this record brush as a free gift, if you place your order today. It's a token of our appreciation for getting your order this week."

Don't be afraid to *give* to *get*. Remember the words of Winston Churchill: "We make a living by what we *get*. We make a life by what we *give*."

The special inducement gives the prospect a reason for buying. After summarizing the benefits, say:

- "If I can book your order today, I'll speak to Norman about special pricing."

- "By ordering during our summer sale you'll get a free case of tape to get you started."

# $E$ASY AS PIE, CRAFTY AS A FOX

Claude Hopkins, one of America's greatest mass salesmen, worked for a Chicago meat packer who dumped a special problem in Hopkins's lap: selling expensive shortening to commercial bakers. The packer's six salespeople in Boston had sold practically no shortening in a month.

"Here is a letter from Boston," the CEO told Hopkins. "I agree with it entirely. They are not making sales and cannot make sales at the price you have fixed on our product."

"They are wrong," Hopkins said. "Real salesmanship isn't concerned with price."

"Can you sell to the bakers in Boston?"

"Yes."

"Can you go this afternoon?"

"Yes."

When Hopkins hit Beantown, he asked the local manager to name the hardest prospect of all. He got the name: Ebenezer Fox, owner of the Fox Pie Company. Fox wasn't particularly eager to see Hopkins.

"I came from Chicago to consult you about a card," Hopkins said, placing a card about five feet away. "This card is designed to picture the ideal pie. It cost us a great deal of money. The artist charges us $1,500 for the drawing. What do you think?"

"That card shows pie at its best," Fox said. "If I could make pies like that, I'd have the largest market share in Boston."

"How many Boston stores are selling Fox pies?" asked Hopkins.

"About 1,000."

"Mr. Fox," Hopkins said, "I'll give you cards like that to go in every store. I will give you 250 of those cards with every carload of shortening you order now, as a special offer."

The prospect signed for four carloads of shortening on the spot. Then Hopkins went to Providence, to New Haven, to Hartford, to Springfield. All in all, he sold more than six salespeople had sold in six weeks.

The local manager was scornful.

"You haven't been selling shortening," he said. "You have been selling a pie card. I'd like to see what you can do without it. Do you think you could sell if you didn't have that card?"

"Of course. Who should I try?"

The manager named a large firm, which Hopkins called on the telephone, only to discover that the prospect—loaded with shortening—was not interested in buying more. But Hopkins didn't allow that to deter him. He suggested a special inducement:

"I want to advertise your pies all the way from here to Chicago. If you order two carloads of shortening, I will place a sign on both sides of the cars. This sign will announce that your pies are made with our product. Not on one side of the car, but on both sides, so everyone for 900 miles, on both sides of the tracks, will know you."

He sold two carloads to an overloaded customer. He knew how to use Something for Nothing. A smart card got him to Boston. A larger card got him back to Chicago.

Practically all the great business leaders—and that includes great closers—are astute users of Something for Nothing.

# *F*IVE SUCCESSFUL JUST-SUPPOSE QUESTIONS

At times, rather than flat-out Something for Nothing, try a Just Suppose Question—powerful in its ability to trigger human imagination:

- *Just suppose* I were able to ship this by airfreight for delivery next Tuesday—could you place your order today?

- I've never heard of specs like that! But *just suppose* I can *customize* it. Would you invest another $6,000 to get exactly what you want?

- You're specifying a very unusual color and interior. Can I get it? I don't know. But if *I can*, do I also have your commitment on this business?

- Just suppose I could get you a full year of free maintenance. Would that shift the decision in our favor?

- *Suppose* we could do all your corporate tax work and prepare the 1040s for your senior executives for the budget you now spend for just the annual audit. Interested in hearing more?

## $M$EN'S ROOM DIPLOMACY

If you followed the business methods of the late Howard Hughes—and most everyone did—you know his dedication to doing business in lavatories. Hugh Edwards, president of the Research Guild, Chapel Hill, North Carolina, believes the men's room is also an excellent place to close with Something for Nothing.

Edwards had gone to Minneapolis to sell his research services to General Mills. But he was having a hard time getting to see Jerry Stoneseifer, the decision maker. He had just about given up—after talking with several other receptive but nondecision-making people—when he spotted Stoneseifer on route to the men's room

"Why not?" Edwards said and followed.

At adjacent stands inside, Edwards struck up a conversation and explained his business.

"We've been having a lot of trouble with our exiting suppliers, getting them to understand the General Mills way," Stoneseifer said.

Edwards said he could understand that problem.

"Many suppliers are set in their ways," he said. "And it's hard to change them. But I guess it all depends on how you get started. Now us, we believe in helping you *train* your own suppliers—right from the start—in doing things your way. Remember what Dr. Samuel Johnson said: 'Much can be made of a Scotsman if he is caught young.' With us, you can train your own research group *just as if we were located in the last office on the left.* Of course, the important difference is we're not. We bring you outside expertise and outside objectivity. It's a Something-for-Nothing value you get in working with us."

Well, Stoneseifer said, maybe you've got something there. Edwards went home with an assignment that led to many more. Shortly, he was doing close to $100,000 worth of business a year with General Mills.

"The idea of training his own suppliers *his* way did it," Edwards said. "He felt he was getting Something for Nothing. But somehow it wouldn't have worked in his office. I highly recommend the men's room for certain kinds of closing."

Everyone wants a little something more as the motorist found when he asked the character in Maine: "Have you lived here all your life?"

Said the Down-Easter, carefully whittling a piece of wood: "Not yet."

## $F$REE, YES, BUT NOT THE WHOLE STORE

The late William Wrigley, Jr., was eminently successful because he was continually sending his dealers special inducements to get them to buy more. One time Wrigley sent out a card listing a number of premiums dealers could earn by buying more gum.

Another time he would offer a bonus for orders of minimum size. It was always something attractive, something special, and an inducement to buy.

On a large scale Wrigley was using the same technique you employ one on one—Something for Nothing.

Sure, you give the buyer Something for Nothing—usually a fairly minor concession, but once in awhile, you run into The Dedicated Chiseler who wants you to give away the store.

Don't do it. Never confuse closing with charity. Keep them separate (as important as the separation of church and state). Here are ways to appeal to The Dedicated Chiseler:

- "Would you trust a doctor who offered discounts to get your business?"

"No."

"Well, like other professionals, we charge a competitive rate, and we don't give discounts. But I'll tell you what we do give: top quality service. Isn't that what any astute buyer really wants?"

- "Are you worried someone will get a better price than you?

  I can guarantee that will not happen!

  "Since no one will ever get a lower price or a discount, can we take care of the paperwork on your order now?"

- "Do you give a 10 percent discount of everything you sell? No?

  "Well, we don't either. Why would you expect us to do something you yourself don't do?

  "What is your real reason for hesitating?"

- "Does Mercedes give discounts?"

  "No."

  "We are known as the Mercedes of this industry, and we are already available at Volvo prices. What more could you want?

  "Can we place your order today?"


## INDUCEMENT: BUY NOW OR LOSE OUT

Terry and Sue Muth sell Lincoln Log homes in Haywarden, Iowa. They are also experts in landscaping and plants—their second business.

Sue Muth, who studied horticulture, decided to use greening as a Something-for-Nothing key.

"Buy this log home and we'll give you $600 worth of landscaping free," the Muths tell customers.

It works. "What a relief! I was wondering what to do about the grass and trees. What a nice addition."

Sometimes what would cost your customer $600 can be bought wholesale for $300—well worth it to nail down a big-ticket sale.

The inducement need not be tangible. It can be purely a mental picture. If you can show the buyer he will lose prestige by not buying now, that's an inducement. If you can show the buyer her name will go on an honor roll if she buys now, that is a sufficient motivation.

Or you can turn it around: "You are paying for this whether you are enjoying its advantages or not."

The Something for Nothing key comes in mighty handy. You can often use it when other techniques fail. It tackles and whips the ever-present problem of procrastination—your biggest nemesis in closing. It appeals to that universal hope in everyone—"What's for free?"

CHAPTER SIXTEEN

# *Ask and Get to Close and Sign*

Liam O'Toole, a New York sales executive, sent out this bulletin to his office copier sales force: "Hereafter, no matter what the conversation with the customer has been or how the interview has terminated, the last thing you must do before taking leave (provided he or she has not already bought) is to ask for the order."

Basic? Sure. Had each salesperson been doing it? No. They tried it for a month. It increased sales 25 percent! Asking each prospect to buy brought in a one-fourth increase in business, not an isolated case.

General Electric increased over-the-counter sales of Mazda lamps the same way. After careful experimentation, a sales executive devised a simple closing technique. Retail salespeople were required to ask everyone who stopped to look at a sparkling lamp display to buy a carton of eight bulbs. That was all. Just ask them to buy. One in four bought. Sales went up 25 percent.

If you ask for the order, there are only two things the buyer can do: buy or refuse. Occasionally, the buyer will refuse. No denying that. But even if it happens, buyers develop greater respect—they realize how important they really are to you.

Never fail to ask your customer for the order. It works.

## GETTING DOWN TO BASICS: JUST ASK

Bob Blaney's closing technique was based entirely on Ask and Get. He never used any other. His methods were simple and often primitive:

"Jake, got an order for me today?"

"Joe, are you going to buy from me today?"

"Miriam, how about a half a carload of bacon this morning?"

"Bill, here is a special we just brought out. I think you need 200 pounds as a starter."

To a person—Jake, and Joe, and Miriam, and Bill—usually bought what Blaney asked them to buy.

Yet some selling "experts" say no salesperson should overtly ask a prospect to buy. Nonsense! Asking for business is a very high type of salesmanship, if you ask in the right way, at the right time.

Opponents believe no salesperson should ever ask a favor. But students of psychology know when you *ask* a favor, you really *do* a larger favor. When you ask a slight favor, you enhance her self-importance. She does the favor for you but actually is pleasing herself. Therefore, when you ask a person to buy, you do not weaken your case. You quite often strengthen it.

In fact, for many ace closers, Ask and Get is the favorite technique. But 99 percent urge asking for an order on every call, no matter what other closers are also utilized.

It's simple—come straight out and ask for the decision. Many prospects are just waiting to be asked. They face a basic fear of instigating commitment. You help them make the decision:

- "Can I have your authority to go ahead?"
- "When would you like delivery?"
- "You've thought this out very thoroughly, Mr. Jones. Give me your okay to put this order through, and I can promise you'll never need to defend your decision to anyone."
- "Will it be all right to get going on this, Mr. Jones?"
- "Let me suggest four cases as a practical way to start, Ms. Jones. Just okay this!"
- "Mr. Brown, you and I seem to agree this system will cut your maintenance cost significantly. The sooner we can get it installed, the sooner you can benefit from the savings. All I need is your initials."

- "I'd like to place your order on high priority. With your okay, I'll do everything possible to get your material on the job right away!"

# $A$SK AND IT SHALL BE GIVEN

Oxford Pendleton, a successful sales executive in Los Angeles, sees it this way: "I ask for the order at the earliest possible moment. If he says 'Yes,' I'm in luck. If he says 'No,' I often get 50 words on what's running through his mind. Having found out what he's thinking about, I continue my story until I can again ask for the order. The prospect either says "Yes" or has to think up another 50 words.

"This goes on and on until I close or throw in the towel. At least I can mentally say: 'That customer really had a chance to buy.' Most closing problems in selling trace back to salespeople without guts enough to force an answer. Even the Bible says: 'Ask and it shall be given to you.' You can't beat that for authority!"

Of the many tested closing techniques you place on inventory, each is ideal in its own way. Choose one for almost all conditions that arise. But at times the best closing technique is simply asking the buyer frankly and openly for the business.

The *time* you ask is important, too. First, decide which closer is the most natural and most adaptable to your selling situation. Then, try to close. Don't be dismayed if you fail with one, two, or even half-a-dozen experimental probes. As long as the opportunity continues, try to close.

If everything else fails, you always have Ask and Get. You'd be surprised at how often it flatters the buyer. Vanity is powerful and ego is a dominant factor. (If your prospect's a psychological problem, you may decide go *start* with the Ask and Get.)

# $N$ICE GUYS ASK DIRECTLY

Eldorado Reed, an office supply salesman in Lake Charles, Illinois, prided himself on simplicity. He called himself a "plain old country boy from Elgin trying to get by in the big city." He employed just one close.

"I'm a nice guy to work with. I sell office supplies at a reasonable price. Whatever you order today, I deliver tomorrow. Please tell me what you need."

Certainly it's not going to work selling speedboats, trucks, industrial equipment, or mutual funds, is it? But there are times and proposals that respond to it. Eldorado Reed proves it. Ask and Get.

## *W*HAT TO DO WHEN OTHER KEYS FAIL

Under many selling circumstances, you'll choose other closing keys over Ask and Get. Most other keys are more positive, less open to rejection than the overt asking for the order.

Occasionally, you meet a buyer who, for one reason or another, is not impressed or moved by techniques (so effective with others). This occasional customer may be

1. A suspicious person with low self-esteem. The buyer is unsure of himself in everything and hence is unable to make up his mind. If your actions increase his suspicions, he shuts up like a clam.

2. Her strong vanity makes her want to be the big number in everything. Your best appeal: play on her sense of importance.

3. The negative personality resents being controlled, guided, or led. Tell him a product is square, and he'll say it's round. Tell him it's black, and he'll swear it's white.

Ordinary techniques do not work with such hard cases. But asking them for business in the right way often does.

Sometimes you must tell such folk (The Contraries) the opposite of what you want. Phil Taggart, who sells a financial relations service to top management in Houston, says: "My Uncle Harry was a Contrary. If his wife wanted to get him out to dinner, she'd call and say she'd like to fix dinner at home. 'Oh, no,' Harry'd always say. 'I want to eat out.' "

"If she wanted to visit relatives on the East Coast, she'd suggest to Harry that they go West. 'Oh, no,' he'd reply. 'It's high time we went East.' The only way to get him to take any action: suggest the opposite."

The corollary in closing: suggest to The Contrary he or she cannot afford to buy at this time or that perhaps this product isn't right.

One chief benefit of Ask and Get: it makes difficult customers realize their self-importance. Each of us has this sense. In difficult customers, it's more highly developed. When you ask a difficult buyer for his business, you never need demean yourself. Ask for business in the right way, and you're doing the buyer a favor.

We all enjoy doing favors more than we enjoy receiving them. Doing a favor, provided it doesn't cause too much expense or trouble, brings us far more good than it brings the receiver. It protects and buoys the ego.

## *W*HEN OPPORTUNITY LOOMS: GRAB IT

You've made an appointment to see a prospect. You called to confirm and everything is okay. But when you arrive, Teresa Target walks briskly out saying: "Sorry, something came up at the last minute. I have to catch a plane."

What to do? First, you show your understanding. "I'll book another appointment. Have a nice trip," you say as you walk alongside her. Ask where she is going. A lot depends on the kind of relationship you build in advance. If she responds, what about asking for the business? What can you lose? Try for a close!

"Mrs. Target, why don't I just go ahead and install the system now? We can work out the details when you return. And, of course, we won't bill you until everything is in place and you agree it's working like a charm."

What to lose? She might say yes. At worst, you can always make another appointment.

Henry I. McGee, dynamic president of Dallas Airmotive, always told his executive staff: "Never let me hear about you making any call to a customer or prospective customer without asking for the order—no matter what stimulated your original call."

Jerry Grossman, likable manager of Wurlitzer's New York store, said it differently: "If you don't ask, you don't get."
Whatever your style, ask.

## $W$*HEN TO SKIP THE PRESENTATION STEP*

At times, skip the presentation. A presentation is a means to an end, not an end in itself. Some closers forget that.

For years, Clarissa Roget wanted a set of *Encyclopedia Americana*. One day she called to ask the Peoria office to send a representative. She told rep Junius Scale she had long wanted his product. Yet Scale went through a one-hour presentation before writing the order. Perhaps he felt he was giving better service! In this case, all he wasted was time. With other prospects, he might have wasted a sale!

If you close 10 percent of your encounters just by asking for the business, you can invest the saved time in more presentations. If you have any reason to believe your prospects are disposed to what you are selling, *ask them to buy!* On your way in, ask. Ask often. On your way out, ask again. Other ways to ask to get:

- Start with a close: "Would you like to own this fax-workstation?"
- Ask for a test: "Try one dozen of these on a test basis."
- The testimonial: "The Miller Company saved 10 percent in energy costs on this machine."
- The Door Knob Caper: act defeated; almost leave; return; then throw facts, statistics, examples into the game.
- Place a call so your prospect can talk to a satisfied customer.

## $A$*SK CLIENTS: WHAT ELSE DO YOU WANT?*

Mehdi Fakharzadeh, the millionaire insurance salesman you met earlier, takes the Ask and Get further. When he runs into a roadblock, rather than asking for the order, he asks: "Why *else* do you want to buy?"

Once Mehdi worked for weeks to get a difficult client to agree to a $250,000 policy. The backing-and-forthing was unusually long. Finally, the man agreed to take his medical examination. Even this took longer than usual. At last the answer came from the underwriting department. "Rejected. Applicant uninsurable."

A severe disappointment to Mehdi? All that work for nothing? Mehdi didn't see it that way. A believer in person-to-person encounters, Mehdi went to see the applicant. He explained the rejection in detail. He expressed his honest regret. Then he probed the man's motives.

"I know a lot of reasons why you want this policy." he said, "and they're good reasons. But isn't there something else you were trying to do?"

The client, an import-export executive, said: "Yes, I wanted to provide for my daughter and son-in-law. Now I can't."

"There is another way to do it," Mehdi said. "Suppose I come up with a plan (he always talks *plan*, never *insurance*) that provides tax savings in the event of your son-in-law's or daughter's death. I'm sure you'll agree this is desirable."

The man was interested.

Mehdi analyzed the estates of the son-in-law and daughter. Soon he came back with two policies totaling $550,000. The father signed the initial check, and policies have been in force ever since.

Mehdi more than doubled his commission over the original policy. He saw problem as opportunity.

Ed Trabulsy, sales manager at Mehdi's Metropolitan District Office in Manhattan, explains this ability:

"Closers like Mehdi just don't think negatively. Mehdi never broods over setbacks. He looks at every problem as an opportunity. He glories in problems because he's sure he can find the way out. He always does.

"He starts with native charm, and he capitalizes on it all the way. He's sincere, never tries to fool anyone. He motivates himself. His product knowledge is astounding. He spends time on each objection and he resolves it. He's the finest salesman the company has ever had."

The same principles are available to you. Analyze each problem to find the opportunity. It's always there somewhere.

## $D$ON'T FORGET POLISH AND SOCKS

Kinney Shoe stores carried socks and shoe polish for some time displayed behind the register. Some customers motivated themselves by asking for socks or polish as they checked out their shoe purchases.

Then one day an enterprising regional manager (he was new, not burdened with all the reasons why things won't work) said: "From now on, we're going to *ask* each customer to buy socks and polish. Just ask. Nothing more."

Each retail salesperson started doing just that: asking. No product benefit. Just "Would you like to pick out a pair of socks? Would you like black (or brown) polish for those shoes?"

Now as professional salesfolk know, that's not the best appeal in the world—far from it. But would you believe socks and polish sales jumped 50 percent in the stores insisting on this Ask and Get policy?

Did it cost anything? No. Did it take extra time? No. The customer was at the check-out counter anyhow. But it sure sold the product.

People will buy *if* you ask. So ask!

## $F$IVE WAYS TO HEAT UP YOUR COLD CALL

The cold call (you just drop in) is part of Ask and Get. You walk in unannounced to make an instant presentation and secure an immediate buying decision. Certainly you can't use it under all conditions or with all proposals. But where appropriate, it is powerful. Here are the five steps:

1. *Skip the formalities.* Don't introduce yourself. Start talking about your product or service at once. Pull out some strong benefit of

your product or service from the middle of your presentation, and open with this benefit: "I know that if I can show you how to eliminate losses you now incur from employee theft, you will recognize the money saving right away. Here's what I mean . . . ." Then go into your presentation.

2. *Hand the prospect a sample.* The surest way to prove reality is to reach out and touch it. The more of our five senses that are mobilized the more convinced we are. Your prospect *hears* you, she *sees* a picture or a drawing that confirms what she hears. When she *touches* it, she believes much more.

3. *Leave your business cards in the car.* When prospects ask for your business card, don't be surprised at the next comment: "We'll call you when we need something." Whop! Your card goes in the trash before the door has closed.

   Yet ignoring a request for a card is rude. Say, "Of course, I'll get you a card out of the car before I leave. By the way, may I have one of your cards." This puts the initiative back in your hands. If your prospect hands you a card, say: "Miss Jones, thank you. Before I go, there is just one thing I feel you'll want to know about . . . ." Continue with your presentation.

4. *Stick to business.* Don't be sidetracked. You may run into a person who likes everybody and talks about everything except your proposition. Keep bringing the conversation back to business.

5. Never treat cold calls as Missionary Work. Great closers do get sign-ups on the first call. You never know until you try.

# *H*UMAN NATURE AND EXPERT CLOSER

One of the nation's greatest closers, Georgeson Hodge, always said he'd been too busy closing to learn much about salesmanship. This man was a millionaire. He may not have called it closing. But he knew a great deal about human nature. Whenever he made a call, he always asked the customer to buy.

Many customers turned him down. They were not in the market. His prices were out of line. Hodge never talked back. He'd slowly pack his samples and reluctantly prepare to depart. Almost at the door, Hodge would turn back and blandly and graciously ask the customer for his business. This he did, not as a beggar, but as friend asking friend. Many, immediately after dismissing him, turned right around and gave Hodge an order.

Ask and Get, like the other closing techniques, is valuable only when practiced consistently. Asking one prospect to buy and then failing to ask the next three or four won't build your business. But asking every prospect to buy will!

# $W$HEN TO USE ASK AND GET

Is Ask and Get always indicated? No, but neither are the other closers. Further, Ask and Get is hardly ideal for certain conservative temperaments. Said Horace Lorimer, a gentleman of the old school: "At certain times, when you feel you've exhausted all other possibilities, confront the prospect and literally ask him for the order. Since its use demands a yes or no answer, use it as a last resort. After all, other closing keys are less threatening. However, given a choice between asking and not asking for the order, always ask."

Conservative Horace suits methods to his persona. But even he says: "When chips are down, ask."

Now you have your inventory of major closing keys. You're ready to add special keys.

## CLOSING LAB

*KAT:* Well, Cray, can we review the major closing keys?

*CRAY:* Sure. Remember Henry Ford told his friend, "I didn't *buy* because you didn't ask." That's *Ask and Get.*

*KAT:* Yes. I heard Jack Chase tell his sales force "You want the prospect to hit you over the head with a hammer? Then sign the order, and put it in your pocket? You do your job, let the prospect do his. Ask for the order. Ask to get." Another key is *Beyond Any Doubt.*

CRAY: You take it for granted the answer's *yes*. You are 100 percent certain—you can imagine no other outcome. The more you demonstrate this belief, the more likely the buyer will buy.

KAT: Now I have a question about *The Little Question*. Why not the Big Question?

CRAY: You ask a little question to keep the prospect from stewing about the big question—whether to buy in the first place.

KAT: Something of secondary importance (master bedroom's shape in a house). Not whether to buy the house. *The Little Question's* an action step.

CRAY: Just like the next key—*Do Something*. Nine sales in 10 should be closed by physical action.

KAT: *The Coming Event*. Are we buying futures here?

CRAY: Just the opposite. The buyer buys to *avoid* the future. The coming event is often an *undesirable* event to the buyer. But it can be highly *beneficial* to the adroit closer.

KAT: Another key—the *Third Party Endorsement*. Sounds like politics.

CRAY: It's politics and business. You get *someone else* to tell your customer to buy your product. The more respected the endorser, the greater the motivation. Get referrals from happy customers. Say: "Don't take my word for it. Listen to what happened to Joe Weaver!"

KAT: The final key taps into the most basic of human emotions—*Something for Nothing*. It's often a small concession of no great value. Free delivery? Free freight? We pay the tax?

CRAY: Right. Let's walk through the major closing keys. I'll say the key and you give me a short one-liner to remember it by. Key number one: *Ask and Get*.

KAT: If you don't ask, you don't get.

CRAY: *Beyond Any Doubt.*

*KAT:* Assume you'll get the order—act as if there's no possible doubt.

*CRAY: The Little Question.*

*KAT:* Action closes the sale.

*CRAY:* Number Five: *The Coming Event.*

*KAT:* Buy now—because the event upcoming will make you lose money or time or power.

*CRAY: Third-Party Endorsement.*

*KAT:* It's not what *you* say—it's what *they* say that counts.

*CRAY: Something for Nothing.*

*KAT:* Capitalizing human desire to get something free.

## CLOSING LAB

*KAT:* Do champions develop a sixth sense about when to close? When in doubt, try to close: it can't hurt and often works.

*CRAY:* Yes, sell yourself and then your product. First learn *when* to listen and *how* to listen. The right kind of listening is a golden foundation. Even the 25-year-pro still practices closing presentations every day. So must you, if you want to continue to make progress.

*KAT:* I'm also impressed that every buyer has an Achilles' heel. Attack where the defense is weakest. The more you know about human vulnerability, the better you close sales.

*CRAY:* And as Bob Schiffman proved in selling Cadillacs, convert your benefits to money advantage, and you're well on your way to closing.

*KAT:* I assume we will not often use all seven keys as Dave Boue did. But learn *when* to use *what* key. And be prepared to use any key as the need arises.

*CRAY:* When you get knocked out of the box, start to go and then come back to say, "Oh, one more thing." Some closers call this *The Balk.* They stop the action and start a different topic entirely. The first thing the buyer knows, he or she is back on track, okaying the order.

*KAT:* For every rule there's an exception: Ellery Jordahl stayed for dinner long after closing. He felt he'd closed too fast. He wanted to solidify with empathy.

*CRAY:* Recall Tom O'Ryan did it by being a young and innocent who didn't know you couldn't keep coming back day after day.

*KAT:* Dick Considine created an event on the spot—his trip to Rochester. But Dick's technique illustrates another key— he also was using the *Do Something* key.

*CRAY:* Frequently ace closers draw on more than one key in the same close. Tom Tierney, who sells a business consulting service, announces he'll have four people there tomorrow: *The Coming Event.* But he gets there by calling on several other closers—the *Beyond Any Doubt* key and a variation on the *Little Question.*

*KAT:* Doesn't the Albert Lasker story illustrate capitalizing on *The* (unavoidable) *Coming Event?*

*CRAY:* You might also be interested in his closing appeal to the chairman at that meeting. Lasker said: "I'll make you *rich.*

*KAT:* Wasn't the chairman already rich?

*CRAY:* Remember what Babs Paley said: "You can never be too rich or too thin!"

*KAT:* There you have it: complete advice and experience from the best closers in America. Go get 'em!

## PART THREE

# THE MASTER CLOSER IN ACTION

You're now fully equipped with tools. In this part, you're ready for the *field*—going out into the territory with the best closers. You'll experience cracking the hard cases, the dedicated holdouts, the creative nay-sayers. In the process, you'll see why the champion closer becomes an accomplished business actor—how power words turn prospects into buyers. This leads you into *conversational* and *consultive* selling, the diplomatic branch of "the world's best paid hard work."

Now you're armed with theory, technique, and field experience—ready to make your own luck in closing sales.

# CHAPTER SEVENTEEN

# Twenty-Nine Special Closings That Rock Holdouts and Crack Hardcases

Rudyard Kipling's advice on how to compose a poem: "There are nine and sixty ways of constructing tribal lays, / And every single one of them is right."

Ditto with closing sales. Anything that works is good.

Thousands of successful salespeople use hundreds of closing methods. One characteristic they all share: the willingness to try, try, try again.

Joe Bowlin of Fort Worth's unusual method: he carries a Polaroid color camera in a special pocket. At closing time, he sticks an order blank under the prospect's nose and says:

"I want to leave you a picture of the most important thing you did today."

It works.

A. H. Rosenthal, the great salesmanship scholar, told of a salesman who began to sob at closing time *because he was doing the prospect such a favor.* Strange? Yes. Not applicable often? Right.

Put your special—sometimes strange—closers on file. You already possess seven major secret keys—the great motivators. Add these special closers. Draw down on this cache as and when needed.

Start by smoking out objections. You can't really start to close until you get a path to follow. Objections come about because

- The prospect won't part with money until he's sure he's getting his money's worth.

- The prospect resists change. She must be given good reasons for change.

- No objections means no interest. The more genuine the objections, the greater the interest.

So only after you've uncovered objections do you start employing these closing keys:

**1. The Direct Close.** Simply ask for the order: "I've approved the specifications and the price, Mr. Smith. Read this and okay it right here. I'll give you a copy." Or more subtlely: "Is there any reason why we can't get together on this right now, Mr. Smith?"

There is nothing offensive about asking for the order. Faint heart ne'er won fair maid.

**2. Give a Choice, not a Chance.** Instead of giving the buyer a chance to buy from you, give him a choice. Don't ask him *if* he will buy; ask him: "Which color do you prefer?" "Would you like to pay for this in 30 days or 90?" "Shall we ship by truck or air?"

After all questions are answered, all voiced reservations resolved, assume the prospect is ready to sign. Instead of asking directly, ask roundabout: "Would you like us to handle the financing?" "What would be the most convenient time for installation?" A positive response to any of these questions is almost the same as signing.

If you're still not there, ask for objections. Most will be minor. However, if you persist, your questioning will usually elicit the big one, the really important roadblock to the close. Try to get the prospect to talk about *the* objection. Ask: "Besides this, is there anything else standing in the way of a decision?" (Of course, this key is a variation on two major keys: Beyond Any Doubt and the Little Question).

**3. The Blitz.** This approach put undecided buyer on the spot with a spate of questions. Place her in a position difficult not to say yes. Ask: "Do you want six dozen of these, or do you think you can use eight dozen?" Keep firing questions: "Do you want this in the large or the small size?" "How soon must you get delivery?" Confusion in the buyer's mind (you put it there) works in your favor. When she answers yes, she will buy.

Or ask direct questions. Prospects feel comfortable answering because they think you're on the way out. You just want to know why your prospect has decided not to buy.

**4. *The Half Nelson*** is a contingency close. Prospect: "Maintenance costs are too high." Closer: "Just suppose I can get you one year of free maintenance—would that shift the balance in our favor? If I can solve this problem for you, do we have an agreement?"

This question implies *reciprocal* commitment. "Yes" means "yes" to the sale. Clever maneuver? Maybe. But you're dead if you renege on *your* solution—that's part of the bargain!

**5. *Mention Money Casually.*** What's more natural than closing on a money note? Say: "I'm sure you want the cash discount!" Ivan Daughtery, of Elmira, New York, taught his salespeople to ask: "Do you want to pay by credit card or check?" Sales increased 13 percent.

**6. *The Ego/Profit Close.*** "It's obvious you know a great deal about the grocery business. You've orchestrated every square foot of this store to make a profit. Ms. Stevenson, our products also provide you with a good profit margin. In fact, our profit will exceed your store's average profit per square foot. And they sell like hotcakes. This high turnover will further increase your profits, which is important to you." (Pause, when no response, continue.)

"Given your store traffic, and our projected sales of these products, I suggest you buy (products and quantities). This will meet customer demand for the next two months, plus the profit you expect out of your products. May we go ahead on this?"

**7. *Puppy Dog Demo.*** Walking past a pet store, you're stopped by a small quivering puppy with big black eyes. Before you know it, you're inside. The astute salesperson hands you the puppy. That's the puppy dog close.

An appliance dealer sold television sets using this technique. He insisted that friends and neighbors take home new TVs for a couple of weeks! When the store owner called to see how they liked the product, could they tell him to pick them up? No more than you could hand back the puppy!

Get your product in the prospect's hands for a free trial. It's magic.

**8. *The Name Spelling Close.*** The language's most charming word is the prospect's own name. Wise closers spotlight the name-spelling close: Does the prospect want full name or initials? Does she use Ms., Mrs., or Miss? Few prospects can resist this.

**9. *The Win-Win Negotiation.*** Most sales negotiations focus on two major themes: value and price. In their quest for more value at lower cost, prospects often put heavy pressure on the salesperson. When this happens find ways for everyone to get a piece of the pie.

- "If we could find a way to eliminate the need for a backup machine, would you be happy with this arrangement?"

- "You know I can't give you a discount, but I could defer billing until the end of the month. That I'll be happy to do."

**10. *The Columbo.*** The prospect has said no. You're getting ready to go. At the door Columbo-style, you say: "Oh, by the way, Mr. Watkins, one more thing. I almost forgot to mention something very important. If you place your order this month, you'll get one case free. You simply cannot afford to pass up a savings like that, can you?"

**11. *Appeal to Pride.*** Paint a picture: the customer occupying a place of pride. Make it vivid: "Imagine how you feel driving up in this family van!"

**12. *Future Dating.*** Prospect is not ready to buy now? Sew up an order for the future. Pin down delivery three months or even a year from now. Better than letting a competitor walk away with it.

**13. *The Pure Profit Close.*** You've been working on the close for half an hour. The prospect seems sold, but keeps trying to put you off. Try this: "Mr. Prospect, you and I are both involved in an effort to make money. I don't deny it. If I conclude this sale, I make a profit. My profit, however, will be small compared with your profit, which will be continuous. Your profit will accrue as long as you continue to use this product.

"Your reason and judgment are satisfied. Your deepest feelings tell you this is the decision you ought to make. Your judgment is your court of last resort. And any time you fail to act in accordance with your own good judgment, you fail to serve your own best interests. (Pause) If you were my own brother, Mr. Prospect, I'd say this to you: 'Buy this.'" If he still vacillates, continue:

"Really, Mr. Prospect, don't hesitate. He who hesitates in the face of a sure and certain course of action deprives himself of countless benefits. Okay this now, and you'll get the satisfaction of knowing you've done the right thing. You will have treated yourself with justice."

**14. *Do Something Special.*** Many buyers, seeing themselves as Master of the Universe, require something special—a price no one else is getting. For example, say: "Since you are such a big buyer, Mrs. Brown, I'll tell you what I am going to do . . . ."

With some buyers this is the best technique of all. One buyer told Sandra Compton unless he got a price lower than anyone else, "forget about it." She showed him the list price and then quoted him a lower cost—exactly the price she had intended for him all along. He signed.

In fast-moving financial negotiations, a bird in the hand is worth *at least* a bird and 10 percent in the bush. (The *present value* of money over the value of the same sum at some date in the future.) This is also true in other selling.

**15. *Pros and Cons*** (also called The Ben Franklin; in the United Kingdom, The Duke of Wellington). With analytical buyers who have difficulty making up their minds, take out a sheet of paper and write the pros and cons of your propositions, side by side. Naturally, you favor the pros. But no whitewash.

Tell the customer you realize he has an important decision to make and he wants to make the right choice. So encourage him to write "Yes" reasons on the left and "No" on right. Help him remember the "Yes" benefits—he's on his own for the "No" list.

Make sure the prospect agrees with each listed item.

Admit certain shortcomings, but more than offset them with pluses. He wants evidence. Give it to him in full measure. After a while, it becomes apparent: the negative reasons were not that important after all. He buys.

**16. *Socratic Syllogisms.*** These sometimes convince stubborn buyers.

"It *must be* clear to a man of reason," Bob Pachter says (and who can resist such flattery?), "that if such and such is the case, thus and so must be, as day follows night. Therefore, there's only one thing for us to decide—how soon do you want these books in your library? Will next Wednesday be soon enough?"

When the buyer starts asking questions about delivery date, color selection, length of contract, or installation cost, she's thinking seriously about buying. Accommodate her. Tie the knot on the package.

**17. "If the Office Approves, Do We Have an Agreement?"** One of the cleanest ways to dramatize a discount to your prospect is call your office. If you can get "permission" from anybody, literally *anybody*, this somehow sanctifies the transaction.

Janice Mueller uses this. She's called nearly everyone including the firm's president to get "permission" for a price break. Sometimes she has trouble with the maintenance man, but no one else ever refused her. Before calling, she always boxes the client in: "If they approve this, do we have a deal?"

**18. Summarize all your plus points,** even to writing them down. Say: "This is what you get." It is impressive. The prospect sees an array of benefits marching toward him.

"What more is there to say?" you ask. "It's all here in black and white. You're responsive to benefits like this, aren't you?"

Or "Ms. Customer, let me put all the parts back together for you. Remember when we first met, I told you that my company knows what it's doing, and that we have the best product anywhere. Well, now I think you can see and understand what I was talking about. Not only have you looked at the benefits, but you've actually seen them with your own eyes. Wouldn't you agree that my product is the answer to your need (profit, cost savings, production efficiency, etc)?"

Or "Let's look at this decision from the benefit angle, OK? The first benefit you get is the higher trade-in value—that means no down payment. The second benefit you get is our maintenance contract free for the first year, which saves you $450. The third benefit: this machine will produce at a 17 percent higher rate, which means you earn more money every single week. Aren't these three benefits enough reason for going ahead with this? Or would you like me to go on?"

### 19. The "I'll think it over" close.

Motorist: I'll think it over.

Saleswoman: I'm delighted. I'd hate you to make a snap decision about an important thing like this. And you wouldn't be thinking it over unless you were really interested.

Motorist: Yes, that's right.

Saleswoman: So you'll have all the facts in your mind while you're considering, perhaps you could tell me what it is I haven't satisfied you about? Is it fuel consumption?

Now you're back to overcoming the remaining objective—and on to your close.

People love stories. "I can appreciate how you feel, Mr. Prospect. In your position, I'd feel that same concern. I do remember, just last year, when Colman Handy felt that way. But he decided to lease our vehicle for six months, and within the first few weeks the most amazing thing happened..." You *put the prospect into the picture*, to stress the success of the earlier buyer.

**20. Callback Close.** You're back for a second try. Start: "Last time I was here, there was something important I forgot to tell you." Then tell the prospect something new, adding, "Let me review briefly the things we talked about last time." Then make the entire presentation again. Use comments like "as you remember" and "you'll recall" and "we agreed that." Then proceed with a normal close and ask for the order. (Never ask if she *did* think it over! Whatever her answer, you can't win!)

**21. The Whispering Close.** One high-volume purchasing agent says an effective supplier whispers at moment of closing, as if letting the buyer in on a dark secret.

"I leaned forward—not wanting to miss a word," the buyer related. "The salesman continued to whisper. I continued to follow his words. Before I knew it, he asked me to buy. Before I knew it, I whispered I would!"

**22.  *The Physical Action Close.*** You ask the prospect physically to do something: "Check the features you'd like" or "pick the locations where you want to initiate the system." Depending on prospect temperament, choose:

- "Let me call the office to see if we can ship the merchandise next week."

- Or: "Now I'll call the office . . . ," and so on (more assertive).

**23.  *The "Why Not" Close.*** After several closing attempts, try "Why Not." It often isolates the one real objection:

- "Mr. Daniels, if I understand you correctly, you like our convenient access, flexible delivery, ease of operation, and full message security and backup. But there seems to be something troubling you. Tell me what it is, and I'll do my best to clarify."

- "Ms. Garson, if I understand you correctly, you like our style, our deliveries are good, and we offer superior markup and discount programs. But there seems to be something troubling you. Please tell me what it is, so I can clarify it."

Once you isolate and resolve the principal cause for delay, the buyer usually moves on to sign.

**24.  *Lost Sale Close.*** "Before I leave, may I apologize for being such an inept presenter. I still have a lot to learn. I am convinced this product could benefit you, but I cannot find words that express what I feel. That is unfortunate because you stand to benefit—if I could just say it! One favor that would help me: tell me what I did wrong, so I don't make the same mistake again."

The prospect tells you the reason for not buying. You respond: "You mean, I didn't cover that point?" You apologize—*mean* it—and answer his concerns. Then, of course ask for the order again. When you apologize, be sincere. Otherwise you lose credibility and are soon out the door.

**25.  *Sharp Angle Closing.*** Too often we answer a question too simply. Questions are actually buying signals. If you answer too quickly, you're scuttling a wonderful opportunity to close.

Question: Can I be billed weekly? Answer: Do you want to be billed weekly?

Can I start with the basic package? Answer: Would you prefer to start that way?

**26. *"I Want to Think It Over" Close.*** "That's fine, Ms. Johnson. Obviously you wouldn't take your time thinking this over unless you were really interested, would you? I'm sure you're not telling me this just to get rid of me, so may I presume that you will give it careful consideration?"

She agrees to do so.

"Just to clarify my thinking, what phase of the plan do you want to think over? Is it . . .?" Get that first "is it?" out *before* you pause. Otherwise, she says "the whole thing" and you're dead! Your "is" question technique now becomes a summary close. Reduce "I'll think it over" to a *specific* objection you can handle. You cannot handle an intangible "I'll think it over."

**27. *The Silent Close.*** One sundries salesman demonstrates power of the silent close. From morning till night, Gus West (I swear it!) didn't say a dozen words. He merely shows merchandise. He points to this feature and that. He demonstrates. He lets the products speak for themselves.

Then he starts writing up the order and inquires: "How many?"

Bob Pachter is a strong advocate of silence. As often as not, after completing his presentation, he takes out an order blank, marks an X on it, and says: "Here."

Simply start filling out the order! It makes it *easy* for the customer to buy—and requires action *not* to buy. Anytime your prospect finds it easier to move forward she's likely to proceed toward your goal.

You believe in your product or you wouldn't be selling it. You know when a sale is made, *both* parties benefit. That being the case, you owe a responsibility to your prospect—to help her buy.

So don't make your close a sudden drastic step. *Glide* into it! Or, as Pachter sees it, "Sell with robotic transmission." "Crowd them with silence and they will sell themselves," Bob explains.

Always remember, too, in closing you can't lose what you don't have. When in doubt, ask for the order.

**28. *Bring in the Brass.*** Some prospects are terribly impressed by authority. The very same offer coming from someone higher up sounds better to them. Further, your sales manager may see or hear something you overlooked. At very least, bringing in your manager is an excellent reason to make one more attempt to close.

Besides, nobody wants to look like a numbskull in front of the brass. That's true for your prospect. It's true for *you!* You'll do a better job of selling while your manager is present. In the strictest sense, your sales manager may not solve the problem. However, the *presence* can alter conditions. Maybe the prospect can now speak from a different feeling. Maybe different rapport with this new person. Or a more creative *outlook.* Maybe the prospect will think of resources not considered before.

**29. *Use an Honorary Sales Manager.*** Auto salespeople use this device. The salesperson does everything possible to close. Just before the customer walks out, he says: "Just a minute, please. This is the best deal I can make you, but let me get my sales manager. Maybe she can do better for you." Then the "manager" comes on with better financing. With different customers, the two roles will be reversed.

In using these techniques when you ask a closing question—keep totally silent. Don't say a word. There is no pressure like silence. If you don't speak first, the customer must. He will either say *yes* or *no.*

By now you possess the equipment to become an expert closer. Your next step: use your closing keys until they become a natural function second only to breathing.

# CHAPTER EIGHTEEN

# How to Close When All Seems Lost

So far in this book, you may have thought: "We're treating prospects like pawns to be pushed around on a chessboard at the salesperson's whim."

Let's admit it right out: prospects often prove they're not pawns—they're flesh and blood. Your buyers are often cantankerous, difficult, unreasoning, implacable, mysterious. Sometimes, instead of yielding to your closing logic, they set up barriers. They won't buy.

There you are, feeling as useful as a side pocket on a pig, merely a conversationalist, not a salesperson. That's your predicament until you learn how to retrieve the lose sale. A good closer can breathe life back into a dead sale, turning a prospect's flat *no* into a gratifying *yes*.

## YOUR ACE IN THE HOLE: ASK WHY

The most important factor in reviving dead sales is *persistence*. It has proved its mettle time and again. If you are positive enough, persistent enough, forceful enough in an acceptable way, the buyer will often buy—even if he or she fully intended not to buy. But Hamlet said it for us all: "Aye, there's the rub!" Unless your persistence is *adroit* and *skillful* and *inoffensive,* you may annoy the buyer and blow your chances of closing.

Too many salespeople believe that merely hanging on makes sales. It doesn't. But if you are *smilingly* persistent, you will not offend the buyer. If you submit new ideas, new reasons, and new arguments, you can intrigue the buyer.

Your prospect has just said she doesn't want to buy—with emphasis. She leaves no doubt: she means it. But are you, a wise salesperson, downcast? Not for a second. You know it doesn't mean the sale is lost. It only means you must bring in new sales ammunition, new ideas, interesting new angles. Say something new. Don't tiresomely repeat the same appeal over and over again.

To pull the sale out of the fire, be prepared with both a primary and a secondary presentation—the first to win initial interest and to try to close, the second to shift gear if she decides not to buy. Launch a reserve attack when your first onslaught is turned back.

When a customer says he doesn't want to buy, don't take this refusal personally. A simple question—"Why not?"—can often uncover a prospect's reason. Your customer may have misunderstood the terms. Or imagined a problem that can be easily resolved.

That little word *why* is an ace in the hole. Ask *why* the buyer believes such and such, *why* she isn't ready to buy. *Why* is a pleasantly persistent word. It pins the buyer down to cases, and then usually disarms her.

Other valuable questions: "What can I do to change your mind?" or "Are you satisfied with the quality discount I quoted?" Or:

# $A$SK: "WHAT DID I DO WRONG?"

Joe Skinnerbaum, a $50,000-a-year salesman, always asks the no-buyer this question while packing up to leave: "Ms. Carlson, would you mind doing me a favor?"

Usually the prospect says: "Not at all." We all like to do favors. Besides, in this case, the prospect feels the danger of buying is past. After all, isn't the salesperson packing up to go?

"Would you mind telling me what I did wrong?" asks Joe. "The fact that you didn't buy was my fault entirely, I am sure of it. I know you've decided against buying, so I am not going to mention that anymore. But if you'll tell me what my weakness is, it might help me talk to others. Believe me, I'd appreciate this as a personal favor."

Two out of five of his buyers, by actual count, sell themselves in the process of telling Joe why they didn't buy.

Another way to retrieve lost sales takes more courage: turn the buyer's refusal into scorn and ridicule. Use it with great finesse or it'll turn against you. John Barnhart uses this technique deftly in selling top-of-the-line encyclopedias to mothers.

The woman says she decided not to buy. John says nothing. He just stands there as if dazed. Then he says: "Mrs. Johnson, you've just told me you're not going to buy these reference books for your children. Do you know what you're really saying? You're actually saying you're willing to let your children struggle on without every help you can give them. Who knows, you may be needlessly handicapping them in getting on in the world. You're telling me you're willing to let those children struggle against odds! When just ten cents a day would give them a better chance!

"But I don't think you meant that, Mrs. Johnson. It's a dime a day against the handicap of inadequate preparation. You ought to be willing to invest that to give those children a right start in life."

Strong language? You bet, but what does he have to lose?

"Most don't seem to resent it, and it saves one sale out of five," John declared.

Mack Binney uses this same technique in selling office equipment. "No, of course, you don't want this equipment," Mack says. "If you did want it, you'd be using it now. But, tell me, do you really know *why* you don't want it?"

*Why* again.

## *T*AKING CALCULATED RISKS

When Robert Hawkins, who sells radio communications systems for Motorola, was presenting to the field service organization of a national equipment supply house, he insisted that Motorola's one-way paging system could improve service and cut work force needs. A purchasing agent shrugged him off. Hawkins went above him to a vice president and got grudging permission for a one-year study of the company's service coverage and performance in 20 cities.

When Hawkins completed the study, which showed the need for a paging system, he still didn't receive an order. So he offered a follow-up: an intensive three-month test of the paging system in a single city.

"For 90 days," says Hawkins, "a day never went by when I didn't spend some time with the prospect." Hawkins even helped the dispatcher design more efficient routes, while soothing the ruffled servicemen. "They were afraid the dispatcher would become an ogre in controlling their every move," he says. Finally convinced, the company decided to go nationwide with the Motorola paging system. A lost sale revised, not once but twice.

Sometimes, such indecision can go too far. At times, like the veteran poker player, you must say: "Mister, I'm calling your hand." That's what Olivetti's James Schlinkert did.

"To close a tough sale," he says, "you must establish yourself—not the buyer—as the authoritative person." Schlinkert ran up against a small corporation of five people who needed an accounting system.

"We had them all at our office one evening and presented our solution to their problem," says Schlinkert. "They were a hard-nosed lot that had evaluated every other accounting system available. After a couple of hours of haggling over a $15,000 sale, I finally shut off the machine, put the key in my pocket, and threatened to throw them out of my office. Immediately, they became docile and signed the contract. I had to take a calculated risk. The need and solution had been established."

In the words of World War II's flamboyant General George S. Patton, Jr: "I do not believe in taking chances. I do take calculated risks, which is not the same thing."

## *C*LOSING THE FEMALE WRESTLER

What do you do when your prospect *looks* and *sounds* like a female wrestler?

Says Gregory Jaworowski, quality home remodeler based in Gilbertsville, PA. "Give her plenty of line, let her wear herself down."

In Wayne, PA, Jaworowski rang Roz Fenstermacher's doorbell. A neighbor had said: "She needs work done on her house."

The front door burst open to reveal a 6-foot-3/270-pound behemoth. Jaworowski gulped. The homeowner growled, thrust out a giant paw, and shouted: "Call me Roz! I'll tell you right off: just because I'm a widow who lives alone, you're not going to *cheat* me!"

Jaworowski immediately seized on "the only possible strategy"giving Roz lots of line. She grabbed it:

- She wanted a new picture window installed
- Plus exterior siding
- References from past customers
- Names of building remodeling suppliers

She then adjourned the tourney for a week "to get you checked out."

Most prospects check one reference or none. But Roz called every customer and asked pointedly: "Did he cheat you?"

At encounter number two, the remodeler found Roz out back operating post hole diggers. She reported—grudgingly—that "nobody said anything bad about you."

"The window you want costs $943," Greg told Roz. "We don't mark this up. But we need the $943 now to place the order. It takes three to four weeks to get delivery."

"I'm not *paying* you *nothing*," Roz said, crouching.

"That's fine, Roz," he said. "Here are the measurements. You buy your own window. We'll put it in." Jaworowski recalls: "For the first time she believed I wasn't trying to cheat her."

The window came. "How much did you pay?" Greg asked. $1,100," Roz said.

He *could* have pointed out his quote was only $943. But at times, *silence* is a wonderful choice. He installed the window and the siding on a $1,971 job. Roz paid. She also gave him fine referrals. All became customers.

"They were afraid *not* to," Jaworowski concludes "fear is a powerful motivator."

In all fairness, he recalls, "we barely broke even on the Roz sale"—because of the time she took. But the referrals were solid gold.

So when you run into behemoth buyers, keep giving them line as long as you keep getting closer to closing.

# Relate a running narrative

When the buyer says no with a steel eye, stop the action and tell a story.

Ellerbe Hobbson, one of the nation's master salesmen, supplies sales aids to retailers. The buyer, George P. Jones, has just told Hobbson he's decided not to buy.

"I am glad you're so candid, Mr. Jones," Hobbson says. "I admire a forthright person. Besides, your conviction shows you've thought about what I was telling you and are honestly convinced you do not need this service.

"That reminds me of the time I called on Abel Clemenson of Clemenson Motors. He brought up the same point. He's a Victory dealer same as you are. He has eight people working in sales, a few more than you do.

"Mr. Clemenson said: 'Hobbson, I don't think my crew will read and apply your material.' Then he said, 'Just a moment, I see it's different from other services. I like its pocket size and indexing features. It gets right down to real problems. If only one idea gets across to one of my people, it'll make a big profit on my small investment.' Mr. Clemenson bought of his own free will.

"Now, Mr. Jones," concludes Hobbson, "what this service is doing for Mr. Clemenson, what it's doing for Mr. Grimm in Chicago, what it's doing for Mr. Hackett in Grand Rapids, what it's doing for all these organizations—it will also do for you. Will you just initial this form for me, please?"

The running narrative brings prospects around to buying, perhaps better than any other technique. The narrative revives the sale and closes it.

The good closer doesn't cringe when the prospect delays buying or decides not to buy. Recognize *no* for what it is—a lack of understanding. Then get to work, fill the knowledge gap, rescue the sale, and close it!

# COMBATTING "I'LL THINK IT OVER"

Really good closers make only one call per prospect. They don't think about callbacks. Bob Pachter says frankly to his prospect: "We are going to decide this today. I won't see you again."

When closer Patricia Barry hears "See me later, I'll think it over," she sees it as a challenge.

"Most sales are made because you don't take the first 'come back later' seriously," Barry says, "Your prospect is hesitant because he's undecided. Push his 'come back later' right into his face. Ignore it. Move in with a profit idea.

"Accept the challenge. Convince the prospect he cannot afford to wait. You can do this if you've analyzed his needs. Your prospect is interested in *his* needs—not yours.

"A genuine interest in fitting your product to his needs will prove you want him to benefit from what you are offering. If he continues to hesitate, keep showing him where it's to his advantage to buy now. Determine when you have aroused enough desire to make the sale."

*I'll think it over* is not an honest resistance. Refuse to take it seriously. Keep pushing, pushing, pushing until you get the order. That's what topnotch salesfolk the world over do.

# THE VALUE OF PURE REPETITION

A salesperson selling a special tool to oilfield construction crews called on one cantankerous foreman 19 times—no sale each time.

"Young feller, I'd like to know why you keep coming to see me since I never buy," the roughneck chief asked.

"That's why I keep coming back," the determined seller said. "And I'll keep on coming until you buy. I'm convinced you need this tool."

The prospect gave up.

"Enough!" he said. "I suppose you may as well send me a trial order. Looks like I've got no choice."

P.S. He's still using the tool—which turned out to be a boon on the job. Chalk up one for pure repetition.

Joanne Newport is an energetic young seller of ad space in Charleston, West Virginia. She closes by assuming the prospect didn't understand—never that he or she doesn't want to buy.

The buyer has just said *no* and is ushering Newport out. She stops him.

"I guess I didn't make it clear," she says. "I'm sorry. Now what this is—." She then starts her entire presentation from the beginning. Often that does it, and Joanne walks out with a signed ad order. Some buyers still say "no." Patiently, she starts again at the beginning and goes into it all again. After three times, even the stalwarts falter.

"It's my fault," she says. "I should have been clearer. Now what we have—."

Doesn't she rub some prospects wrong? Theoretically, perhaps. But she's very well liked. She sells a lot of ad space by assuming her buyer didn't understand and, once the buyer does understand, will buy—naturally.

## $C$*LOSING WHEN EVERYTHING GOES WRONG*

Would that every sale wanted to be closed! But some sales don't want to be closed. You know that. But you can fan the breath of life into such a sale—and then close it.

Folksinger Burl Ives sings an old English ditty where "every durn thing went wrong, went wrong, every durn thing went wrong!" You and I know sales where "every durn thing" goes wrong. Instead of being compliant, the buyer is stubborn. Rather than doing what she should do, she goes off on a tangent and upsets your plans. Instead of saying *yes* when bringing the matter to a head, she turns you down flat.

In spite of all your knowledge of how to close, you draw a *no*. Your problem is to revive interest and get the buyer back on the track, in spite of the unwillingness. How?

Often the best way: simply refuse to hear the "no." Go right on with your presentation. You've already learned it's important to assume you're going to close and keep that attitude right on through the sale.

When if you ignore the *no* and keep right on, something you say the second time may intrigue the buyer. Many times you *can* close after a definite rejection, provided you courageously get the buyer back into the picture.

Sometimes, however, the buyer bristles at your insistence. Reduce this risk by keeping your demeanor strictly professional. If the buyer give you a firm no a second time, do not ignore it any longer. Here are other ways to stay in the ball game:

# $A$PPLYING THE CLOSING BALK

In baseball, the pitcher walks up to the mound, goes through the motions of starting a pitch, stops midway, throws the ball to a base—trying to trap a runner. This is a balk.

In closing, you apply the balk much the same way.

The buyer says no sale, not once but twice, and that's that. An unwise salesperson argues, making the buyer more determined not to buy than ever.

The smart salesperson never runs that risk, but applies the balk. When the buyer says no for the second time, get to your feet and say: "Well, you're the doctor."

Start packing samples. You appear to be in a hurry, which gratifies the buyer. The buyer knows as long as you're on the scene, he may buy something. Start for the door, put your hand on the knob, and then, as if you just remembered something important, say: "By the way," and launch into a subject far removed from the product or the sale—some subject, if possible, you know will interest the buyer. Before you know it, you've switched the subject back to business, and before long you're seated at the buyer's desk, unpacking samples!

# $H$OLD BACKUP PLAN IN RESERVE

In selling sales promotion ideas, it's good practice to base your recommendation on carefully acquired trade and consumer information. If it is a real humdinger, it may carry the whole presentation with it.

On the other hand, it is risky to stake your whole capital on one bet. So have some other ideas in reserve, in case, as the presentation progresses, your pet idea faces hard going. Be quick to recognize the inevitable, and slide smoothly into idea number two.

But don't abandon your position too fast. Prospects have a disagreeable habit of raising objections just to see if you mean what you say. One big automobile dealer's standard reaction to any idea presented was "It stinks." Then he'd sit back and see how the seller would handle *that*. He'd roar with laughter when the closer stuck to her guns. He usually ended by buying the idea, too.

Closing requires tact, knowledge of people, a sure instinct for when discretion is the better part of valor, but also ability to push the hang-tough button.

Chuck Fears, a leading life insurance salesman, is indomitable. When he runs into a situation where the sale seems lost, Fears uses shock treatment.

"Before the prospect is ready for it, I flash an application and ask him to sign it," Fears says. "Quite taken aback by my rush, chances are he signs."

"Then I tell him it's not a contract until I have a check. I ask him for one. Usually he draws the line."

"Then I play my ace card: 'Here, you take this application blank. I want you to put it in your safe deposit with your own other valuables.'

"He wants to know why. My answer: So your wife can see how close you came to relieving your family of all financial worries. So your children can see how close you came to providing them with a college education."

That usually does it. The prospect is glad to make out a check.

"I don't know how many sales I have closed this way," says Fears. "It must run into the thousands."

It does take courage. But without courage, what right have you to call yourself a closer? As that great American film personality W. C. Fields once said: "The time has come to grasp the bull firmly by the tail and look the situation square in the face."

# $A$DMIT THE UNTHINKABLE

Irving P. (Swifty) Lazar, a four-decade legend as a showbiz agent, is a lawyer by training, but he describes himself as a salesman. In the 1950s, Lazar bet Humphrey Bogart he could close five deals for Bogart before dinner one day.

He did. Bogart paid up and gave Lazar his famous nickname—Swifty.

Says the diminutive Lazar: "I'm proud to be the prince of pitch. I'm a salesman. When I'm in New York, I'm worried about who's selling what in Hong Kong. When I'm in Hong Kong, I'm wondering who's selling what in Moscow."

In selling book rights to publishers, Lazar takes a hard line: "Before I go back to the Coast, I want a firm offer." If the publisher turns him down, which happens even to a legend, Lazar voices the unthinkable:

"What's the worst thing that could happen, Mr. Publisher?" he says. "The worst is we don't sign an agreement. You'll still be around. So will I."

By appearing offhand, in effect, saying who needs his sale anyhow? Lazar whets the buyer's appetite. After all, if he's not eager to sell, does he have a competitive offer just as good? (In poker, veteran players say: "Scared money cannot win." The same holds true in selling.)

Lazar then bounces right back and starts talking about the values of his property. He's a champion closer.

"If you keep moving, you won't get hit with a hunk of pie with a brick in it," he says. "If you stop, someone's going to get you. People who stand still are liable to get run over by people who don't."

# $W$HEN TO USE MONEY: THE UNIVERSAL LANGUAGE

Pam Pearson is a dynamic saleswoman who offers decorative accessories to retailers in Texas. Pearson closes sales after other reps have packed up and left the retail fray. One department store buyer was downright rude.

"I don't like your products," she said. "I'll never buy."

"Well, you may not, Miss Grimm," Pearson said. "But the public does. So much so, they sell themselves."

"Humph!" said Miss Grimm and terminated the conversation.

Once a month, for the next 15 months, Pearson called on Miss Grimm—each time with another story about how well her products were selling in such-and-such a store.

Finally, it became clear: personal dislike aside, it was not good business to ignore a product other stores were making money on. Miss Grimm placed her first order.

At last accounting, Miss Grimm had bought $113,000 worth of products in one year—and volume continues to rise. "She's become my largest customer," Pearson says.

When the buyer doesn't like the product, talk money—the universal language. It closes sales when all seems lost.

# CHAPTER NINETEEN

# Closing on Outrageous Objections

Sometimes experienced salespeople get turned down cold where a novice—not knowing better—will win. When all else fails, return in manner to those innocent days. It often works.

Tom O'Ryan is a legendary salesman in transit advertising. He rose to become the best-known name in his industry. It wasn't always that way. Back when O'Ryan first started selling transit advertising, for instance, he was assigned a territory in Georgia and the Carolinas. O'Ryan will never forget his first prospect—a bakery famous for Craig's Honey Bread. On Monday, O'Ryan called on the president.

"Young man, we've never used your advertising, and we don't intend to start now," the baker said.

On Tuesday, O'Ryan was back with a smile—and a new advertising idea. No sale.

He came back Wednesday, Thursday, and Friday.

On Saturday, he arrived at noon. The proprietor was getting ready to close for half holiday. At this point, O'Ryan didn't even know all the advantages of his service.

"I've been taught to answer all sorts of objections," he said, spreading his sales literature on the table. "It's all in here somewhere. Anything you ask I'm sure we can find—even if I don't know the answer."

It was a naive statement. No experienced salesperson would have said it. Yet the baker looked at the literature, back at the determined O'Ryan, then sighed: "Well, this looks like something I'm going to have to have. Reckon you'd better sign me up."

O'Ryan wrote up his first customer.

"After that, I started *selling* advertising," O'Ryan said. He soon turned his Irish brogue into a plus. People remembered him. He became a distinctive personality and sell he did. Soon, O'Ryan ranked number one in the nation. He didn't know novices aren't likely to lead the pack.

"Nobody explained the averages to me," O'Ryan recalled. "I tried to sell one contract a day. I thought that was expected."

Ace salesman or not, O'Ryan always retained some of that early innocence. It's a good quality to go back to when you get a turndown.

Ask the buyer what you need to do to sell him. Ask what benefit you should be stressing. Be naive. It closes sales.

# BASICS FOR SCOTCHING OBJECTIONS

Real objections, gold to the skilled closer, establish the floor of reality all successful negotiation must be based upon. The prospect may indeed be checking out three or four suppliers and you are first. Perhaps the price really is much higher than the prospect anticipated. Many people do not dare to make an important decision without consulting a boss or spouse. Should you interfere with these practices? No. Real objections are open invitations to help.

Your first task is to help the prospect articulate the real reason for hesitation. If you assume you know the cause, you'll be wrong a good percentage of the time. So ask. If the objection is real, answer it and close. If the objection is a smokescreen, get the real objection out where you can deal with it and ask: "You must have a reason for saying that. May I ask what it is?"

No one with a legitimate buying need will refuse to answer. Asking for the prospect's reason will often air the true objection. Then you can ask: "If I can solve that problem, can we move ahead with my product (or service)?"

You will get either a yes or a no. If yes, close the sale. If no, ask why again. This time express puzzlement and ask for clarification. Remember, you are helping the customer to ease discomfort. The win-win game is to resolve the customer's doubt by helping him or her decide.

When prospects fear they won't get the best possible deal, you must win their trust. Even the most difficult customers will buy once they trust you. Express your genuine concern. Ask them to explain themselves!

"Let me be open with you and share how puzzled I am. When I came here today I really hoped to reach some level of agreement with you. I'm very confused about how to proceed from here. What can we do to make this a productive meeting for both of us?"

Suppose you—horrors!—know the prospect is lying. Say this: "I hear you saying _____, but let me share with you my reaction to what you're saying. It doesn't sound true to me. I don't feel you're being as open with me as I am with you."

Said one prospect: "As a matter of fact, I'm not. Here's the problem."

Use this valuable way of telling people they're lying without insulting them. It works.

## *H*OW TO CURE THE COMMON STALL

The common stall, like the common cold, will always be with us. But there are ways to ease the pain:

1. "I haven't had time to think about it."

    You: I know how busy you are, but just a few minutes can clear the whole thing up. For example,

2. "I've got to talk it over with my partner."

    You: Fine, a wise decision. Now let's get the whole thing boiled down so your partner can clearly understand it.

3. "The price is too high."

    You: I know companies that sell it for less, and I'll explain why they do.

4. "Business is bad right now; I'll have to wait."

    You: I'm sorry to hear that, but we certainly can work out satisfactory terms...

    Adapt and adopt these stall-masters to suit your product or service.

# NOTHING TO LOSE? GET DRASTIC!

George Garmus believes in drastic action when you've been turned down, when there's nothing to lose.

"Why not?" says George. "You've already lost the sale. A drastic step just might shock the buyer into action. At the very least, you're no worse off."

George had been calling on Walter Hogan for several months. Walter needed George's product, but he never would get off the telephone long enough to talk turkey. He had a classic case of telephonitis.

George walked in one day and Walter asked him what he wanted.

"Just a few minutes of your time," George said.

"Can't do that," Walter said, reaching for the telephone. "I've got to keep things humming around here."

He dialed a call. Walter's action was a turndown, similar to past turndowns. This is it, George said. Now or never.

He waited until Walter finished the call. Then he grabbed the telephone, dialed the company message center, and said:

"Please hold Mr. Hogan's calls until further notice."

Walter was aghast. George took control.

"Walter, three months back, we had a meeting like this—and I never did get a chance to tell you about this product. You bought another brand and I happen to know it didn't work nearly as well. That was *your* day. Today's *my* day. Will you agree to that?"

Walter, feeling undressed without his telephone, agreed—but looked at his watch. George then outlined the product benefits in a short fact-filled presentation.

"Okay, George, you win," Walter said. "We *should* try it. Now can I have my telephone back?"

George shook his head.

"Not until you sign this purchase order," he said. "I don't dare let you get on that telephone again."

Walter signed the order.

"It's a good product," he said. "I just wish I'd heard about it before."

That was a comment George decided he should *not* answer. After all, he had the order. He'd rescued a lost sale.

"Drastic all right," George said later. "But I wasn't getting anywhere the other way. This worked."

When you don't have anything to lose, you may as well shoot the moon.

## $E$XPOSE YOUR COMPETITOR'S WEAKNESS

In the hotly contested travel agency business, each company goes after big-ticket corporate business—the kind of travel that bills $10,000 or more per month.

"The problem," says Hokan Leo, New York travel agent, "is that such clients usually already have one of our competitors providing this service."

When this happens, Leo says with a shrug, "There's only one thing to do—take it away from them!"

Recently John Drewson, CFO of a global drug company, had just changed jobs. He wanted to bring Leo along as his travel supplier.

"But you've got to provide me some evidence," Drewson said. "Internally, I can't just say, 'These are my people'. I need hard facts."

Hokan Leo requested the company's international travel schedule for the last complete month—with prices paid for airfares attached.

Item by item Leo made a comparison: *Their price* versus *our price.*

When he finished, his list came to $8,431—a 25% saving over the company's current agency. Drewson made the switch.

Asked "Isn't this pretty tough competitive practice," Leo reverts to his native Swedish: *"Det ar en djungel dar ute."* Translation: "It's a jungle out there."

When you're negotiating with an adversary, draw on your word inventory for polite putdowns to objections.

One day Harry Truman told his aide, "Get me a one-armed economist." Naturally, the aide asked why. "So he won't be able to say 'on the other hand' all the time," said feisty Harry.

Sometimes it pays to voice the unthinkable. Ad agency pioneer Claude Hopkins did it when a prospective advertiser said: "I don't know if I'm wasting my ad money."

"I do know," said Hopkins. "Your advertising is utterly unprofitable. I could prove it to you in one week. End an ad with an offer to pay five dollars to anyone who writes you that he read the ad through. The scarcity of replies will amaze you."

A week later he got the account.

## *F*IVE STEPS IN OVERCOMING OBJECTIONS

Objections are wonderful. Without objections, few sales would evolve. With objections, close after close is possible. There are only two reasons why customers raise objections:

1. They require more information (an indication of interest)
2. They're blowing smoke

To master objections, follow these steps:

1. *Hear the objection out.* Listen with empathy.
2. *Feed it back.* Repeat the objection back in an inquisitive fashion.

   Prospect: The sun room is too small.

   Salesperson: How small is too small?
3. *Answer the objection.* The content of your answer must be one of these: feasible, plausible, practical. It must also be understandable and believable.
4. *Confirm.* Be sure that the answer you've given is acceptable.

   Objection: The interest rate at 12% is too high.

   Salesperson: Mr. Smith, the net effective interest rate after tax advantages, considering you're in the 30% bracket, will really be only 8%. An 8% effective interest rate is acceptable, isn't it?

   Prospect: Oh, yes.
5. *Move on.* "By the way, let me show you this . . ."

# *F*IGHTING ONE MORE ROUND

Your prospect says *no*. Now it's time to rebuild the sale. See if you can bring your prospect to the closing point once more. Don't give up without a fight.

Reporters asked James J. (Gentleman Jim) Corbett: "How does a man become a champion?" Said the heavyweight champion: "You become a champ by fighting one more round."

Fight one more round with your tough buyer. Try another of your closing keys. Then if you simply cannot close, say goodbye in the most advantageous way possible. Be a fine sport. You are disappointed, of course. But don't show it. You are vexed. Don't show it. You are mad clear through. Don't show it.

Instead, follow Walt Whitman's advice: "Let your soul stand clear and calm." Smile. Show the buyer you are as big in defeat and in disappointment as others are in victory.

Thank the customer for her time. She thinks she did you a favor by granting an interview. Tell her she did. That you enjoyed talking with her. Ask permission to call back at a later time. If she grants this (and chances are she will) when you do go back (and you *will* go back), you'll be an invited guest. This gives you a much better entree. It adds to your self-assurance. You will probably get her initials on the dotted line next time.

# *N*EVER APPEAR AS ANXIOUS TO SELL AS YOUR CLIENT IS TO BUY

Lloyd Allard, sign salesman par excellence, asks for orders everywhere he goes. You'd be surprised how well this pays off— often over outrageous objections. In an Amarillo, Texas, motel coffee shop, he introduced himself to the owner, Mishra Patel.

"I'm a sign man, Mr. Patel," Allard said.

Patel brightened. "Ah yes, I need a sign."

Allard convinced Patel that a new sign would bring in enough new business to pay for itself in a short time. Further, Patel was convinced he'd be getting a bargain. He was ready to buy. Then he threw the curve.

"I tell you what, Mr. Allard," he said. "I will buy the sign, but first I must show it to my older brother."

"Mr. Patel, I thought you owned this motel."

"I do," he responded, "but out of respect, I must first show it to my big brother." This wasn't part of Allard's game plan. He was heading for Tennessee. Not buying *now* meant not *buying,* period. Slowly, Allard packed everything. He shook Patel's hand and said: "Well, I can't wait around for your big brother, Mr. Patel, but frankly I hope he isn't anything like my big brother."

"What do you mean?" said Patel, uncertain.

"Because," Allard said, "if your big brother is like my big brother, and he finds out what a fantastic offer you turned down, he'll kick your tail all over this parking lot for passing it up."

Patel thought for a moment. Then he sat down and wrote a check for $850.

Allard cites this closing principle: "Never be more anxious to sell than your customer is to buy. Don't ever attempt to sell from weakness. Your customer must be more afraid he's going to lose out on a great deal than you're afraid of losing the sale."

## *T*HE FEEL/FELT/FOUND MATRIX

Arnold Schwartz, the astute Long Island sales trainer, believes fervently in the 3F matrix—feel/felt/found—in closing:

- "Mr. Barnes, I understand how you *feel* about changing terminals and retraining your operators. Don Blakely over at Superior Financial *felt* the same way when we first talked. But since using ABC's service for only three weeks, he's *found* his system never ran better. I'm sure you'll enjoy the same results. Let's get started so you can begin benefiting as soon as possible."

- "Mr. Peters, I understand how you *feel* about changing to the new 8mm format. Bob Long over at First Security National *felt* the same when we first talked. But after working with this new technology for a short time, he's *found* it was a good move. You'll get the same results. Let's get started so you can begin benefiting from reduced mailing costs and better quality."

This works in dozens of closing situations where the prospect tells you how she *feels* about the product or service. Arnie Schwartz says: "When you hear *feel*, trot out the *felt* and *found*. Collect 3F stories. You'll always find them helpful in closing."

# $P$ERSISTENCE PAYS

Studies show that 80 percent of buying occurs after the fifth call and 80 percent of salespeople quit calling *before* the fifth call! To get more than your share of business, keep on calling and trying to close—it's that basic.

Your prospect might seem dead today, but conditions change. Time works surely and steadily in your favor. The need that didn't exist today may be a pressing demand tomorrow. So keep on calling.

Each time, try to close. You are selling only when you're trying to close. In between calls, maintain contact with your prospects and customers—a letter, a telephone call, anything that keeps you in touch. These contacts build confidence. Even though he's an ace closer, Jim Halbert gets turndowns that he cannot, then and there, turn into a sale.

He called on one bank every week for eight years without getting an order. Eight years is a long time. But Jim thought it worthwhile to keep right on calling, keep right on trying to close.

Finally, he closed the sale. And the order—his largest—made up for the time he invested. It also reflected his judgment: he knew this prospect was worth keeping on his active list.

Some would have quit at the end of a year. More at the end of two or three years. But Jim kept right in there.

This *is* an unusual case. But most good closers can show you customer names sold only after repeated calls.

When the buyer turns you down cold, you face the true test. After all, anyone can be in good spirits when sales are closing the way they are supposed to close. But sometimes they don't. Remember the advice of John W. Gardner: "The prospects never looked brighter. The challenges never looked greater. Men and women who are not stirred by those statements are probably too tired to be of much use in the years ahead."

It takes courage to keep right on calling and get nothing but turndowns. But good salesfolk do it. They know it pays off. The important point: make your callbacks in the right way. Keep in touch with prospects the way you do with a friend you respect and admire.

## *E*XPOSE OBJECTIONS AS ABSURD

In many fields, a prospect can make a technically true comment that is still out of whack with reality. (In insurance: "The only way I can win is to die.") When consultant Ben Helms, of Wingate, North Carolina, faces the *perhaps* true but not *right* objection, he tells this story:

"A woman hired a well-known author to research and write a book about her ancestry. The researcher discovered that her great-grandfather had been electrocuted at Sing Sing. The woman insisted on the truth, "but phrased positively." The author wrote it this way: "Her great-grandfather occupied the chair of applied electricity in one of American's best known institutions. He was very much attached to his position and literally died in the harness."

True? Technically, yes. Misleading? Decidedly!

Tell your prospects: just because something is technically *true* doesn't make it *right*.

## *D*ON'T BLAME THE BUYER

When you call back, never refer to previous failure—as Kurt Wiggins did. Kurt tried to sell Brook Turner office equipment. Brook had a perfectly logical reason for not buying at the time. Two months later, Kurt Wiggins called to try again.

"You will remember, Mr. Turner, that I tried to sell you this once before, but didn't make the grade," began this inept salesman. "So I called today to see if I'd have better luck."

Well, he didn't. You make your own luck.

A good salesperson rebuilds the sale in his or her mind. Try to point out your own errors to yourself. Then correct those errors as you present.

You may decide the closing key was wrong for this prospect. Try a key better suited to person and/or situation.

Review the sales conversation in your own mind. Analyze it step by step. Where did you lose control of the interview? Not a complete enough story? Not developing desire before you tried to close?

Four faults to avoid:

1. *Being too eager.* Buyers resent that. When an overly enthusiastic salesperson goes too fast, buyers go into a shell and refuse to buy.

2. *Waiting too long.* A premature close is better than waiting too long. If you delay your close, the buyer may cool—and it takes superhuman strength to rekindle.

3. *Wrong method.* Because you misjudged your buyer's temperament, you applied the wrong closing technique. You reached for a close and got thrown for a loss. Try another key altogether.

4. *No proper foundation.* You were building a house before you poured the cement slab.

## HELPING BUYERS WITH WIN-WIN QUESTIONS

Ninety-five percent of people work for a boss who makes the major decisions. They have little practice in making decisions. You must help them with win-win alternate questions:

- "Would you use this product inside or outside?"
- "Would you place your couch by the window or the door?"
- "Would this bed be for your son or your daughter?"

1.  *Replace an objection with a benefit.*

    - "I know you want _____. However, isn't it true that _____ is more important?"
    - "I know you're concerned about _____, but wouldn't you prefer _____?"
    - "While _____ seems vital at this moment, in the long run isn't it true that _____."
    - "I know how you feel about _____ but if I can prove this _____ wouldn't that be more important?"

2.  *Don't run away from an objection. Face it squarely:*

    - "Why should I buy from you when I can get a similar product for much less?"
    - You: "Mr. Prospect, in your business, don't you have a competitor who sells for less? How do you suppose he's able to do that? In this case, how much do you want my company to do for you—as *little* as possible or as *much* as possible?"

3.  *Try the feedback formula on objections:*

    - "It's really a concern to you, isn't it?"
    - He either drops the objection or validates it. If he validates the objection, you say: "I can see how you feel about it and I understand. But have you thought about _____."

4.  *Question the objection.*

    - "I know you want a product that will do _____. However, isn't it true that a product like that would be prohibitive in price? And would it really give you that much more?"

5.  *When the prospect brings up the same objection twice, say:*

    - "What's so important about that feature you keep bringing up? What real benefit will it give you?" (But say it pleasantly!)

    Most prospects will be happy to give you answers. Just keep on being a friend who's helping them make decisions.

# *I*T MAY BE CHEAP, BUT IS IT QUALITY?

When Mehdi Fakharzadeh, one of the nation's top-selling insurance salesmen, gets finished explaining a policy to a prospect, sometimes he hears: "I have a nephew in insurance. I feel I should buy from him."

Says Mehdi: "Let's assume you go to your physician and, after a thorough examination, he recommends open-heart surgery. If your brother, nephew, or classmate is a doctor, would you go to him for the surgery, or would you try to find the best doctor in that field?"

"Invariably, the client says he'd go to the best doctor. I explain that the same holds true when buying insurance from me."

When the prospect says: "Yes, but he can get it cheaper," Mehdi asks him what kind of car he drives.

"Regardless of what he tells me, I bring into the picture a less expensive car. If he says he drives a Mercedes, I mention a Chevrolet. If a Chevy, I mention a Hyundai. And I ask him why he did not buy the less expensive car, and I wait for his answer." (Many a sale has been lost because the salesman talked too much.)

"Invariably, the client will tell me he buys the more expensive car because it has a better name, is more prestigious or of better quality, or offers better service and more extras. I tell him that this is precisely why he should buy his insurance from me."

Mehdi makes it work. He believes in his answers and it shows.

# *S*IX WAYS TO SIDESTEP PURCHASING

Many a salesperson has butted heads with the purchasing depart-ment, usually not the best place to try a new idea or to shoehorn in a new supplier. What to do?

Jeanette Amboy says: "Avoid the purchasing department. You can always do better with someone else." When you next hear, "see Purchasing," Amboy suggests that you fire back your choice of these power answers:

- "If my recommendation saves your company $_____ a month, who should be the hero, you or the purchasing manager?"

- "Purchasing? *This is an executive-level decision.* I need to talk with you."

- "Your purchasing manager? You don't think this opportunity is worthy of your attention? May I take two minutes to explain why it *is*?"

- "Talk with someone else? Why do you think I called *you*? It wasn't by chance! *I have information for you only!* After you hear it, if you want me to talk with _____, I will."

- "Your purchasing people are known for their competence. However, this information is for the person responsible for bottom-line profitability."

- "My company doesn't allow me to talk to purchasing managers. I must either talk to you or no one in your company will hear about this opportunity. Can we talk?"

Are these answers pretty tough? "Sure they are," Amboy says. "But P.A.s are tough on salespeople. And if you know the P.A. is not the way to move your product, what do you have to lose?"

It works a good percentage of the time. Amboy's five-figure income proves it.


# COUNTERING "YOUR PRICE IS TOO HIGH"

There are three basic reasons for a price objection:

1. Your prospect believes your price *is* high.
2. Your prospect may have a lower bid from another service.
3. Price as an automatic brushoff, no matter what the true objection is.

Take these reasons one by one.

**1. Truly believes your price is too high.** Obviously, your first move is to determine why. Ask, politely and tactfully. But ask.

Her answer may startle you. In many cases, she doesn't understand your product. Or the value of extras she requested (these vary industry to industry). Or that her last quote was four years ago (a problem in many cases). Whatever the reason, your job is to discover it! Only then can you handle the objection.

*2. Lower quote from another supplier.* The first step is to make certain you are apples-to-apples in size, height, components, and so on. Your prospect may not understand the differences between your product and someone else's.

Make the distinction between your product's benefits versus the inferior product. Your prospect must understand the contrast.

*3. Price as standard brushoff.* How do you expose the brush? Again, ask polite, gentle, probing questions:

- "Ms. Jones, to what are you comparing my price?"
- "My price is very competitive. Why do you feel it is too high?"
- "When did you last price this service?"
- "I'm surprised to hear you say my product is too high. Do you have a price in mind you feel is fair?"

In most cases, the price objection will turn out to be an outgrowth of other problems:

- Fear of making a wrong decision
- Not understanding your product's benefits
- Fear that buyer may pay more than your lowest price

Most objections occur to delay decision. People find decision making painful. Your prospect is no different. It's not a rejection of you. Or the product. Or the price! It's simply a means to delay! Continue selling yourself and your product until the prospect is convinced.

Learn what his fears are. Deal with them. Dig out what he doubts about your statements. Again, ask questions:

"If the price was just right, Mr. Smith, is there any other reason why we couldn't put your order on schedule today?"

All this assumes the product or service you sell *is* worth the money. (If it isn't, you're obviously selling the wrong product.) If you're selling the right product at the right price, be thankful it costs more than your competitors'. Selling a quality product is always easier and far more rewarding. If all you're offering is a cheap price, the minute someone else comes along with something cheaper, you're out of business! In the long run, quality beats price every time.

A low price, by itself, means absolutely nothing. Even cut-rate discount stores advertise top-quality nationally advertised brands. Everyone wants the best he or she can get. Be happy you're providing it.

## *GO BACK TO BASICS*

When you get turned down, go back to basics. After all, when you're closing sales right and left, there's no need to review fundamentals. When you're on a roll, keep up the momentum. But when sales aren't closing, despite your best efforts, it's time to review the block-tackle-run side of selling—the indispensable cornerstones that makes it all work.

Walter H. Johnson, Jr., former president of Sales and Marketing Executives International, calls this a "return to sharp-thrust selling." You sharpen your selling thrust by using timeliness, demonstration, research, alertness to trends, and pure closing power.

Says Johnson: "Knowledge is power. Knowledge of your product. Knowledge of your prospect's needs. Knowledge of how to bridge the gap between the two. This power is developed by experience, analysis, and concentration.

"Confidence is power. Confidence in yourself. Confidence in product quality and value. Confidence in your ability to meet the customer needs.

"Expression is power. Mastery of words is essential in influencing others. When you face a customer, your ability to speak is crucial. Know the emotional power of words. Dress up your ideas with colorful, descriptive words. Develop power of expression by reading, practicing, and collecting powerful words and phrases.

"Being affirmative is power. Prospects respond to a positive attitude and a can-do presentation. This is developed when you have pride in your product and when personal attitude is positive."

Basic? Sure. But many otherwise lost sales could have been winners with these fundamentals. When you get a turndown, go back to block, tackle, and run.

# CHAPTER TWENTY

# Champ Closer As Business Actor

*The Consultant* presented industry statistics to his prospect. Figures pointed to new corporate strategy. The prospect became the customer.

*The Apprentice* just wanted the veteran buyer's advice on positioning a new product. Part of this advice called for shipping a trial order—to that buyer.

*The Seasoned Veteran* offered to help his career-oriented buyer prepare an internal company presentation. It worked, enhancing the buyer's stature within the company. Result: the buyer consolidated all his purchasing with the Seasoned Veteran's firm.

Consultant, Apprentice, and Seasoned Veteran, when offstage and playing themselves, are also called *closers.*

So it goes each business day in the larger-than-life business theater. Salesfolk also play *psychologist, priest, mother, daughter-he-never-had, big brother, coach, teacher, companion,* among many other roles. Ace closers are business actors.

"Sure, we cast ourselves in various roles." says Ron Fletcher, former actor now champ closer. "And the roles vary as widely as customer problems. You go in, analyze the situation, and start playing the role required."

## *T*HE SPELLBINDER AS CLOSER

Ad man Bruce Barton (the second B in BBDO), also author and newspaper columnist, heard that his client U.S. Steel was planning to cut its institutional ad budget. Barton got hot under the collar. He scheduled an emergency client meeting, all geared up to play *evangelist*. He rose slowly, looked at the committee, shook his head sadly.

"Gentlemen, you can *cancel* your national advertising—that is, if you mean canceling the limited fraction of your advertising you originate and place.

"But the overwhelming fact is that today, neither you nor any other big corporation can really halt its advertising. You can only suspend the small part over which you have control.

"The part you do not and cannot control will roll on in ever-increasing volume. It is the advertising given you by politicians with axes to grind, by demagogues who may point you out as typical of all that is bad in big business, by newspapers that hope to build circulation by distorting your acts, by labor leaders misrepresenting your profits, by all other operators in the field of public opinion, some unfriendly and many merely misinformed.

"Thus you are going to have national advertising whether you want it or not!

"The only question you have to decide is whether it is worth a little money, a fraction of 1 percent of your annual sales, for advertising of your company that will be factual, informative, and constructive.

"Or whether, in the present state of world politics, where the electorate is the court of final appeal in *all* business decisions, you can afford to take the risk of having all your advertising emanate from sources beyond your control."

Barton sat down. U.S. Steel reinstated its institutional ad budget. The master business actor had spoken.


# CLOSING TIPS FROM HESTON/HOLBROOK/SCOTT

Since you're going to draw on acting techniques to sharpen your closing skills, let's see what you can learn from veterans of stage and screen. For starters: your spoken words must be first rate—in context and in style.

To become a business actor requires practice and dedication. You must develop self-discipline. You must learn to *listen*. You must be gracious in victory and courageous when the applause isn't there.

The actor, Charlton Heston once said, has three (and only three) assets—voice, body, and personality. But what powerful tools when harmonized correctly! With voice, tone, stage presence, and body language, the skilled thespian moves you to laughter or tears, transports you to another time and place, puts you inside another person's psyche.

The unusual effective performer (recall Hal Holbrook as *Mark Twain Tonight* on the stage or George C. Scott as *Patton* on the screen) can play the audience the way a musician plays an instrument.

Experienced performers use classic techniques again and again. You can master those techniques until they become second nature. Soon effective closing becomes a reflex. In time, power speech emerges—almost automatically—when you need it, at the right time, in the right way.

Once you become aware, you'll be more atune to a society awash in poor speech. Los Angeles talk maven Lillian Glass says we spend 80 percent of our lives communicating—and much of it poorly.

Did you miss out on the long-awaited promotion? Was it your breath? No. But it could have been your breathlessness. The way you speak—exhaling profusely like Marilyn Monroe, for example—can make or break you.

"Women have a lot of problems in the corporate world when it comes to communicating," Glass told *USA Today*. "Many little-girl voices are difficult to take seriously."

How to improve? Eliminate the *ahs, ums*, and *buts*, Glass says, keep your chin off your chest, "flow out your tones," be enthusiastic, and learn to listen.

As a child, you learned to talk. But most of us developed speaking and listening in remarkably haphazardly fashion. You've learned from parents, relatives, playmates, schoolteachers, street urchins. Over the years, you've listened to movies and TV, picked up by reading (comics to classics). When you analyze this mulligan stew, it's not surprising that some speaking habits are poor, some good, most in between.

As a business actor you must learn to take regular inventories of your oral communication—then capitalize on the techniques, that work, improve indifferent habits, unlearn and expunge the clunkers.

## *W*HAT YOUR SPEECH SAYS ABOUT YOU

In the performing arts, speech is an invaluable shorthand in providing the audience a quick fix on a character's background and destiny. In the film *An Officer and a Gentleman,* Debra Winger tells Richard Gere: "And I don't think you have what it takes to be *no* officer." Her double negative instantly establishes her factory girl background.

In *On the Waterfront,* Marlon Brando tells Rod Steiger: "Cholly, Cholly. You shulda looked outfa me, Cholly. I coulda been a contendah. Instead, I got a one-way ticket to Palookaville." This portrait speech coupled with Brando's marbles-in-the-mouth delivery, tells us all about the past and probable future of longshoreman Terry Malloy.

Novelist John O'Hara put all his character chips on dialog. His precinct cop picks up the telephone: "Wukkan I did fya?" When O'Hara's teen from Bryn Mawr or Wellesley says: "Robert didn't come with she or I," her grammatical error tells us about her breathless need to appear grown-up.

If such shorthand is widely accepted about fictional character, why should real life be different? It isn't, of course. A pig dressed in a tuxedo still looks like a pig. Similarly, a blue-collar accent coming from a financial consultant? Your listener will think you're not real. Speech will betray you every time.

In England, speech has always been *the* class establisher. The laboring class can say *bloody* every other breath, but the proper person does not utter That Word except under the most dire circumstances. The dropped *h* in *'otel* is perceived a scandal coming from respectable middle-class types.

In American society, as power closer you must know how to use language to defend or attack, when and how to admit you're wrong, and how to vary speech when addressing a group. Remember, listener needs, not *your* needs, dictate content.

# GUIDELINES ON SAYING IT BETTER

An excited first-nighter spotted playwright George S. Kaufman in the lobby during intermission.

"Mr. Kaufman," he said, "you don't know me..."

"That's half of it," Kaufman riposted.

To the closer, *what* to say is half of it. *How* to say is the other half:

**1. Discard regional accents.** The power closer usually wants people to listen to *what* he or she says, not the *way* it's said. So cultivate standard American: it sounds right all over the nation. Control regional accents unless you're using them for a purpose.

**2. Learn to be eloquent.** Scintillating conversationalists do not spring full-born from the forehead of Zeus. The Effectives deliberately work at eloquence. Collect apt words and phrases. Dole them out the way a miser hands out gold. Choose the single best nugget to meet each moment's pressing need.

Make short speeches. Use short sentences and short words. All are harder than long. But short pays greater dividends by adding muscle to your speech.

**3. Be a sloganeer.** By originating (or collecting and adapting) memorable motivating phrases, you become an influencer. On the antismoking front, no one has ever topped Horace Greeley's "Fire on one end, fool on the other."

And the dollar value of American Express's "Don't Leave Home Without It" is beyond calculation. Apt phrasemaking raises funds, elects presidents, averts nuclear war, moves mountains, and most important of all, closes sales.

**4. Become a great storyteller.** Collect anecdotes: apply liberally to selling. Stories—windows that allow your audience to "see"—also entertain, inform, inspire, make people listen, and initial on the dotted line.

**5. Become a persuader.** The ability to persuade is the ability to succeed—in management, the law, in selling. Give your persuadee a choice between something and something—never something and nothing. The key to persuasion? Preparation. You cannot bore and persuade at the same time.

**6. Keep them laughing.** Funny stories support points, connect sections, build rapport. Never read a story. Tell it with feeling. Put yourself into it. Make jokes come as close to the truth as possible. Constantly test jokes: keep the audience-pleasers, weed out the duds. With practice, you can be funny—much of the time.

# *P*RESENTING WITH ENTHUSIASM AND PRESENCE

You can say 9 out of 10 things correctly and still fail if you lack *enthusiasm.*

Enthusiasm—knowledge on fire—is available to you free of charge. So whatever you say, say it with enthusiasm. Henry Ford II recognized the power of enthusiasm:

- Enthusiasm is the yeast that makes your hope rise to the stars.
- Enthusiasm is the grip of your hand, the irresistible surge of your will, your energy to execute your ideas.
- Enthusiasts are fighters. They have fortitude, they have staying qualities.
- Enthusiasm stands at the bottom of all progress. With it, there is accomplishment. Without enthusiasm, there are only alibis.

Lee Stanley, president of Solar Additions, Inc., Greenwich, New York, considers command presence vital in closing sales: "In high school debate, trying to accomplish objectives by using the English language, I was fascinated by idea presentation. I never envisioned it useful in making a living. But today speech is a tool I draw on hour to hour in selling.

"When I was in the Army, we called it *command presence.* If you talk, and some people listen, that's command presence. If you talk and nobody listens, you don't have it. The Army considers effective speech absolutely necessary for leadership.

"In presenting our product (sunspace add-ons to homes) you must convey *building a dream*. You do this with words and tone to establish comfort and rapport with the homeowner. Command presence and effective speech makes it happen."

# REQUIRED: QUICK ROLE-CHANGES

The business actor learns to play Macbeth one day and Macduff the next. Further, he or she may play both at the same time, as Norman L. Simpson reported to Bill Safire.

Simpson's story: A politician in the 1920s was pressed for his stand on whiskey (when wet/dry was issue number one). Said the politician: "I'll take a stand on any issue at any time, regardless of how fraught with controversy it may be. You have asked me how I feel about whiskey; well, Brother, here's how I stand.

"If by whiskey, you mean the Devil's brew, the Poison scourge, the bloody monster that defies innocence, dethrones reason, creates misery and poverty, yea, literally takes the bread out of the mouth of babes; if you mean the Evil Drink that topples men and women from pinnacles of righteous, gracious living into the bottomless pit of despair, degradation, shame, helplessness and hopelessness—then certainly I am against it with all my power.

"But if by whiskey, you mean the oil of conversation, the philosophic wine and ale consumed when good fellows get together, that puts a song in their hearts, laughter on their lips and the warm glow of contentment in their eyes; if you mean that sterling drink that puts the spring in an old man's steps on a frosty morning; if you mean that drink that pours into our treasury untold millions of dollars to provide tender care for our little crippled children, our pitifully aged and infirm and to build our highways, hospitals and schools—then, Brother, I am for it. This is my stand."

Politicians are also actors, constantly trying to "close" voters. As an effective closer, use the *if-by-whiskey* straddle when forced into controversial comment. You'll need it.

Says a female bank vice president in *The Wall Street Journal:* "Be aggressive but not repulsive." Take a stand. And Will Rogers said: "Even if you're on the right track, you'll get run over if you just sit there." Society is critical of nondecision makers.

# COLLECTING SPARKLING STORIES

When Groucho Marx toured the South Pacific for the USO during World War II, he reached an army orderly room (company HQ) just in time to hear the telephone ring. Since the company clerk was goofing off, Groucho picked up the receiver and said crisply: "World War *Two!*

He emphasized *two* to let the caller know precisely *which* war. A match point—doubled.

Back in Hollywood, at a party at Groucho's, a departing guest told The Leering Mustache: "I'd like to say goodbye to your wife."

"So would I," said Groucho.

Ah, yes, you say. If only I could be as clever as Groucho!

Turnipseed! What you mean: "Too bad I don't work as hard as Groucho at collecting and remembering material."

Julius (Groucho) Marx was a voluminous cataloger and learner of jokes, quips, descriptions, colorful words. His hilarious ad-libs were carefully drawn from his lifetime inventory. If you work just *half* that hard, you can be a sparkling conversationalist.

This does not *mean* asking: "What's new?" "How've you been?" "How's tricks?" "Whaddya say?"

Robert Riley, vice president of Baird, Inc., Little Rock, Arkansas, loves collecting plural nouns (it helps make him a power closer). Says Riley:

> Three English gentlemen were sitting in their club watching the passing parade. Three ladies of the evening strolled by and the gentlemen sought to discover proper collective nouns.
>
> The first gentleman suggested a *jam of tarts*. The second suggested a *blare of strumpets*. The third suggested an *anthology of pros*.

This is a productive vein. On the business front, consider a *territory* of salespeople, a *delay* of production men, an *agony* of call reports, a *frown* of purchasing agents, a *chart* of researchers, a *gabble* of conventioneers, and a *froth* of inspirational speakers.

# *U*SING DISTINCTIVE SPEECH IN SELLING

When you don't have much time to make an impression, use distinctive speech. A cameo performer on Broadway knows this. (If you're unknown, it's a bit part. If you're a star, the same role's a cameo.) In Broadway's *You Can't Take It with You,* Colleen Dewhurst played Olga, the Russian grand duchess who arrives at the last moment to cook blintzes.

Dewhurst enters the zany Sycamore family's cluttered living room. Everyone ineptly pays proper homage. "I am most happy to be here," she barks like an agitated bulldog. "How soon is dinner?" That one line, spoken as a command, tells us Olga retains her imperious grandeur but "hasn't had a good meal since before the revolution."

An accent that suits the role is often memorable. Dr. Walter Kempner, the teutonic wizard of Fat City (founder of the rice diet in Durham, North Carolina), retains an unforgettable German accent. It's perfectly suited to threats, exhortations, and clucks when he talks to the Ricers (dieters) from all over the world.

"Geef us more time," Kempner says when a Ricer announces his length of stay in Durham. ("No matter," one Ricer relates, "if you've agreed to stay *for several years.*")

Dr. Kempner's accent is a component of his total presentation. He has no plan to change it. In fact, his American staff picked up German pronunciations. It goes with the territory, or, as they perceive it, with the power.

Cary Grant, an actor of moderate ability, parlayed distinctive style into world acclaim. His own name came out *Kerry Grent* when processed by his unique vocal apparatus.

John F. Kennedy and his brother Bobby had a habit of telephoning Grant, sometimes interrupting his lunch. "They'd just ask me to talk," Grant said. "They wanted to hear Kerry Grent's voice."

"The best way to say something smart," said Sam Levinson, the urban folk philosopher. "Think of something stupid, then say just the opposite." Fine. But if it turns out *good*, remember it for continuing use in building distinction.

# WHY SELLING MEANS PUTTING ON A GOOD SHOW

Putting on a good show and making a great closing presentation share features in common. Harken:

- Don't present unless you really have something to say that is not generally known.
- Talk about something the listeners need to learn about and are interested in knowing.

To open a sales presentation, tell the audience an interesting or surprising fact. Humor is wonderful. But don't overdo it. Too much humor in a serious presentation indicates you don't put a high value on the listener's time. Demonstrate to listeners that you revere their time and don't intend to waste it.

Shakespeare threw currants of humor in heavy drama batter as comic relief—to wit the drunken porter in MacBeth right after the bloody murder of Duncan. But only as relief. Soon Willy the Shake got back to serious. So should you.

Think of your presentation as a coat rack. Hang all the important ideas on it. Relate everything to the single most important message you've hung on the top pole. In a play, this is called *the premise*. No play can succeed without a premise that all actions and speeches enforce and develop. Sound like a good presentation? It should!

Maintain eye contact at all times. Don't use props that draw attention away from you (called "upstaging" in the theater).

In boardroom or on stage, don't begin at too high a pitch—leaving nothing to build up to. Start on a low key. Make the audience strain to hear you. A noisy crowd? Speak softly until listeners gradually become more attentive.

End it by reinforcing the premise you established in the beginning. Said playwright Anton Chekhov: "If you show a revolver in Act I, it must go off in Act III."

## $S$AY IT JOURNALISTICALLY

The exceptional business actor knows—and all must learn—to present information in journalistic form. Spit out the most important facts first, then work down. Give them *who, what, when, why, how*— and add the *wow* for listener interest.

In verbal reports, presentations, and speeches: tell what you're going to tell, then describe it in detail, then summarize what you said. In your closings, be a top-down speaker.

Say it with distinction, panache, enthusiasm, courage— qualities most effective when based on knowledge, delivered after practice (with dramatic gestures), and punctuated by strategic pauses.

At times, say it with understatement and a smile. At other times, command presence is your best tool.

Let's hear it for *the pause*, that powerful ingredient of distinctive speech. But badly placed pauses result in cluttering (the Germans call it word-salad). Your words run together in a mad jumble. Pause at the right time, or you'll give listeners the impression you're a breathless chowderhead.

John Wayne, who started as a movie stuntman, grew to screen greatness as Rooster Cogburn in *True Grit*. Gravel-voiced Duke explained his style simply: "I cut each sentence in half. I say the first half, stop, and then say the second half."

Al White, an army journalist, in impressing his boss with the amount of cooperation he expected from company headquarters, said: "If I call in here for a portable typewriter mounted on the port side of a jackass, I expect it to be provided."

He got attention. He spoke with panache. Tone of voice can move mountains.

# $A$D-LIB: YOUR SECRET WEAPON

Like stage actors, be prepared to ad lib in emergencies. Lloyd Allard made it work selling signs to Betty's Beauty Shop.

"Betty had pretty much given up on the business and didn't care about the future," Allard relates. "After a short while, she told me the reason for her depression. Her husband had run off with one of her beauticians.

"I tried everything I could think of to get Betty to see the value of keeping the business going, but she simply wasn't buying."

Finally, Allard took her out in front of the shop, drew a sketch of the sign, and showed her where it would fit on the building. Then he told her:

"Look up and imagine how your ex-husband and that beautician would feel when they drive by and see that new sign. He'll say, 'Gosh, it looks like she didn't even miss me.' That bimbo will turn green with envy."

Betty looked at Allard. A wry smile crossed her face.

"Put it on rush," she said.

# $C$OMMONSENSE GUIDE TO BUSINESS ACTING

Sometimes otherwise promising stage performances fall apart because commonsense is lacking. So too it is with business theater.

*Don't knock competitors.* It's counterproductive. Most buyers become intrigued with a product or company under assault.

*Don't question a customer's final decision to buy competitive merchandise.* Instead, increase your own selling efforts.

*Don't oversocialize.* When a buyer begins to expect such treatment, withdrawing it becomes painful.

*Don't complain to buyers about job or domestic problems.* ("Half the listeners don't care; the other half are glad you got what's coming to you.")

*Don't overtalk technical information.* Buyers are more interested in what a product or service can do for them.

*Don't try to impress customers with your professional qualifications, education, social status.* Some buyers resent this. Learn about each buyer's personal history and adapt your conversation accordingly.

*Don't overdress.* Extreme fashions call attention to the wearer. Conservative clothes are always safe.

*Don't be a gossip.* They are universally distrusted.

# LACK OF INTEREST? LETHAL!

Bergen Evans, the great Northwestern University English professor and TV personality, was once asked in rather academic language how his teaching method differed from the norm. Evans wrote simply:

"I have tried to be *interesting!*"

A small, but vital, distinction that made him a personality on three TV shows and much in demand on the lecture circuit. His advice:

- Read everything. Almost indiscriminately. Learn to read fast, and to skip. Digest trade papers and professional journals, the things your bosses read.

- Learn to speak properly. Watch for all the little things. Above all: practice. Presenting is theater. Act it out, persuade. Do not try to be dry, impartial, solemn. Rehearsal is the key to learning to be a good presenter.

- Half the time, when people present, they do not know all the facts. Don't let this happen to you.

Try to be interesting! Tell your stories so well the human-interest-hungry prospect will gladly listen. Telling stories well is an art. Some salespeople narrate with spontaneity and interest. Others belabor and bore you to tears. Stories that drag, miss the point, or tire are not going to help you close sales. Say it with style and leave your audience with a smile. (In Owen Wister's *The Virginian*, Trampas calls our hero a "son of a bitch." The hero logs eternal fame by replying: "When you call me that, *smile.*")

Learn to collect humor to sprinkle into your speech. Test jokes out before you use them. To tell stories well, *practice*—hours, if need be. The business actor must rehearse just as carefully as a stage actor. Tape yourself. If you don't like what you hear, take a public speaking course.

Back before TV, staff radio announcers read commercials. When TV emerged, announcers were soon replaced in commercials by actors. Today a coterie of actors does nothing but TV commercials— along with famous performers who do commercials in addition to screen and stage work.

Says Peter Walker, popular New York actor known for his American Express and Coca-Cola commercials: "I work just as hard or harder on my selling roles as on a stage part. The point is to make the character believable and interesting. Once I've done that, the product—assuming it has basic merit—comes across fine."

The actor must create a favorable impression. So must the salesperson. Be convincing. The best closers insist on the same routine—rehearsal and more rehearsal. A champion salesman's wife described her husband's antics:

"He'll walk for hours in front of the mirror," she said, "going through his act. He smiles, not at all self-consciously, becomes serious, uses gestures, taps his palm, sits down, arises. He demonstrates for the mirror in the bedroom."

That careful preparation pays dividends. When he tells his stories, people flock to listen.


# *O*RCHESTRATING THE STORY CLOSE

If you tell a story that shows how a customer enjoyed your product or service, or a before-and-after story, you can easily tie story end to sign-up.

Start collecting success stories. Example: a small-business person who installed automated machinery. Tell the story; then add: "I think you know successful people like this don't buy or replace such equipment lightly. May we install this on a trial basis to see what it will do for *you*?"

Also collect failure stories about customers who persisted in using antiquated or worn-out equipment to "save money," until more efficient competition moved in. Close with: "May we help you to avoid this?"

In using a story to close a sale, make it a memorable. Most accomplished narrators rarely let the truth get in the way of a good story. But keep the *nucleus* true—especially when talking about real people. This still leaves much room for poetic license.

End your story with straightforward restatement of the point, then say, "This is why I strongly suggest—" and move into a closing question.

When you tell a *real* (albeit dramatized) story about *real* people like your present prospect, the buyer will project himself or herself into the title role. With richness of detail, warmth, and color, your prospect will see the scenes and feel the action. Thus your closing question—"What days of the week will your family be using your weekend property most?"—follows naturally.

# *T*HE EMPEROR'S CLOSE

Nearly all great leaders have paid more attention to perfection in their presentations than the average person ever dreams possible. Napoleon, as self-assured a person as ever lived, realized the necessity for special training. Before being crowned emperor of France, he hired the best actor available. They spent hours rehearsing what he would say and do on his great day. He ran through every gesture, perfected every word, under the performer's eagle Gaulic eye. When Nappy got in front of the multitude, he told an enthralling story.

So will you, if you pay attention to perfecting your closes.

Jorge Santiago, a Detroit sales manager, puts young salespeople through a dramatic course after they demonstrate initial ability. This doesn't come cheap. Occasionally, management gets on his back about costs. But he always demonstrates that each dollar spent in dramatics training is worth $100 in profit.

"Most new salespeople are inarticulate in facial expression," Santiago says. "They need training. The sales trainee learns first how to control words. But unless he or she gets professional training, they'll never learn to control facial expressions. You must not register disappointment, anger, distrust, or any state of mind—so effective in driving orders away.

"My salespeople get to be actors so they can control expressions and not reveal what they're really thinking."

Learn to communicate—or not—what you're thinking (and when to do each). Many powerful closers are also good poker players. It's *not* a coincidence.


# How DEMOS HELP TO CLOSE SALES

Why are demos so helpful in closing sales? Because you're creating live theater right in the prospect's office or home. Your business theater must

1.  Catch the buyer's interest
2.  Fortify your argument
3.  Help the prospect understand the proposition
4.  Communicate your own enthusiasm for the product
5.  Use objections as platform for building value
6.  Usher you into the close

The buyer may not be fully convinced by your words. A lively demonstration often swings her over, but just as there's no free lunch, there's no crackerjack demo without sweat equity—in advance. Remember:

- The most elaborate equipment in the world is of no value if you're unprepared. If you don't *know*, don't *show*. Check out the equipment before using it. An inept demonstration can kill a sale in the worst way—stillborn. Nothing chills a prospect as quickly as a screen that doesn't pull, charts in the wrong order, or a model with missing parts. And don't forget that extension cord and an extra projector bulb!

- "Stage business" is what actors do with hands while they talk. (Roger Ebert and Gene Siskel, TV's popular movie critics, talk to one another with animated hand gestures that add sinew and heart to the show. "Tie their hands and they'd both be mute," a producer said. Actions support words. Charts and slides give you something to do with your hands while you are talking. Make sure word and deed are coordinated. One plus one must add up to three.

- Your handling of your product, for example, can be turned into a supreme act of showmanship that melts the hardest buyer. Hold the product as you would a precious stone. The prospect will think of it that way. Remove samples as if they were rare paintings. But later, if you want to show toughness, fling your product against the wall.

- A salesperson dressed quietly in good taste, with a charming voice and smile, is a walking/talking example of business actorship. Some actors cultivate a personal prop like a walking cane (Keith Michell on Murder, She Wrote) or a fresh boutonniere every day. Business actors must be distinctly remembered, too.

# *W*HAT NOT TO SAY (AND WHEN NOT TO SAY IT)

When you're unsure of your facts, uncertain of the proper tone needed, or too angry to speak properly, cool it. Say nothing until you're on firm ground. When Ma Ferguson was governor of Texas, Spanish was proposed as a second language in Lone Star schools. Said Ma Ferguson: "Not while I am governor! If English was good enough for Jesus Christ, it is good enough for Texas children." She missed a real good chance to keep quiet.

As soon as you ask a closing question take a tip from the French: *Ferme la bouch! (Close the mouth!)* Don't speak, don't fidget, just keep quiet and calm. There's no pressure like silence. If you don't speak first your prospect will—by either agreeing to buy or stating why not. If it's an OK to buy, write up the business. If you hear *why not*, go back to re-presenting and a different close. Either way, your silence wins.

# *W*HEN TO OVERSTATE, WHEN TO UNDERSTATE

Power closers *under*promise and *over*perform. That way, you always exceed expectations. The *over*promiser and *under*performer is always in hot water.

Overstatement invites skepticism. A commuting train passenger told his seatmate: "I heard the funniest story yesterday—you won't believe it!" After he told the story, his friend assumed a distinct ain't-so-funny look.

Give the listener the facts. Then let *him* tell *you* how impressed he is. Seldom do scandals trace back to too *little* talk. Yet too *much* talk is a classic problem. ("Loose lips sink ships.")

Boasting and lying are costly. If you have a good thing going, keep your mouth shut—lest you mar your fortune. Another excellent reason for putting your talk on leash: it provides vital time for listening. Good actors, stage and business, are gauged by how well they listen. Says Sonny Harris, builder of the growing Window Man franchises based in Durham, North Carolina:

> Before you can listen to a prospect, you must flip your attention switch. Set it on full attention. Acknowledge what she says by word, gesture, or facial expression. Focus on *ideas*, not facts alone. Don't make the mistake of trying to remember a list of facts. Listen for *keys* to needs, wants, desires. Listen. Really listen. It's the key to closing the sale.

# *B*E BRIEF, BE BRIEF, BE BRIEF

Wordiness is a liability that afflicts many. Avoid the heavy use of superlatives and adjectives. Don't talk for 15 minutes to say what could be better said in 3. Don't be a bore. As columnist Sidney Harris says: "Everyone is a bore on some subjects. The genuine bore is tedious on the subjects he knows best."

London publisher John Camden Hotten left us with this epitaph:

Hotten
Rotten
Forgotten

As a result, he's *not* forgotten.

When you think you've reduced brevity as far as possible, think about Victor Hugo. Interested in news of how *Les Miserables* was selling, Hugo penned this card to his publisher: "?"

The publisher, quick as the uptake, wrote back: "!"

Let *that* be your model for brevity.

Can you summarize your product or service benefit in a dramatic as compelling sentence? If not, better start working on it. This poetic statement by Sonny Harris (no relation to Sidney) puts it bluntly:

Tell me quick and tell me true,
Or else, my friend, to hell with you.
Less of how your product came to be,
And more of what it does for me.

Precedent is all on the side of brevity.

- The Lord's Prayer has 71 words.
- The Ten Commandments have 297.
- The Gettysburg Address has 271.
- The legal marriage vow has 2.
- General McAuliffe at the Bulge made his point in 1: "Nuts!"

# *B*E A WORD-MISER

When President Lyndon Johnson was rushed to the hospital for his operation and lay minutes away from anesthesia, an aide asked him: "Any last advice for vice president Hubert Humphrey?"

"Yes," said Johnson. "Tell him to keep it short."

Humphrey, a famous extemporaneous speaker, produced many long fire-and-brimstone orations. (As Maxie Schwartz, a New York deli counterman, said: "A speaker he is, but a short speaker he's not.")

Ergo, LBJ's last words to a man then a scalpel's breadth from the presidency: "Keep it short."

Humphrey, effective as he was, could have been greater if he'd been a word-miser. If you need daily inspiration, catch the evening news any night—for *sound-bytes*. Today's interview source must be equipped with a very short sound-byte—a message capsule that diminished in average length from 43 seconds to 8.9 seconds in a recent 10-year period, *The New York Times* reported. That's *short*.

So short that satirist Mark Russell reported George Bush's New Hampshire sound-byte message thusly: "It's great to be here in New Hampshire. Jobs, jobs, jobs. God bless you. Goodbye."

It's funny because it's (almost) true. And instructive to the closer. People today expect to get the quintessence of your per-suasive message in *sound-bytes*. Does the effective salesspeaker dare ignore this? Your sharpest competitor won't!

# CHAPTER TWENTY-ONE

# *Power Words That Close Sales*

Since we all use words in selling, there must be certain words with more motivating muscle than others—power words. So let's learn power words for closing sales.

You now possess tested closing keys. The nation's greatest salespeople employ these techniques to become infinitely better, more successful, more prosperous. If you study and master these major and special keys, only one thing can result: more sales.

However, often the *manner* of closing is more important than the techniques themselves. Power words, tested in the crucible, get at the *manner* to make your major and special keys drastically more effective.

## *Y*OU ARE WHAT YOU SAY

Two competent closers are equal in product knowledge and sign-up savvy. Yet A does better than B. Why? Power speech often provides the cutting edge.

The muttering Bowery bum and the articulate TV spellbinder both draw on the same word inventory. Words that are free to us all—they're in the Bible, in Shakespeare, in your dictionary. But *which* words you choose to do *what*—and *how* you use those words—ah, that makes a world of difference. Knowing *what* to use *when* (and *why*) separates the power speaker from the dese/dem/dose types.

Power speech can move you into the top rank of closers, to the forefront of professional organizations, yea even to the White House. Basically, it's a matter of *what to say* and *how to say it*.

# WHAT TO SAY

Once you make word collecting automatic, you're on your way to mastering the awesome power of speech.

1. Whatever your product or mission, *file away motivating words,* ready for instant use. Be careful what you collect. Avoid trite and hackneyed phrases that irritate listeners. Hoard the winners, expunge the sinners.

2. *Suit message to audience.* The world's best words/phrases are the worst if unsuited to your audience. The prospect's needs (not your needs) dictate content.

3. *Cut words to fit fashion.* In the ebb and flow of the mighty American language, words move in and out of influence— heroes in one context, bums in another. You insist on dipping into the well-worn barrel? At least be creative and adapt.

4. *Never miss a good chance to shut up.* Pauses are powerful. Often the contender who speaks last wins—by saying "just your initials here please." Underpromise and overperform.

5. *Use speech to defend* (but know when to choose the rapier and when the baseball bat). Lesson from a master:

   *Gladstone:* My opponent will either die on the gallows or as victim of a loathsome social disease.

   *Disraeli:* That depends on whether I embrace my opponent's *policies* or his *mistress.*

   Do these speech rules sound overly idealistic? Maybe, but next time you watch an impressive closer, you'll hear an astounding number of these qualities!

# HOW TO SAY IT

That popular Friday night TV show *Washington Week in Review* invited a *Wall Street Journal* reporter as a panelist. He joined Charles Corddry, Jack Nelson, Haynes Johnson, and Paul Duke, the moderator.

In his opening statement, the reporter logged in six *yuh nos* and eight *uhs*. He swallowed his words and didn't project his voice out where the viewer could get at it.

Not only were his fellow panelists concerned for him, but home viewers felt embarrassed for him. We all breathed easier when the show rolled to end credits.

That same day, in New York, a Boston banker spoke to a press conference, representing an association of 40 banks. Unlike the *Wall Street Journal* reporter, the banker was confident—but maybe he shouldn't have been. He pronounced dais as Dy-us rather than DAY-us. He said *boutique* as BOW-teek, not the preferred BOO-teek. He talked about being INNA-restered instead of IN-trest-ed. Knowledgeable audience members winced.

These two unrelated incidents—and hundreds like them— prove the vital importance of power speech in modern society. When your speech is shabby, you get demerits, despite expertise in your own field.

The reporter is a rising star in Washington journalism—a respected and talented writer. He won the Raymond Ciapper Award for his congressional coverage. Does he get credit for his stature with *Washington Week* viewers? Not at all.

The banker was elevated to association office by his peers (a notably hard-nosed lot). Did he reflect these credentials at the New York media event? Not with his pronunciation gaucheries. Listeners started waiting for the next gaffe.

Portrait of two professionals getting lower grades than professionalism alone indicates. But that's just the problem: your professionalism in closing sales doesn't stand alone. Your credentials are linked securely to your speech—as incontrovertibly as two roped-together mountain climbers inching up the slope. Each depends on the other for life itself. If one falters, both plunge into the abyss.

You *are* the way you sound. The B student in life who sounds like a C student will get a final grade of C. The B student who sounds like an A student often gets an A. Effective speech can upgrade your professional status. Tawdry speech can drag you down.

Which is for you? It's your choice. Power speech is available. It is learnable. Will you take the time and invest the effort to acquire this vital asset to sign-ups? You'd better! Your competitors *will!* Listen to Daniel Webster: "If all of my possessions were taken from me with one exception, I would choose to keep the power of speech, for with it I would soon regain all the rest."

## Motivating Words: Key to Influence

Suppose you opt for power speech as tool in closing sales. This means standard American English. *Substandard* is the speech of uneducated groups—punkers, mountaineers, dock-wallopers, migrant field hands, rustics with no interest in "book learning," people not interested in changing their ways. A person from such a background who wants to become an effective closer must *lose* substandard speech and acquire standard.

People are more hampered by speech they *think* is *right* than by *disregard* of speech they know is *wrong.* The Boston banker, for example, assumed his pronunciation correct. Otherwise, being bright and accomplished, he would have changed it.

Power speech encourages others to follow your ideas and directions. Without exception, charismatic leaders are effective "me-to-you" speakers. Napoleon achieved his dominance through the power words. At the pyramids, Napoleon said to his army:

"Soldiers, 40 centuries are looking down on you! I will lead you into the most fertile regions of the world. There you will find flourishing cities, teeming with riches."

The Corsican who conquered most of the world unlimbered verbal artillery to match his field guns. In another campaign, he said: "You will return to your homes, and your neighbors will point you out to one another saying: 'He was with that army in Italy.' "

Man is a word animal. Speech conveys our thoughts, gives us confidence, relieves our tensions, encourages good human relations. Speech is the main connector between people. Closing sales is a competition between you and many other qualified sellers. Napoleon said: "God is on the side of the big battalions." The big battalions in closing are *words* adroitly and properly deployed.

Words are bricks that build your thoughts and feelings, desires and dislikes, hopes and fears—everything that makes up *you*. The more words you know, the closer you come to saying precisely *what* you want to say, *when* you want to say it.

Besides clarity, a large vocabulary provides variety, the basis for discrimination. You choose from a large number of tools. A hammer won't do when a saw is called for, and a nail file is inadequate when you need a rasp.

A varied vocabulary makes you more interesting, helps you avoid the dullness of repetition. Your speech demands attention. The interesting person is almost always persuasive. People endure dullards with secret distaste—wondering how soon they can escape. Clearly, a versatile vocabulary is part of the ace closer's arsenal.

Says Dr. Bergen Evans in *The Word-a-Day Vocabulary Builder:*

> Words cannot be separated from ideas. They interact. The words we use are so associated with your experiences—and what experiences mean to you—that they cannot be separated. The idea comes up from our subconscious clothed in words. It can't come any other way.

> We don't know how words are stored in our minds, but there does seem to be a sort of filing system—controlled by a perverse if not downright wacky file clerk. Everyone has tried to remember a word and been unable to. Sometimes it is a common word, one that we know we know. Yet it won't come when we want it. It can be almost a form of torture trying to recall it. Then usually some time later (when it's no longer useful to us) the word comes to mind readily.

# *H*OW YOUR LANGUAGE SKILLS PAY OFF

Millions use English as a second language. And although English may be the toast of Paris and Peking, back home in River City there's trouble, trouble, trouble. The shortcomings of U.S. schools, waves of immigrants, and addiction to TV are all taking a toll on our linguistic skills.

A survey by the National Opinion Research Center shows that the language ability of the U.S. population has dropped ever since the 1950s. Doubly worrisome: the ranks of the illiterate and marginally literate are swelling at the very time rapid technological change makes proficiency with words and concepts more and more important. Today, many college graduates have a weaker command of language than their parents do.

"In its short lifetime, television has become the major stumbling block to literacy in America," says Jim Trelease, author of *The Read-Aloud Handbook*. This problem, alarming sociologically, has a personal impact on the man or woman determined to master speech in closing sales. Effective speech—much more in demand—will now be rewarded more than ever.

Of course, throughout the ages, men and women who make impressions on society have been unusual speakers. (*Clothed* speakers, evidently. Mark Twain warned us that "naked people have very little influence on society.") Demosthenes, an ancient Greek orator, said: "As a vessel is known by the sound, whether it be cracked or not, so men are proved by their speeches whether they be wise or foolish."

The White House has always given speech top priority. Each president since Franklin D. Roosevelt has retained speech writers and often coaches on delivery, "says speech coach Dorothy Sarnoff:

"All through history, people have been more quickly perceived and accepted as leaders if they could speak persuasively. The superb quality of Reagan's speechmaking, refined through the years before he took office, had tremendous impact on the nation."

On the downside, Nicholas Gage (in *The Wall Street Journal*) tagged unfavorable speech as instrumental in retiring Lyndon B. Johnson:

> Now it can be told. Here's why President Johnson decided not to run for reelection. It was because his voice had become so grating to so many ears that his popularity had fallen dangerously low. He no longer sounded like a President. The more people heard his voice, the less secure they felt about him.

Anyone who doubts the importance of speech in swaying political audiences need only look at the furor over Geraldine Ferraro. As a congresswoman, her New York accent was accepted without comment. As a candidate for vice president, her speech attracted attention. *The New York Daily News* headlined in pure Gothamese: *TO HEAH HUH IS TO KNOW HUH.*

*The Daily News'* Stuart Marques pointed out that New Yorkers say "berl the erl!" and "I sawr huh." Although Ferraro doesn't go that far, she does say *daughta* and *supporta*. Further, she uses New Yorkish expressions such as "stand on line" and "I'm here for ten years" for "I've been here for ten years." During the campaign the question was not how would New Yorkers respond, but how would Ferraro's speech play in Peoria.

Ronald Reagan, on the other hand, was a speech clutch-hitter. When queried on the age issue, Reagan turned on his familiar grin and pointed out he'd made a decision earlier not to use "my opponent's age and lack of experience as an issue" in the campaign. Bingo!

# *D*ON'T REPEAT THE CANARD

For examples of what to do—and not to do—in competitive speech, catch the evening TV news.

"Tell me, congressman, why are you against the Aid to Grade School children bill?"

*Inexperienced congressman:* Against the grade school children aid bill? Why no! I'm not against the grade school bill, why—

Score so far: three to nothing against the congressman. The audience has heard *against* three times. Contrast this with:

*Experienced congressman:* (taking care not to repeat the canard): Happy to comment on my progressive plan for U.S. school children. I believe . . .

Score so far: one to one. Every positive point he adds now is a plus.

Move this principle to selling. You're trying to get a prospect in another city to use your shipping service.

*Prospect:* Do you have a warehouse in this state?

*Inexperienced salesperson:* No, we don't have a warehouse here. But what we do . . .

Score: two to nothing against the seller. Now a power-word closer answers the same question:

"What particular features of a warehouse would you find of interest?"

Score: objection derailed without repeating the canard. Prospect now redirected to tell you *why* such a service appeals to him. Now the power-word closer can zero in on *that.*

Persuasive speech! The great entertainers have it. Top executives. Super salesfolk. Influencers of public opinion. Power speech will rivet and hold attention, sell your products, your company, your ideas, *yourself.* It's the most potent weapon available in modern society. Acquire it and you accrue many other abilities. Ignore it, and drab speech will kick you in the slats.

No wonder effective speech is your primary tool in closing sales. The need for correct words doesn't begin with the close, of course. It starts with the first word in your approach and continues through your goodbye. However, right words are more important in the close than any other time. At the close, the buyer's mind is highly sensitized. He or she is irritable, suspicious, and extremely susceptible to word shadings—more so than at any other time.

Weigh every word. Power words build a positive rather than a negative reaction in the customer's mind. Great trial lawyers, evangelists, and sales-closing leaders collect and use these words. They are not difficult. They are, without exception, simple common, everyday words. Every closer will find them invaluable.

## *H*OW TO BUILD YOUR "YES" FRAMEWORK

Get the buyer into the habit of saying *yes* all along. Then it's easier to get *yes* on the important questions.

"You like the pattern, don't you?"

"Yes," the customer says.

"This is a very valuable feature, don't you think?"

"Yes."

"You are perhaps wondering just what this attachment does, aren't you?"

"Yes, I have been."

"This could go well with the drapes in your dining room, couldn't it?"

"Yes, it could."

By asking yes-generating questions during the sale, you build a series of favorable responses. You've conditioned your customer's mind to successful closing:

- "Can I confirm your address?"

- "Do I have your initials correct?"

- "Will you OK this for me?"
  (Always *OK*, never *signature*)

# *A*LWAYS ASK WHY

Without *why*, expert closers' work would be much harder—sometimes impossible. Imagine you're a buyer. *Why* is hard to answer without committing yourself. Yet it's inoffensive. Children are forever asking *why* of parents. We grew up with it. Great salespeople use *why* whenever the sale gets on shaky ground.

Suppose your customer says: "I do not think this is exactly what I want."

Your best defense is: "Why?"

Suppose your customer says: "Oh, I don't know. I just don't think I want it." If you smile, you can ask *why?*

Repeat the word, with charm, to draw out the real reason the customer hesitates. You ask: "*Why* do you ponder, Mr. Rinker?"

Or: "*Why* do you think that is true?"

Or: "*Why* do you want to wait until after April 15, when the price will inevitably advance before that time?" Don't forget that little word *why*—one of the most powerful closing words in the rich American language.

A Chicago psychologist has systemized the sales use of *why*. He calls it the Bounce-Back. You merely use *why* on the prospect after she throws her *why* at you.

You asked the buyer for an order. The buyer counters: "Why should I buy these products now?" Use the Bounce-Back: "*Why* do you ask why?" the most powerful defense is still another *why*.

Remember the schoolyard doggerel:

Y Y U R
Y Y U B
I N O U R
Y Y 4 M E

It translates, as you probably recall:

Too wise you are
Too wise you be
I know you are
Too wise for me

Use it to help you remember the power of two *whys* in closing.

## *L*ET'S USE LET'S OFTEN

Good closers use *let's* to stimulate sign-up.

"Highly useful," ace closer Chris Locke agreed. "Let's is a cooperative word. It's you-and-I-together. It is an unselfish word. When you say, 'Let's do so and so' buyers don't feel coerced. They think the suggestion is as much their idea as yours."

"I might say to a woman: 'Let's you and I see why you'll get more for your money by okaying this today.' How much more acceptable than the dogmatic: 'You'll get more for your money if you buy today.' The conclusion is the same. But that word *let's* makes it more acceptable."

Locke, with annual earnings in six figures, continued: "I often say to a prospect, as a strong powerful closing shove: 'Let's arrange for you to try this in your own home.' Build closing phrases around *let's*. It gets more dotted-line action than the same ideas expressed other ways.

# CONNOTE OR DENOTE?

One good salesman started his presentation with: "We'll now show you *how* this service will save you money." An infinitely better choice than: "You will save money if you install this." *How* arouses curiosity, one of the mind's dominant turn-ons. An opportunity to see *how* something works? Your curiosity is immediately aroused. You lean forward to hear the rest.

On best-selling newsstand magazines, note frequent use of *how* in cover headlines. Look at both ad and editorial pages inside. See also how often *new* and *now* are used. Everyone wants *instant* gratification in a *new* way. Build these words in your closing.

Another magic closing word is *truth*. *Truth* immediately gets attention.

"Here is the truth about that situation, Mr. Roberts," a saleswoman says in countering an objection. *Truth* is strong. It stands for a quality we all respect.

*Right* is a powerful closing word. Robert D. Esseks, a master seller of leasing services to business, employed it to great advantage. In leasing, the interest rate is the prime issue, arrived at after back-and-forth negotiation. Yet the prospect often asks "What's the rate?" at the beginning.

Esseks always said: "Whatever's *right!*" The prospect invariably relaxed. After all, isn't every buyer interested in the *right* price?

Esseks closed dozens of leasing contracts at the *right* price.

William E. Bolster, an advertising agency account manager, also used the word *right* in another way. When a client threatened to cut his budget, Bolster told him seriously: "This isn't *right*."

The client reconsidered. After all, if it's not *right*, who wants to do it? Forestalling a cutback saves reclosing the sale all over again later.

Every word has two meanings. The dictionary meaning of a word is *denotation:* for example, a dog is a quadruped of the canine species. The second meaning of the word is *connotation*, that peculiar personal interpretation based on your own experience. Connotation of *dog* thus means *your cocker spaniel Gloriana, or a neighbor's* dog, a dog *you owned,* a dog that barked at midnight. You give dog your inner meaning.

In selling, *connotation* is far more important than *denotation.* Why? Because 80 percent of all buying decisions are based on emotions. Connotation is the emotional meaning.

In closing a sale, if you tell the customer to *sign here,* the connotation is formal, legal, formidable, binding, fearful. The buyer has been warned about signing contracts, wills, waivers. On the other hand, if you ask for the buyer's name and address, he or she is usually willing. There's no fearful connotation about those words.

## *T*HE POWER IN STATING THE PROSPECT'S NAME

Dale Carnegie taught his students: "If you remember my name, you pay me a subtle compliment; you indicate that I have made an impression on you." Your prospect's name is one of the most powerful closing tools because most of us are more interested in ourselves than anyone else.

Repeat your prospect's name several times—but don't overdo it—during your sales call. *Connect your prospect's name with the major benefit statements:*

- "This automatic dialing feature, Jim, will save you a lot of time."

- "Our warranty is designed to give you peace of mind, Susan."

Your prospect will not know it. But you are using a powerful psychological strategy called *learned association* or *positive pairing.* By connecting your prospect's name with prominent product benefits, your customer will expect to hear something positive when you next mention his or her name. At the close, use your prospect's name. The name will again produce positive feelings. This little-known secret of master closers will cinch more sales than you ever thought possible.

# ON USING REASSURING WORDS

Many a close is bungled by improperly chosen last-minute words urging the customer to sign. The straw-hat era salesperson disdained such refinements. He browbeat customers, saying: "Put your John Hancock right there on the old dotted line!"

Customers, by not signing in droves, made such salespeople and their methods obsolete. Today we use these refined but powerful reassuring phrases:

- "Your name and address, please."

- "Would you mind looking this over, and if it's correct, put down your name on the next-to-the-last line?"

- "Just write your name and address the way you want it to appear on our records."

Joseph Conrad, the novelist, was an effective user of motivating words. What a salesman he could have been! That keen perception of human emotions and respect for the fine shadings of word meanings—a prime asset!

A friend suggested that Conrad write an autobiography. Conrad refused. He didn't believe he had anything to say in a life story.

Then his friend insisted: "You know, you really *must*."

"It was not an argument, but I submitted at once," said Conrad. "If *one must!* The force of a word! He who wants to persuade should put his trust *not* in the right arguments but in the right *word*. The power of sound has always been greater than the power of sense. Nothing so affecting a whole mass of lives has come from reflection.

"On the other hand, you cannot fail to see the power of mere words, such words as *glory*, for instance, or *pity*. Shouted with perseverance, with ardor, with conviction, these two alone have set whole nations in motion and upheaved the dry hard ground on which rests the whole social fabric.

"Of course, the accent must be attended to. The right accent. That's very important. Don't talk to me of your Archimedes lever. Give me the *right* word and the *right* accent and I will move the world!"

An illustration of "the right words in the right accent" came during a large heating, ventilation, and air conditioning (HVAC) trade fair. A near-10 salesman worked outside a display. He was in complete charge each minute of his presentation. He motivated the crowd exactly as he wanted to—with masterful salesmanship via master wordsmithing.

During a lull, a business reporter asked him how many times a day he gave his presentation.

"Five times an hour, 12 hours a day."

"Sixty times a day?"

"That's right."

"Have you been giving it long?"

"Three years."

Each time he gave that talk—without ever changing a word or altering an accent since both were perfect—he made sales or got good leads. Yet the talk contained exactly 237 words.

"I didn't write the talk," he said. "The customers did. I tried telling them and watched results. Whenever I'd think of an improvement, I'd try that. Some worked. Some didn't. Whenever I found a word or phrase that increased sales, I added it. In time, I got a presentation that really brought them in. That's what I wanted.

"Every word in that talk is important. I wouldn't change one word. I couldn't afford to. I'd lose money."

The right words are golden.

One hard-bitten sales executive, a respecter of words, lacked Conrad's finesse. But what he said will live long after Conrad's fine words are forgotten. Each morning he said:

"Worship words, you fellows. If you ever stop using 'em right, you stop eating. Remember that."

## PRACTICAL GUIDELINES ON WORD MASTERY

How can you ensure the right word at your tongue tip when you need it? Wilfred J. Funk, who spent his life among words, believed: "The man or woman who's master of words is a master of people." Dr. Funk's suggestions on word mastering are particularly helpful in closing sales.

*Listen* to cultured people. Hear them on TV, at lectures, in church, in conversation with learned men and women. Listen. Notice how they choose their words and how they use them. You can do it too.

*Spend* 15 minutes a day in serious reading, not comic books or mysteries, but classics by word masters.

*When you encounter* a new word, look it up at once. Not "later" which never comes. Now.

*Add two new words* to your inventory each day. Learn their meanings. Use them in writing or speaking several times. Make them yours.

But don't overdo it!

Peter Hockstein, vice president of Ogilvy & Mather, New York, has words for salespeople on words: "The following inputs, "said the account executive fresh out of business school, "should be sufficient for you to generate a sales presentation."

What he meant to say, of course, was "Here's the information you need to write the presentation."

Here are astounding ways to get so gobbledygooked you'll be *sure* to be *mis*understood:

1. *Use buzzwords* from mathematical and computer sciences, misapplied to business—words like *parameters, inputs,* and *generate.* Instead of saying, "Let's make up a prospect list," say, "Let's input a probability sequence within firmly limited parameters."

2. *Use nouns as verbs,* for example, "The cancer scare will impact our market."

3. *Use gobbledygook.* Here are well-known quotes rendered in gobbledygook. See if you can translate them back to the American language.

I would optimumly prefer to proceed from confirmed models in the decision-making process than to have the chief executive officer's options to implement decisions. *(I'd rather be right than be president.)*

Hopefully, if they input their caloric requirements with pre-sweetened high-yeast-content baked goods products, they will have an affirmative nutritional experience of adequate dimensions. *(Let them eat cake.)*

I am faced with the options of continuing to function as an entity or to abort the process and terminate all operations. *(To be or not to be, that is the question.)*

Proceeding according to acceptable strategy, and on the basis of visual inputs, I launched the strike potential under my authority, thereby effectively relegating the manned enemy subsurface vehicle to a condition of permanent downtime. *(Sighted sub, sank same.)*

All male heads of household have an inherent right under established common law principles to an upscale, multileveled, primary dwelling unit of impermeable construction, accessed by implementing a retractable passageway across an aqueous perimeter. *(A man's house is his castle.)*

At 2 A.M. this morning, a battalion-sized unit of colonies-posted infantry cold-bloodedly launched an aggression against several unprepared and unprotected civilian hamlets and are now proceeding without the support of the oppressed indigenous population, evidently intent on subjugating the legitimate democratic aspirations of marginal agribusinessmen and small commercial entrepreneurs. *(The Redcoats are coming! The Redcoats are coming!)*

As a manager of this functional aggressive mobile marine combat entity, I have ascertained we should continue standard operating procedures for combative maneuvers under favorable conditions, despite questionable projections by our adversaries regarding our progressing to fruition. *(Don't give up the ship.)*

Get the point? The classic phrases are famous because they *move* people to actions, to meet objectives, to need the bidding of celebrated motivators. Which versions are best for closing sales? You know the answer.

## *F*LATTERING WITHOUT OVERDOING IT

Many are the commercial uses for flattering words—to make a rose by any other name a lot more impressive. Rock Lubin, real estate maven, says sales soar or droop on the way you describe the house to the buyer.

Lubin exhorts real estate salesfolk to use *year-round comfort control, husband's retreat, slumber area, countrylike atmosphere, extra touch of quality, indoor/outdoor living, country-style kitchen, programmed family comfort.*

"Semantics can turn an ordinary floor plan and community into a highly attractive place to live," Lubin says. "The consumer must be romanced."

Take a hard look at the way you describe your products, services, company, or industry. Are you giving your enemies free points? Don't.

Remember, a prophet is often without honor in his own country; you buy Kansas City steaks in New York and New York strip sirloin in Kansas City; an expert is a person with a briefcase 50 miles from home.

*We* is a power word with potential for both good and bad. When an accountant sees a client and talks about *our* problems (meaning the client's), that's good. He's being part of the common family. When a doctor or nurse asks a patient, "How are we feeling today?" it's childish and patronizing.

And while we're snuffing pointless diddle, help kill off the affected saleswomen in ladies' clothing shops. A perfect stranger walks in to hear:

"Come in, *sweetie.*"

"Yes, *honey,* what can I show you?"

"Yes, *dear,* did you have something in mind?"

I've polled 50 women, and I've yet to find one who likes this mawkish twaddle. Since no one wants it, why do it? This is power in reverse. Overfamiliarity in public to a stranger is a sure way to win the booby prize—even if you do sell lingerie.

## *A*VOIDING TURN-OFF WORDS

You've seen how certain words are turn-*ons.* Conversely, other words are turn-*offs*—not only do they fail to push your case forward, they actually set you back.

Topping the turn-off list is "you know." This fad has reached gigantic proportions. One teen was heard telling another: "You know, I don't know, you know."

Inserting, "you know" between every few words is deadly. The salesperson must arrest it: it's wanted for murder.

One salesman was heard recently using "to be honest with you" four times in one presentation. His prospect aptly said: "Anybody who keeps saying, 'To be honest with you,' scares me. What else is he supposed to be but honest?"

Whatever you do, avoid the tired, hackneyed, fad figures of speech. Why be the 14th to say "Have a good day!" before 10:30 A.M.? That's not the way to close sales. It is the way to sound like an unimaginative moron.

## $H$OW TIE-DOWN WORDS PROMOTE BUYING

Tie-down words literally tie the prospect to a buying commitment. To understand why they work, understand the base theory: closing is a participation, not a spectator, sport. If you make a statement, the prospect may well disbelieve. If the prospect makes a statement, he or she *believes.*

Here are four useful tie-downs:

- Wouldn't it?
- Doesn't it?
- Don't you agree?
- Isn't that right?

Create tie-downs that suit your product or service. Here, for example, are questions adapted to housing:

- "Do you think this is the sort of community you'd like to live in?"
- "Do you think you'd be comfortable living in this home? If we could work out a good purchase price (financing agreement, etc.), do you think you could decide today?"

- "Now that you've selected a home you really like, would you like to put down a deposit to guarantee your home (lot) I'd really like to see you get this home before our next price increase. Are you ready to get it started today?"

Lee Stanley uses this tie-down in selling sunroom additions: "If I can show you how to get an $8,000 sunroom for $1,500, will you feel comfortable giving me a small commitment today?"

## *R*EPLACING INFLAMMATORY WORDS

Inflammatory words block sales. Avoid *if* in most conversations. All too often it leads to a negative. A much better word: *which*.

"*Which* of these two finishes do you prefer?" is a strong safe closing phrase. Use SOS—Something Or Something. Avoid SON—Something or Nothing. (Not to be confused with Something *for* Nothing, one of your major closing keys.)

You must also avoid playing the prospect's game with inflammatory words. Don't get suckered into pouring gasoline on the fire.

Ace housing salesfolk know this do/don't list by heart:

| **Never say:** | **Instead, say:** |
| --- | --- |
| Buy | Own or get involved |
| Sell | Help you own |
| Monthly payment | Initial equity to get you started |
| Price | Total investment |
| Subdivision | Community |
| Lot | Home site |
| Contract | Paperwork |
| Deal | Magnificent opportunity |
| Final house or lot | One available transaction |
| Problem | Challenging |
| Commission | Fee for service |
| Standard | Included features |
| The company | We (not them) |

Memorable words, properly applied, close sales. Make sure your word power is first rate.

# CHAPTER TWENTY-TWO

# How to Close for Keeps

Think your work is finished when the buyer signs the order? *It's not.* One more vital step remains: nailing the sale down for good.

One-shot Finnegans are salespeople who close a sale once and never go back to the same customer. They don't wear well. They close by deception, too much pressure, or misrepresentation, or they fail to build ongoing confidence.

One-shotters are not good salespeople. The man or woman who can make a sale, call on the customer later, and continue to increase the volume—here's the salesperson who makes big money and gets promoted to a better job.

Let's examine the closer who sells for keeps—professionals who make a sale, and make it stay closed, can call back and get more business, time after time.

Sales have a habit of backsliding just when you believe everything is closed. The slippage is sometimes a cancellation, sometimes a reduced order, sometimes a postponement.

Even odder things happen: Ms. Decision-Maker is transferred and her replacement comes in with a clean broom. It happens.

No matter what causes the slippage, guess who's nominated to put traction back under the wheels? You're right—the Old Dependable. You.

Your job is to reclose the sale and lock it tight. You'll need additional closing strategies for encore work.

Sometimes the backsliding's just simple buyer remorse. For you, the close is a victory. You're elated. For the buyer, it's an uncertainty. Buying fears, momentarily overcome, are back.

The buyer thinks: "Did I make a mistake? Will I get my money's worth? Could I have done better elsewhere? Will these be what I really need? How do I know the firm is reliable? What will the stock market do? Am I going to lose my hard-earned money? Am I crazy?"

These fears turn the buyer into a doubter. The same person who willingly signed your order now withers you with: "I've been thinking. Better hold up on my order for a while. There are some factors I didn't think of when we met. I'll call you."

This doesn't occur occasionally. It occurs often. Buyer's Remorse is seated backward in the saddle, charging to the rear at a full gallop.

# *H*OW TO PREVENT BUYER REMORSE

The best way to handle computer virus? Don't let it get a toehold in your software programs in the first place. Ditto buyer's remorse. Prevent the seed from being planted.

First for starters, a good closer doesn't linger longer than absolutely necessary once the sale is closed. One fine salesperson recommended: "Get in—get through—get out." Good advice.

Get out as quickly as you can. But don't run like a bandit. Obviously, jumping out the window arouses distrust and ill feeling. However, don't dawdle and engage in social conversation one minute longer than necessary. Don't give the buyer an opening to think about cancellation or postponement.

Express that most beguiling and valuable sentiment on taking leave: gratitude. Many salespeople slur over this step, treat it as inconsequential, pay it little or no attention. That is wrong. Thank the buyer cordially, sincerely, and warmly—even if you had to fight every step of the way for that order.

Say "Thank you!" and mean it. Smile! Show the buyer you appreciate the business. We all want appreciation. We all like to feel our business is important and vital. We like to think our purchase keeps a department store operating, an insurance company in business, an airline flying. Stoke the idea in the buyer's mind.

Do I hear catcalls out there? "Smile and a shoeshine! Right out of Willy Loman and *Death of a Salesman!* Get current, brother!"

The reason some clichés last long enough to get tiresome is fundamental: they're true (or as Jack Point tells us in Gilbert & Sullivan's *Yeomen of the Guard:* "There's a grain or two of truth among the chaff!").

So it is with smile power. And new research supports it, Lionel Tiger reports in *The Pursuit of Pleasure.* Roger Masters of Dartmouth College and his associates have published research on the facial expressions of human politicians. Those who smile more do better. Smiling appears to be a critical factor in attracting voters, women as well as men. Constituents may be irritated or intimidated by grim-faced leaders but reassured and enhanced by the smiling variety. Happy smiling faces are also an asset to entertainers, who must control the attention and enthusiasm of their audience.

Bill Miller, a mobile home salesman, used the "I appreciate you" technique in nailing down sales with Joe Conforti, one of his dealers.

"You're my biggest customer," he said to Joe. "I'm going to buy you a steak."

Joe Conforti was flattered. "I had no idea my business was that important," he said beaming.

Small thing? Sure. But do you think any of Bill's orders were likely to come unglued?

## CONGRATULATE YOUR BUYER ON CHOICE

Sincere thanks is fine for many buyers. But for the more sophisticated, take an added step: congratulate the decision maker "on making a profitable choice for your company." After all, that's the reason *why* of her decision. Sure, she'd like to feel appreciated—even more so by her boss. So when buyer sophistication allows it, *congratulate* more than *thank*.

Henry Schapper, ace Manhattan head hunter, always wrote a letter to the newly placed employee, timed to arrive on the new hire's first day.

Congratulations to you and to the company on getting together. An excellent choice! Best of fortune in your continued career advance!

Henry

A great inoculation against the scourge of buyer's remorse. His placements (and payments of fees) rarely went awry.

## $T$URNING DISASTER INTO TRIUMPH

Sometimes gratitude leads to repeat sales, even when the first sale went kaflooie. Lynn Doyle had been contracting only three months when he unearthed a large prospect. Only a youngster, he was enthused that tycoon John B. Phillips let him quote on a million-dollar project.

Lynn gave Phillips the best he had. But his experience just wasn't solid enough. The business went elsewhere. Naturally, Doyle was discouraged but not beaten. He called Phillips and thanked him cordially.

"But what have I done?" Phillips said. "I placed the business elsewhere."

"I know that," Lynn told him, "but Mr. Phillips, you're the first highly respected developer who had enough confidence to let me quote on an important project—an enormous boost to me as a new company. I want to thank you. I am deeply grateful."

Nothing happened for three days. Then Phillips called Doyle over and gave him a contract for a smaller building. "The attitude of the gratitude" pleased Phillips. He expressed his pleasure by assigning Doyle a different piece of business.

Before you leave a closed customer, make a short pointed reassurance talk—the shorter and more pointed the better. Highlight the advantages. Reiterate to your customer the profit and satisfaction he's going to get.

"I congratulate you on your choice, Mr. Wilsie," Johnson Benn says. "You will enjoy months and months of satisfaction from this equipment. And you will save money, too—the market is definitely headed upward. Thirty days from now it would have cost you $75 more to duplicate this model."

As she leaves Millicent Braun says: "Mr. Wells, to a man of your business judgment, I needn't even say this—but it's wise you're placing this order now. As time goes on, you'll be more and more satisfied." Then out she gets.

One retail clerk got the postsell theory right but missed the application. When a poker player bought playing cards, the clerk said: "Thank you very much. I hope you win with these."

"Thanks," responded the local Amarillo Slim. "I just hope you don't say that to each customer."

"Sure I do," said the clerk, seriously, "the playing card company tells us to say it. It makes customers feel lucky."

As sales trainers know, you can't win them all. As the native New Yorker said to the inquiring tourist: "Radio City? It's easy. Watch me and get off two subway stops *before* I do." Oh, well.

## $S$*TRESS BUYER NEEDS, NOT YOURS*

Hubert Bermont learned the value of selling for keeps when he trained in retailing. Says Bermont:

> When I was a young salesman, a top-notch colleague always went home with the biggest commission check. He had 30 years' experience. Having armed myself with product information as the old-timer had, I went into combat with customers: wheedling, cajoling, charming, telling jokes, and even threatening them with consequences of not buying.
>
> I was the good guy trying to make sales to support my new young family. They were the bad guys trying to prevent me from making sales. After each infrequent sale, I was emotionally exhausted.
>
> Mr. Experience had no such days. He was easygoing and calm and lost very few sales. One day, he took me aside and said:
>
> "Kid, I like you. I'm going to explain why you have the wrong approach and the wrong attitude. These customers aren't your

enemies. They don't wander in by accident or to come out of the rain. They come here because they want something.

"You act as if they're here to give you a rough time. As if it's your duty to remind them they came in to buy something. They have a genuine need for what we sell, but they're frightened. These are tough times. They work hard for their money. They are terribly concerned about buying something they don't need nor want.

"Your job is to calm them and help them part with money. Your job is not to fight them and try to grab their money because of your own needs. Their needs come first."

## $T$AKING THE UNHURRIED CLOSING ROUTE

Ellery Jordahl runs River City Furnace Ltd., in Mason City, Iowa, the city known for flamboyant salesmanship as the fictional River City in *The Music Man*. But a greater contrast between Jordahl and Professor Harold Hill would be impossible to find.

Jordahl is low key and sincerely believes in supplying a quality product. He was his company's initial salesman for River City's Hot Shot furnaces. He believes in selling for keeps. After all, his Hot Shots last 10 years or longer. Jordahl wanted to sign Dave Wetzel in Waterloo, Illinois, as his distributor for the state.

"At the time I didn't have a product to deliver," Jordahl recalls. "Yet I had to collect a $9,000 deposit on my word alone so I could start building the furnace. I had never met Dave or Rita Wetzel face to face. They had never been furnace distributors before."

Formidable barriers, indeed! Jordahl decided on an unhurried we're-all-friends approach.

"I decided to make them aware I was selling this product across the whole United States and that distributorships were going on a state-by-state basis. Hot Shot was a hot opportunity."

Jordahl drove from Eau Claire, Wisconsin, to Waterloo. He arrived at the Wetzel farm late one afternoon and had dinner with Dave and Rita. He took it slow. After dinner, he took the Hot Shot prototype out of the box.

"They were astonished," Jordahl says. "They'd never seen anything with such attractiveness and quality."

Again no rush. He told them he wanted a deposit of $9,000 for the Illinois distributorship.

The Wetzels wrote out the check. But Jordahl didn't consider the sale finished—far from it. He wanted to nail it down; he was selling for keeps. To establish trust, he emphasized a common experience: farming. One farmer can trust another.

"I told Dave I was willing to give him a chance in a new field. He never had any experience. When I started out, I never had any experience either. I told him I knew farmers get up with the birds and they work until work is done. It's hard for eight-to-five people to be successful."

Jordahl kept talking for a couple more hours, emphasizing trust, nailing down the sale.

"I had faith in Dave and Rita and showed it," Jordahl says. "In return, they had faith in me. They wrote out a check strictly on my word. Honesty makes people credible to me. And my honesty came across to them. These people were farmers. We were talking about farming. I meant what I said—and it showed."

Wetzel became Hot Shot's largest distributor, accounting for 1,000 units a year, via 90 dealers in Illinois and Missouri.

Jordahl, the master salesperson, knows when to break the sign-up-and-get-out rule. When you're building a big-ticket long-range relationship based on trust, stay as long as it takes.

(Are closing rules contradictory? You bet! The aces know *when* to apply *which* technique!)

# *H*ELPING BUYER SELL SELF

Robert Connolly closes for keeps via customer involvement. The sale is nailed down because the customer comes to believe he made each critical decision along the way.

"When you convince the buyer the purchase plan is *his* idea, remarkable things occur," Connolly says. "Once he accepts praise for a procedure, he'll defend it. So he is convincing you and thus selling himself."

Exciting? Yes. But, like most sophisticated closing principles, it takes time and practice to master.

How to credit your prospect? It may fall into place. One way: simply pretend it was his idea. React as if the idea had just occurred. Show a growing enthusiasm for it. Then he will start to sell you.

Start the process with a statement: "You know, you really have quite an idea there."

Or try this: "What is your judgment on the best course of action here?"

This whole technique is based on human vanity. If your prospect believes *your* idea is *his* idea, he'll defend it to the end.

You're selling a line of commercial supplies. You write your regular size order then ask:

"Do you feel it would be good planning to reserve an additional quantity for delivery during May? Of course, we will confirm before delivery."

After a yes answer, but before leaving your prospect, say: "You know, I like your idea for planning future deliveries. It makes a lot of sense."

You're selling homes. After you feel you have made your basic points, say: "I'd like to get your judgment on this matter. Do you prefer the *convenience* of the 20-year installments or the greater *savings* of the 15-year-installments? What's your idea on that?"

Then later you say: "You've got a good thought there. We'll set it up just that way."

# *D*ON'T NEGLECT YOUR CUSTOMER—EVER

Use each customer as a source of additional business. Your closing-for-keeps job is not to make *sales* but to make *customers*. Keep in touch with the customer. Find out how the product's working. See that the buyer is kept pleased and happy.

A shrewd businessman in Detroit once sat down and wrote out his business credo. The sale, said he, *starts* when the order is signed.

After that the seller must see that the customer gets the utmost profit, satisfaction, advantage, and use out of the product. That man was Henry Ford I. That credo did extraordinary things to the small business Henry Ford headed. It will do wonders for you.

The sale is truly closed only when your customer knows how to use the product or service, when he is satisfied. Your job as a closing specialist: drop in on your customer within a reasonable time. See how it's working. If you cannot look in on him, call. Ask if there is any further service he needs.

If you want to keep the customer, keep in touch. Customers resent neglect. A chief cause of lost customers: failure of the salesperson to follow the sale. Don't let this happen to you.

One veteran salesperson, asked for the most important principle of all, said: "Never forget a customer. Never let a customer forget you."

Closing sales is much more than the vital act of "your initials here please." Your job is closing ongoing customers. Such is the route to repeat business *and* to powerful Third-Party Endorsements. An actor in off-Broadway's *Song of Singapore* stops the curtain-call applause to say: "If you like us, tell your friends. If your don't like us, tell your relatives!" Nailing down the sale, pure and simple.

# CHAPTER TWENTY-THREE

# Closing with Consultation Plus Conversation

Clinton Bird sells men's clothes in Manhattan's trendy SoHo in a store "as much show business as retailer," complete with dogs, cats, parrots, a live jazz combo, and one pet monkey as mascot.

Theater though it be, salesfolk are still judged at day-end by closed sales. And in this vital tally, Bird excels. Why? Because he achieves instant rapport as he consults with 15 to 20 buyers each day, people he's closing—and meeting—for the first time.

"My drive is to close at least 15 buyers per day," Bird says. "But the goal is all *underneath*. On the surface, I'm a *consultant*—choosing the right clothes for each buyer, wearables that enhance each person's presentation to the business, professional, and social world.

"Buyers lack objectivity about what they should wear," Bird says. "You view this need as consultation. To them, it's relying on an *expert friend*.

"It's taken some years to become a genuine expert on men's wear," Bird says. "But I establish myself as a friend in the first three minutes. Without rapport, there's no friendship and no sale—that's the short formula."

How does he do it? First, by whom he selects as they come in the door. The store specializes in "suiting the counselor to the customer." (The multinational store's 30 salesfolk look like a UN committee—blacks, Latinos, Arabs, orientals—each alert to corresponding customers.)

"And don't forget the real minority—the *WASP*, me," says Bird. "I watch for the superpolite snotty Princetonians." Such a couple entered one afternoon, dressed in clean but worn informal yacht clothes. ("They could have just docked from a Bill Buckley world cruise," Bird thought.) The monied set doesn't always go to Bloomingdale's—sometimes they go slumming in a search for quality and good prices.

Bird introduced himself, embassy reception-style, carefully noting the names—Dr. and Mrs. William T. Hamilton—and offered them a choice of juice or seltzer. The couple graciously took one of each. ("Good idea to *give* the customer something early on," Bird says. "After all, that's what friends do!")

Everyone settled in comfortable consultation chairs. Mentally noting they called one another Bill and Millicent, Bird played his first card:

"I noticed the club crest on your shirt, Dr. Hamilton," Bird said. "Isn't that the Zanzibar Club in Florida?"

"Why, yes, it is," the customer said. "We're from Naples, Florida. Taking our boat up to the Finger Lakes for the summer. This is a stop en route." (Not far from the Buckley cruise, Bird thought, also noting Millicent's $30,000 worth of understated jewelry.)

They swapped mutual friend Club Z stories. Then Dr. Hamilton asked about a suit he'd seen in a newspaper ad, his reason for coming to the store.

Bird didn't think that suit was right for this customer and said so.

"But I do recommend you now look at the double-breasted below-navel-button garbardine just in," he said. "I believe it will do something rather startling for you."

He got the doctor before the try-on mirror.

"Look at yourself in these colors—light gray, black check, and deep brown," Bird said.

The prospect tried on the three coats, and then Bird turned to Mrs. Hamilton: "Which *effect* do you like best?"

"Bill, the brown is really you," she said.

Bird now knew that each purchase must suit her. She never criticized what she didn't like—praised what she did.

"There are good ways to complement this suit," Bird added. "Take a look at these four ties." He fanned the ties out in the water-fountain style on the table. On impulse, he asked her: "What color do you tend to avoid?"

"Green," she said. "Makes him look sallow."

"Excellent judgment!" Bird said.

He then brought out a blue blazer cut in nautical style.

"I could see you on the bridge with this."

While the couple were looking in the mirror, Bird spread three pairs of mix/match slacks on the floor. He arranged them like cloth sculpture at the Museum of Modern Art. Mrs. Hamilton nodded in approval as she tiptoed through the floor art.

"Bill, this blue twill has *savior faire*," she said, again never knocking the others.

At that point, Bird made a silent calculation on the approved stack of clothes: two suits, three pairs of separate pants, three shirts, and four ties ("$2100, give or take a few dollars").

Dr. Hamilton then took out a vest-pocket calculator designed like an expensive cigarette case and started punching. Money discussion on the starboard bow! Time for friend-to-friend talk.

"Is that the new computer from Great Britain?" Bird asked. "I've heard about it. It's not on the market here yet! I hear it does absolutely everything!"

Flattered, Mrs. Hamilton made a "it's nothing" gesture. The doctor chimed in: "Our neighbor's a computer nut. Brought it to us from a London trade show."

Bird grabbed the cue.

"No wonder Robert Frost told us to help our neighbor build a fence!"

Both Hamiltons smiled, icy polite, as if to say: "We *know* Robert Frost. Lots of people don't."

Dr. Hamilton went back to checking his computer.

"Let's see. Your ad said 10% discount today."

Bird held up a hand.

"Yes, before 2 P.M. But our store sticks strictly to advertised sale time. Tell you what I *can* do—rush the alterations. That normally takes ten days. Where are you staying.

"Hotel Mark on the Upper East Side."

"Fine," said Bird. "Make out your check and I'll personally deliver your clothes tomorrow."

"Before noon?" Bird agreed. "But on one condition: you log me and the store into your database. Nothing is more valuable than keeping in touch with rare friends."

When Bill and Millicent said good-bye to Clint, they all regretted concluding a highly unusual party. Even the parrot sqawked: "Style leader! Style leader!"

P.S. Clint Bird's day continued, fueled now by closer's high. By day-end he'd sold $5,000 worth of clothes—via his powerful instant rapport with strangers, the cornerstone of closing via consultation.

# KEY TO RAPPORT: "WE'RE IN THIS TOGETHER!"

The first step in business-to-business selling—with rapport—is to find out how buyers in your industry operate. Sound basic? It may be more basic than you know. Mark Blessington found this out the hard way fresh out of business school.

Business was off for Blessington's client, a small screen-printing company specializing in putting designs on glass for slot machines and arcade games. The economy was down, and kids were turning to home video games. The company needed to find another outlet—quickly. Blessington's brainstorm: furniture.

"Instead of printing dragons, they would be printing inlaid glass effects, like a cat peering out of the front of an Early American cabinet," Blessington projected.

He wrote a marketing plan and started to call on furniture companies. "I told them about our design capabilities and our quality," he said. But he drummed up very little business. The floundering company folded.

The reason, he finally discovered, was that the furniture business consists of a small network of decision makers based in North Carolina. "They all know one another and here I am with this sophisticated sales approach that didn't get me anywhere," he said. "I was still an outsider."

"Selling through a network can be a slow process. But in many industries, the only way to sell is through the relationship game. Had I done a little thinking ahead, I'd have saved a lot of time and effort."

# *W*HAT TO DO WHEN THEY WANT TO THINK IT OVER

"Isn't all this business about consultation just effective closing dressed up in new language?" one veteran closer asked at a sales rally.

Three answers:

- *Yes*: good closers become consultants when effective.

- *No*: sometimes ace consultants go beyond normal closing to sign the toughies (read and heed).

- If you can add new closing techniques to your inventory, who cares about the label? Rejoice in the better results.

Take Patty Bryant, ace closer of sun rooms for Solar Additions. You could call her work "adroit answering of objections." She calls it "consultation to aid the undecided."

Prospect: We want to think it over.

Bryant: That's fine, Mrs. Smith. Obviously, you wouldn't take your time thinking this thing over unless you were seriously interested, would you? I mean, I'm sure you're not telling me that to get rid of me. So, may I assume you'll give it very careful consideration? Now to clarify my thinking, what *phase* of this opportunity do you want to think over? (No pause.) Is it the quality of the service my company will render? Is it something I've forgotten to cover? Is it (two or three more positive statements that customer can't deny). Seriously, please level with me: what is it? (Pause.) Could it be the money?

Many times they will say, "Yes, it's the money." Then she handles the objection and begins reclosing.

Bryant believes every consultation has a reverse side. As a student of Biblical parables, she calls on her Lazarus Risen close. "I ask the prospect to consult with *me*." Bryant brings out Lazarus when the sale appears lost—lost that is, to the ordinary salesperson:

"Pardon me, Mr. Smith. Before you leave, may I apologize for not doing my job today? I must have been inept. Otherwise, I would have said and done the things necessary to convince you of the value of our sun rooms. Because I didn't, you and your family will not be enjoying the benefits of our beautiful sun room. And believe me, I'm truly sorry. Mr. Smith, I believe in this company and I earn my living helping people enjoy it. So I won't make the same mistake again, will you please tell me what I did wrong?"

It's dynamite! Recruit the prospect as *your* consultant.

# EASING YOUR BUYER'S TENSION

The consulting closer always works to relieve tension. Only in a relaxed atmosphere can the prospect respond to "just your initials here, please."

Consultative selling is based on this principle: the buyer makes decisions on specific buying criteria (needs, wants, desires). Then you act as a business partner to help the prospect meet those needs.

On TV, Lt. Columbo doesn't seem like a threat. He drives a beat-up car, wears a wrinkled raincoat. When he walks up, the suspect thinks: "This clown's trying to trap me? Impossible." So the suspect relaxes ("nothing to worry about.")

Then Columbo starts asking the right questions and the suspect feels a little tightness. Columbo senses the tension and changes the subject. Columbo is the great interrupter. "By the way," he says, and takes off on a new tangent. Once the tension is eased, he goes right back in.

He may walk away from a suspect six times. Each time, the suspect thinks "It's all over. He's done. I'm in the clear." Then Columbo comes back. The professional at work.

In consultative closing, we do much the same thing—without the battered car and rumpled clothes. We ask questions, not to threaten, but to get next-step information. Questions in a warm and pleasing way. When you see you're threatening the prospect, back off. When the pressure is off, try again.

In relieving tensions, why do you need so many closes? Because you need *more* ways to stimulate *yes* than they know ways to say *no*. If you don't outgun them, they'll outgun you.

Remember Gus McCrae in *Lonesome Dove* deciding not to chase the renegade Blue Duck across the desert: "No point in going after a man when you're *outhorsed!*"

All champions are multiclosers. This doesn't require towering intellect. It does require organizing your time and learning several closes throughly—not a high price. But you must get yourself up each day and put yourself to work. No one makes you do it. The sharp scissors of competition cuts away the incompetent. In this free field, you're free to succeed, free to fail.

# *T*HREE WAYS TO BREAK CLOSING IMPASSES

Closing the sale is the logical windup of the presentation. Here's where you solidify details of the purchase agreement.

"Yes, but some closings don't solidify all that easy," one promising newcomer pointed out. How true! If closing was a shoo-in, it wouldn't call for professional preparation and continual honing of skills. When the close fails to jell, ask yourself why.

Perhaps some earlier problem with a similar prospect brought about a mental block. This may have caused you to stop short of asking for the order. Know thy (inner) enemy. Knowledge is power.

Another closing block (certainly one of the strangest) occurs when a salesperson decides the prospect should *not* buy and doesn't *ask* for the order. For the record, it's the prospect's decision and responsibility to buy or not to buy. Do not make that decision for your buyer.

Finally, the closer may not have worked hard enough developing a customer benefit plan, resulting in a poorly prepared presentation that fell apart. Don't let this happen to you.

Say you're on a hike in the mountains. It's not on your map but there's a creek cutting across the trail. You're on one bank. You need to resume your trip on the *other* bank. What do you do? Figure a way to bridge the chasm. The same with a barrier to closing. Build a bridge. Here's how:

*1. Apologize.* You've pressed too hard. Back off with a quick apology: "I'm sorry. I just got carried away. I didn't mean to move so fast." What you're really doing is apologizing to yourself. Don't worry about it. Now you get a chance to try another of your many closes.

One champion says, "I didn't mean to push you." (A champion doesn't *push*—he or she *pulls* with leading questions.)

*2. Summarize benefits already agreed to, using tie-downs.* Play it safe and aim for minor agreements only now.

- "I know there are still questions in your mind, but this model is the size you wanted, isn't it?"
- "I wouldn't be here if you didn't have a need, would I?"
- "So all I'm trying to say is that the ajax seems to meet your needs, doesn't it?"

*3. Ask a progress question.* "I know we went through that rather quickly, but on those areas we've discussed so far, we've really agreed, haven't we?"

Keep using this technique to roll into your next close. Eventually the prospect will own your product/service.

Why? Because you know more closes than she knows objections.

# $H$OW A SOFT ANSWER TURNETH AWAY WRATH

The alliterative consulting closer commences civilized conversations with customers/clients and commences to convert the consultee. Sometimes it works that way. But on rare occasions, the buyer runs amock.

Jan Suchanek, a consumer goods salesperson, suggested a large drug wholesaler buy a six-month supply of his product. The salesperson explained his company had doubled its promotional spending in the buyer's area—thus stocking up would be wise. Outraged the buyer threw the order book across the room. Suchanek calmly picked it up, smiled, handed it back to the buyer: "Did you want to buy *more* than the six month supply?"

The buyer laughed and said: "What do you honestly believe is a reasonable amount to buy?" (a buying signal). They settled on a three-month supply.

Remember it may be a flare-up—not a psychotic episode.

Don't think rage is solely a modern problem. Back in the gas-light era, Diamond Jim Brady believed that seller wrath quenches buyer wrath. Brady, who sold railcars, tackled the terrible-tempered George Baer, president of the Reading Railroad (known to hate salesmen only a little less than labor unions). For five days Jim camped in Baer's outer office. Finally, Baer could stand it no longer. He rushed out popping with rage: "Why have you been sitting there for a whole week?"

"I've been waiting to tell you, Mr. Baer," said Jim pleasantly, "that you can go straight to hell."

When Diamond Jim Brady left an hour later, he carried a signed contract for $5 million worth of steel freight cars.

Brady was a closer who lived and worked on Flamboyant Street. During economic downturn—"panics" in his day—he remained in character: "Nothing's wrong with this country," he said, "that ain't only just temporary."

And on days when no strategic wrath was needed, Brady went back to consultative closing. His quiet self-effacing manner, his obvious pleasure in diversions of his prospects, his homely talk, his knowledge of the business, his easy, ample style—all added up to rare natural persuasiveness, which in every age, enables gifted closers to command the minds and hearts of others.

Accompanied by section foreman friends, Jim patroled tool shacks, listing needed supplies, and then presented lists to the astonished purchasing agent.

"Here's what you need, John," he'd say. "Me and the boys saved you a little work."

But James Buchanan Brady was much more than a spectacular character. All his outlandishness was not only an end, but a means. He was phenomenal. Everything he did, said, wore, ate, drank, and delighted in fitted into—and enhanced—the closing of sales.

## WHEN (AND WHY) TO OFFER FREE COUNSEL

Al Wall gives his customers Something for Nothing—free counsel. A Hollywood casting director would probably never cast Al Wall as a sales manager. (Movies, like the law, lag reality.) Al Wall is the modern, quiet salesperson who's come a long way from the old stereotype. He's racked up a successful record selling decorative home accessories—so much so he became national sales manager of the MaLeck Group, a leading company in that field.

Al's Something for Nothing is free advice. He meets regularly with group buyers for department store chains—not to sell—but to talk about their problems.

"Funny you never try to sell us your products," a buyer said to Al one day.

"No, I don't," Al said. "I'm here to find out about your problems and to relay solutions I've encountered among other retailers. Now some of those solutions probably include MaLeck. Sell products only and you're only as good as your last sale."

Al Wall calls it reverse selling. His customers feel they're getting an added service for free. No wonder Al's sales rise steadily year after year.

## CONSULTING WITH THREE Rs

John Medick was making his presentation for coffee service to the administrative service manager. As he neared the end, the ASM asked: "What's your price?" John quoted his list price and immediately the ASM said: "Way out—your competitor's price is $10 cheaper!"

How do you work with this objection? It's a road sign not a roadblock. John attacks it with the 3 Rs:

- **R**ephrase the statement as a question.
- **R**epeat the benefits stressing the cost-effective points.
- **R**educe the cost to its lowest factor.

In real life, it goes this way:

Medick: You feel that our price is too high for the quality and service you'd get. Is that your question?

ASM: Yes.

Medick: I know that our competitors *appear* to offer a lower price. But I guess I didn't explain very well all the extras you'd be getting for just pennies per cup.

John details the differences: his product versus competitor's. Quality. Holding power. Service on equipment. He didn't talk about the cost per case, but pennies per cup.

He added a Third-Party Endorsement: "Joe Benson, over in Rockville, wanted the same reliability for his operation. He's had our installation for three years. Why don't you call him and ask if our product pays its way?"

Medick also pointed out the long-range cost versus initial price. His key word: reliability.

"Ours is initially priced higher than theirs, but over a period of five years, our costs to operate are less than theirs due to the energy-saving feature. In fact, over time this will cost you *less* than the competitor's model."

"Your price is too high." Familiar knee-jerk reaction from buyers. Combat it with knowledge of your product or service, your prospect's business, your competitor's products. As the consultant, you can satisfy your prospect: the value she receives is well worth the additional cost.

And always, when you reduce the cost to its lowest denominator ("pennies per cup"), price will seem to shrink.

# Basics of Consultative Closing

Consultative selling is a closing system based on this principle: the buyer makes decisions based on specific buying criteria. The closer discovers the criteria (needs, wants, desires) and then acts as a business partner to help the prospect meet those needs.

"Clearly," says Hokan Leo, the award-winning travel consultant, "it is essential to gain insight into the client's needs, wants, and criteria *before* you sell merits of your agency.

"Through *needs profiling*, you discover the criteria that drives the sale. This enables you to develop a presentation that says to the client: 'Here's what *you* said *you* wanted.'

"In selling most services, you cannot improvise a needs profile on the spot. It must be carefully constructed in advance."

If you prefer not to view consulting so formally, take a leaf from consultant Peter Drucker.

"My greatest strength as a consultant is to be ignorant and to ask a few questions."

Ask questions to help the buyer help himself: What would happen if you *started* doing this? What would happen if you *stopped* doing that? Sure, you've been following that plan for some years. But would it benefit you to *improve* it? *Eliminate* it?

Consulting closers also believe in internal allies. In New York police career talk, popular wisdom says: "You don't get the promotion unless you have a rabbi down at Police Plaza." Translation: Get an internal ally at HQ.

Ace closers use inside allies to overcome obstacles. Once you develop an ally in a customer company, understand your ally's motivation. Only by helping him or her can your ally help you. Every ally ploy must be predicted on win-win.

# How Conversational Closing Differs

Big Bill Broonzy, popular folk singer, disliked the term *folk song*: "Every song is a folk song," he'd tell his audience over his trademark acoustic-guitar chording. "I never did hear no horse sing one."

The closer, like Broonzy, may rise up against the term *conversational selling:* "Show me a closed sale *without* conversation. *All* selling is conversational."

Well, yes and no. It's all a matter of refinement. Steve Thompson, speaker/trainer closely identified with conversational selling, sees it this way:

A successful closer encourages the prospect to participate in a special kind of atmosphere, trust, rapport, and good feelings. It's a bonding process where buyer realizes *needs* and recognizes seller as the ideal *solution.*

Okay, but how does conventional selling (CS) differ from regular selling? Says Thompson: "In traditional selling, the salesperson tries to keep tight control of conversational flow; in conversational selling, you share control. In traditional selling, salespeople *conceal* feelings; in conversational selling, we *share* feelings.

"In traditional selling," Thompson adds, "salespeople simulate attention, while they think about what to say next; in conversational selling, really listening becomes all important. Your genuine listening helps the prospect focus on *her* needs and thus become receptive to *your* solution."

Thompson believes the CS closer must start with a "balanced self-concept." Know who you are, recognize and approve your strengths, clearly identify (never deny) your faults.

After communicating this comfortable, balanced self-concept, you can create a pleasant base for good conversation. Your mission: keep the flow of information free of barriers. Being comfortable with *who* and *where* you are, you feel no threat and no need for barriers. Your customer senses your internal comfort and trusts you with her specific needs.

Keep the entire interaction positive, even objections. Instead of overcoming objections, maximize them. Building your strong bond, you can work positively through objections. One response that works well with the conversational selling is this simple phrase: "That's why I'm here"—no matter what the objection is. This reply shows that (1) you understand, and (2) are fully prepared to remedy the problem.

Two powerful words that improve your negotiation power are *think* and *feel*. Both move directly into emotional centers of your customer's brain. They trigger new thoughts. Your customer says: "This won't work." You: "Can you share with me why you *feel* that way?" This encourages your customer to suspend his logical conclusions and reveal true feelings.

Conversational selling creates the proper mutual trust atmosphere. It also takes the temperature of the sale.

"With conversational selling, you can close any time you see signs of acceptance," Thompson says. "You are not likely to talk past closing opportunities."

## GUIDELINES TO LISTENING SKILLS

"The most important element—and probably least fully utilized—tool in conversational closing is listening," says Dr. Kenneth B. Haas. "Keep the ratio of one mouth and two ears in mind. Listen twice as much as you talk."

Really listening, Dr. Haas says, can:

- Persuade, motivate, guide
- Control a prospect's purchasing activities
- Inflate the prospect's pride
- Learn his needs
- Remove obstacles
- Guide the prospect's thinking

"Listening and questioning work together," he says. "When both are used with skill, they become conversational selling—a rich and subtle art. Many times the prospect would have talked himself into buying if the salesperson had listened more and talked less. When words flooded the prospect's mind, he becomes confused and doubtful."

Why is good listening difficult? Because you:

- Fear losing control of the conversation (same thing: you fear rejection)

- Jump ahead in thinking
- Concentrate on framing what to say in reply
- Fail to hear the meaning behind the words
- Don't analyze body language that accompanies prospect's statements

"Listen with rapt and true attention," Dr. Haas says. "A talking customer is a helping customer. Make sure your buyer talks and that you listen, really listen. Good listening is a priceless asset."

Not only must you really listen, you must *appear* to be listening. One's no good without the other:

Really listening is not always easy. You may be sure you already have the answer to the objection. But if you attempt to reconcile without buyer input, you risk alienating yourself. Take time to really hear what the buyer is saying.

The pause is a silent demonstration of your objectivity. It proves you are truly concerned and working on the objection (in fact, use the pause to think about how to handle it). Start with the buyer's name: "Mr. Buyer, I understand how you feel" or "Mrs. Buyer, I can appreciate your concern." Restate into question form: "Correct me if I'm mistaken, Mr. Buyer; you feel that (objection), is that right?" Even if the buyer says: "No, that's not it," you get the opportunity to rephrase the question and again ask if it's correct.

An agreed-upon restatement of the objection gets it out where you can treat it—conversationally.

# WHEN TO CALL YOUR PROSPECT'S HAND

Real objections are gold to the skilled closer. They establish the floor of reality upon which all successful conversations are based. Your prospect may indeed be checking out three or four suppliers. Perhaps the price really is much higher than she anticipated. Many people do not dare to make an important decision without consulting a boss or spouse. Should you interfere with these practices? No. Real objections are open invitations to help.

Help your prospect articulate the real reason for hesitation. Don't assume you know the cause. If the objection is real, answer it and close. If the objection is a smoke screen, get the real objection on the table. "You must have a reason for saying that. May I ask what it is?" Prospects seldom refuse this request.

After you get the true objection, say: "If I can solve that problem, can we do business?" You'll get either yes or no. If yes, negotiate a solution and close. If no, ask why again. This time express confusion and ask for clarification. Remember, you're helping the customer ease discomfort. The real win-win game is to resolve customer doubt by helping her decide.

When conversation bogs down, openly share your feelings.

## FOUR TESTED CONVERSATIONAL CLOSES

Closing is just the final conversational brick in the structure you've carefully built. Keep it interwoven. Never telegraph your punch to make the buyer feel: "Oh, God, here comes the close!" Try these closing add-ons to your conversation:

- "Can we review why this is the best choice for you? First, you get higher productivity. Second, it will save you $75 per hour in service. And, third, you get our three-year warranty. Doesn't that cover all of your needs?"

- "You've shaped our shipment plan to meet your deadline, and since you insist, we will extend the warranty by six months and you will get the extra 2 percent discount. Doesn't that give you everything you wanted? Congratulations! You are a tough negotiator!"

- "Mrs. Jones, since we agree that our delivery date is satisfactory, our terms competitive, and we seem to have overcome the financing hurdle, would you please initial this agreement?"

- "Let's look at this decision from the benefit angle, OK? The first benefit you get is the higher trade-in. That means no down payment. The second benefit is our maintenance contract free for the first year. That saves you $450. The third benefit: this machine will perform at a 17 percent higher production rate, which means that you will earn more money every single week."

# USING LANGUAGE AS A WEAPON

Experienced conversational closers are always expert users of language. Words are your stock in trade—in addition to your real product or service, of course. When you know and draw on a varied inventory of language, you're way out in front of competitors who don't take the trouble to collect and polish words. Examples:

1. Eisenhower delegates to the national Republican convention were challenging the seating of Taft delegates. Herb Brownell, Ike's astute manager, introduced an amendment to the rules that set Ike's people well ahead. He labeled it The Fair Play Amendment. This reduced Taft supporters to speaking against "the so-called Fair Play Amendment." You do not have to be a political buff to know they were licked before they started. Taft never made it to the White House.

2. In the 1990s, abortion became the explosive issue in American politics. One faction made great capital with its slogan: *Pro-Choice*. Then the opponets riposted by calling themselves *Pro-Life*—a great slogan, impossible to decry. The right word at the right time can move mountains.

3. James Webb Young, a master mass salesman, retired to New Mexico and set about selling apples grown on his own ranch. He sold Uncle Jim's apples by mail as business gifts for Christmas.

   One fall, disaster struck. Just before picking time, a hailstorm hit Jim's orchards, putting small pockmarks in otherwise perfect fruit. At first Jim thought of returning the money to his customers. Then inspiration. With each bushel he sent this note:

"You might see some small pockmarks on my apples this year. They're hail marks. They won't hurt the flavor or texture. They're your proof that these delicious apples were grown here in the high mountain country of New Mexico where the air and soil are just about as perfect as you can find for apple growing."

Not one customer asked for a refund. In fact, for the next couple of years customers wrote to ask if Jim could send genuine hail-marked apples!

# ONE-SENTENCE SUM-UPS WITH COLOR AND CLARITY

If you get assurance the prospect understands everything, move ahead. But don't be too sure even then. Keep fishing for admissions that some phase of our explanation hadn't been more thoroughly clear.

Summarize your advantage points in an abundantly clear short sentence. That great mass salesman, Theodore F. MacManus, was responsible for selling hundreds of millions of dollars' worth of automobiles. MacManus suggests you to take this test: "Can you summarize the advantages to your prospect in one short, simple, crystal-clear, convincing sentence? Do this and you will close more sales."

Like doctors, salespeople may bury their mistakes—in monthly or weekly averages. But mail-order advertising is either a success or a failure on the record. Look at famous money-making ad headlines that have consistently sold products and services. It's a useful exercise in stating benefits in one sentence:

- The secret of making people like you
- A little mistake that cost a farmer $3,000 a year
- How a new discovery makes a plain girl beautiful
- Do you make these mistakes in English?
- Who ever heard of a person losing weight—and enjoying three delicious meals at the same time?

- Another woman is waiting for every man—and she's too smart to have "morning mouth."
- They laughed when I sat down at the piano—but when I started to play!
- No more back-breaking garden chores for ME—yet ours is now the showplace of the neighborhood!
- Imagine me—holding an audience spellbound for 30 minutes!
- It's a shame for you not to make good money—when these men do it so easily.
- A wonderful two years' trip with full pay—but only those with imagination can take it.
- Former barber earns $16,000 in four months as real estate specialist

Dramatic benefit sentences close sales. Make sure you tell a complete story.

Here's where many salespeople fail. It's easy for you, living your presentation 20 times a day, to acquire contempt for some of the simple details.

So little by little you drop essential information. You understand it and therefore conclude your customers understand it. Fatal error! Stick to basics. Summarize. Measure your presentation against this closing wrap-up:

> Now, Mr. Britten, I know you realize from statements I've already made that this product will save you a considerable amount of money, conserve a great deal of your time, and eliminate much unnecessary work. I've proved what it has done for many other users. The facts and figures I've cited prove no expense has been spared in assuring the quality of this product. It's what you would naturally expect from a well-known firm like ours.
>
> But I'd also like you to picture in your own mind why it's so important for you to enjoy immediately the advantages of this product. Surely the saving of $10,000 a year means as much to you as it does to those companies I've mentioned.

Of course, saving an hour a day is probably even more worthwhile to you because of your busy schedule. I'm sure you have many productive things to do with the extra time each day. That is why it's very much to your advantage to accept this opportunity at once. Another reason why immediate action is attractive: at present our company is offering a special discount . . .

If you're not being that basic in your closing summation, you're not being basic enough to become a champion closer.

Seasoned closers use talk words, not write words. Avoid clichés and fad phrases that label you as "nonthink." Power words motivate, captivate, and titillate your prospect. Power words place your prospect in a "Yes" mood. Most are simple words, including *which* (something or something), *why* (the favorite of all great closers), *what if* (the fantasy spinner's workhorse), *let's* (remember Lyndon Johnson's biblical quotation: "Come, let us reason together"), *here's how* (this will save you money or time), *right* (everyone wants what is right), and many more.

Cap out your conversational presentation by adding power words—the vital components that make your speech golden and your pocket green.

# CHAPTER TWENTY-FOUR

# *N*egotiating: The Diplomatic Close

Negotiating ideally is a win-win process, be it global diplomacy or in closing a sale on industrial equipment. When the buyer makes a firm demand, you cannot blandly stick to your cards. But you can't give away the store either.

The secret: give a little, get a little, continue to work toward the long-term relationship. You may think of *negotiation* as billion-dollar deals in board rooms or hostages on hold involving the government and terrorists. It's high time we applied the word to day-to-day life.

We negotiate with children to do homework and chores. We negotiate with people we live with about responsibilities and how we spend time and money. You probably negotiate these matters through trial and error. But what about the prospect sitting across the desk?

Here you need to know your own style as well as your opponent's. (What is style? a combination of personality, body language, verbal clues, and self-esteem.)

Is your opponent Big Daddy? Jungle Fighter? Wavering Wimp? Nonchalant Nellie? Policy Wonk? Sympathy Sally? And which style are you? How does it match/contradict/ruffle/sooth your prospect? Look at cases:

## *R*EDUCING NEGOTIATION TO COMMON SENSE

Williams Construction's major contract had been delayed due to equipment failure. With deadline fast approaching, the company called in Claiborne Rogers, salesman for Alliance Equipment Supply, and requested immediate delivery of replacement supplies so Williams could meet its promised deadline.

Rogers, eager to crack this new account, agreed to (1) generous credit terms, and (2) absorbing airfreight charges to get equipment to customer quickly—concessions that reduced his company's 20 percent net profit to below 10 percent.

"I wanted to be reasonable with this account," he said. "I'm after their future business. I was there when they needed me. They'll remember me later with more business. Concessions were justified."

Robert E. Kellar, negotiating expert and CEO at Brandywine Performance Group, Brandywine, Maryland, disagrees:

"Rogers was up against an astute opponent," Kellar says. "It's the buyer's job to ask for generous treatment (if he doesn't, he's in the wrong job!). But that doesn't mean he expects to get everything he wants!"

In his enthusiasm to gain a new account, Rogers downplayed what keeps his company healthy: profit. With minimal risk, he could have committed to speedy delivery—evidently the customer's chief concern—and resisted other concessions.

Under these rush conditions, he could have taken the policy position: on rush orders the customer assumes all freight charges.

"He needed to say 'no' a few times," Kellar says. "Most likely, the buyer—pleased to get fast delivery—would have given in on his additional requests. Besides Rogers and his company bailed the buyer out of a potentially expensive missed deadline. A great negotiating point!"

# *W*HAT TO DO WHEN BUYER TRIES TO CHISEL

Some buyers feel all's fair in negotiating and war, and this is both. Sometimes (God save the mark!) it gets down to buyer's attempt to chisel!

Jane Jacobs is about to close the sale when the buyer announces: "There's $5,500 worth of breakage because of your lousy packaging.

I'm willing to split it with you if you give the word right now. I've another appointment beginning in a few minutes."

Jacobs suspects breakage traces back to buyer's sloppy handling, but can't prove it.

To herself she thinks: "Splitting the difference is a reasonable way out. I'll agree and get the contract signed." Again, Kellar says Jacobs "caved in too easy and too early."

If Jacobs concedes instead of testing this claim, the buyer will continue asking for dubious concessions right along. What should Jacobs have done?

"Ask to have an independent inspection service assess the damages," Kellar says. "Get specifics about the damage. Arrange for photos if possible. Verify if buyer filed a claim with the carrier."

How to handle the buyer? Jacobs should explain she lacks authority to reduce charges. Be gracious but firm.

If claim cannot be proved or disproved (why did buyer offer to split if claim is honest?), Jacobs should offer a less costly concession. Hang tough with this buyer.

# $W$HEN NEGOTIATING: WATCH WHAT YOU SAY

*What* you say in negotiating can turn and bite you. O. C. Haylard, the real estate negotiating czar, has seen house sale palavers go haywire when negotiating brokers referred to as *kids* rather than children. Ross Perot, in attempting to put his presidential case before the African-American community, lit up TV screens over his term "your people"—a tremendous trifle, it turned out.

CNN, in showing why voter polls differ so much (same people, varying answers), attributed it strictly to language. Example:

1. *Pollster:* Would you be interested in the nation spending more money on welfare?

   - *Yes:* 18%
   - *No:* 63%

2. *Pollster:* Would you be interested in the government allocating money to poverty families?

- *Yes:* 68%
- *No:* 11%

Same question, same representative sample. Different language, different answers. Can you see how language makes or breaks your negotiation? Your successful competitors can. Words can be critical.

So can eye contact, as Bruce Shine found out.

# $A$GAINST THE ODDS: SELLING 1,000 INFURIATED EMPLOYEES

D. Bruce Shine, Kingsport, Tennessee, attorney, won his superior negotiator spurs by selling 1,000 North American Rayon employees on a stock ownership plan they "distrusted and didn't understand." Shine's methods are instructive to all closers negotiating with groups.

North American Rayon, Elizabethton, Tennessee, locked horns on a 25 percent employee payout with the local textile workers union. The financially troubled company had to (1) get employee concessions, or (2) close the doors.

The company suggested a 25 percent pay cut plus elimination of eight (of nine) paid holidays. The union rejected this offer. The vote-down went to the union's international offices for ratification. International called in Bruce Shine as investigator/negotiator.

Shine first concentrated on fact-finding. His outside audit showed true red numbers. The crisis was real—although the company was making appearance mistakes ("keeping four late-model Chrysler New Yorkers on hand for management used to look bad to employees.").

Shine recommended a drastic shift to an employee stock ownership plan (ESOP), where active employees become stockholders able to sell their stock back upon retirement.

"Employees in ESOPs are owners but not managers," Shine explained. "The management reports to a three-person board—two directors and one employee representative."

ESOP could save the company. But only if the potential owners—the employees—signed off on the 25 percent decrease and eight-paid-holiday cut in exchange for stock with down-the-road monetary value.

The problems: 1,000 hopping-mad employees with one reaction: "No way, Jose!"

Shine found the bitterness based on (1) broken company-to-employee commitments in the past, and (2) lack of employee knowledge about what ESOPs are. To attack this, he

- Wrote the ESOP facts out in readable language to hand out at meetings.

- Scheduled employee sessions in groups of 25 or fewer ("Larger is hard to control, smaller they don't speak up."). Meetings ran two days, 7 A.M. to 2 A.M., each lasting an hour or more.

- Made a verbal presentation at each session: the facts and benefits of ESOP. He then handed out printed sheets on key points. ("Employees in each session were encouraged to speak. Generally, the leaders who emerged were anti-ESOP.")

Employees spoke harshly about past broken management promises. Shine admitted past lacks. But he pointed out: "As an owner, you'll get *written* confirmation of your stock ownership. Besides, this is the only way to save your jobs and the economic life of the town."

Several dissident employees called on the National Labor Relations Board to cancel the ESOP. A narrow vote saved it.

Finally, the employees voted 5 to 3 in favor of ESOP.

A year later, management restored the cuts and employees (now owners) turned up the gain on productivity. ("After all, it's their company!") The plant continues in operation. Once-skeptical employees now see retirees selling ESOP shares for real money.

Shine had closed a negotiated sale to 1,000 distrustful buyers. The most important factor?

"Looking each employee straight in the eye during the meetings," Shine says.

# $U$SING THE WHAT-IF NEGOTIATION

Robert E. Baxter of Los Angeles says: "There is nothing so devastating in real estate as to get caught in the cross-ruff between a buyer and a seller." He uses the what-if negotiation. His story:

I got caught this way on my first commercial real estate sale.

Real estate is no different from other selling. Basic methods are the same. People are people with the same curiosity, fears, hopes, and habits.

My sad lesson cost me a big commission.

I had a three-story office building listed for sale. The owner wanted $300,000—$120,000 in cash. The property had a $80,000 mortgage on it. The owner offered to carry a second mortgage of $55,000. A lot of repairs were necessary: air-conditioning system, plumbing, and parking surface out back. I figured if the owner wanted to sell *as is*, the property was overpriced by about $40,000. The actual market value was around $260,000.

For three months, I brought lookers to the property but got no offers. By this time, the owner was softening and beginning to feel he would never get a buying proposal. It had been advertised and promoted.

Then, one day I got an offer of $280,000 from a prospect instead of the $300,000 asked. Of this he'd pay $90,000 cash, not the $120,000. Further, he wanted the air conditioning and plumbing repaired. I had no idea if the seller would accept this. Air-conditioning repairs alone would cost nearly $8,000. It would mean selling at less than market value by my reckoning.

I presented the offer and just about fell over when the owner said he'd accept, provided the buyer split the cost of air-conditioning repairs. In effect, he was willing at $4,000 to take $6,000 less than the market. He was really anxious to sell.

I ran joyously back to the buyer and told him the good news. I was sure the sale was in the bag but it was out of the bag and I was out of a commission.

Why? Simply because the quick reply caused the prospect to think: "Boy! This owner really wants to sell. He came down in price right off the bat and on top of that agreed to nearly all my demands. I'll just hold out for the whole package, including my demand that he pay all the costs of air-conditioning repairs. Maybe there's something wrong with this deal. Maybe there's something I don't see. He gave me no argument." The prospect didn't sign.

So I went back to the seller with the original offer and told him what happened. The owner made a counteroffer which he asked me to take to the prospect and he made a counteroffer to the counteroffer. Next I got a counteroffer to the counteroffer to the counteroffer. See what I mean?

Instead of running back and forth so quickly I should have let a couple of days go by before I took the owner's first counteroffer back to the prospect. In this way, the prospect would think the seller was going to be difficult to convince and make the deal look hard. Above all, I should have remembered to use a wonderful selling technique called *what if!*

When I went back to the prospect with the owner's agreement to accept his offer with only one condition, I should have taken my time and kept the owner's acceptance in my pocket. I should have said: "I am having a very tough time trying to get the owner even to consider your offer. He knows he has a good piece of property. He might lower that price a little, but he balks at paying for repairs. If you are too strong in your demands, he may take the property off the market entirely as far as you are concerned.

"But Mr. Prospect, *what if* I got the price down to $270,000; *what if* I get the owner to pay for the plumbing and parking surface repairs and split the cost of the air-conditioning? I don't know if I can do it, but if I can, would you accept that?"

*What if?*

Of course, all the time I have the exact agreement signed by the owner in my pocket.

This makes the buyer want the deal. He feels he may lose an opportunity. You are in an excellent position as an expert negotiator. The prospect must rely on you. The prospect not only doesn't think of asking for more. He is thinking he will be fortunate to get anywhere near what he originally offered.

So he would probably say: "Yes, I would accept that kind of agreement. See what you can do." Then wait a day or two before you bring back the owner's agreement which you had all along.

When the buyer signs, he feels he's a clever fellow who's driven a hard bargain.

*What if* you use this simple little technique next time you get caught between buyer and seller in any field? You close the sale. That's what!

# THREE BASIC TOOLS OF NEGOTIATION

Information, time, and power are your basic tools of negotiation.

*1. Information.* It always seems like the other person knows more about you than you know about him or her. Whoever possesses the most information comes out ahead.

*2. Time.* The other person always seems to know what your deadline is, and you've forgotten to ask what his or hers is. Therefore, the person with the deadline loses.

The Japanese excel in hammering out agreements with Americans. The Japanese *appear* to have decades to decide. Americans often work against a short deadline. The group that appears blessed with open-end time holds trump cards.

*3. Power.* If you have the power and don't *know* you have the power, you *don't* have the power. If you don't have the power but *believe* you do, then you *have* the power.

In addition, your opponent may win with sympathy:

- "My brother's in the hospital, and my mind is not on buying insurance right now."

- "We're just a small retail shop, and the way business is this year, we're afraid to invest the money in your plan, even though we agree it could help us."

How many times have *you* felt sorry for your prospect and agreed to come back in a few weeks? Whether you realize it or not, *you* are being sold. You are buying your prospect's excuse. You've lost the negotiation. Hang tough.

# *H*OW TO BOOMERANG OBJECTIONS INTO BENEFITS

Adroit negotiators often turn objections into closes.

"I'm glad you mentioned the heavier weight, Mr. Briggs. We *have* strengthened the frame. We've insisted on a heavier-duty motor in this model. Sure, it weighs a little more. But its heavier construction assures you of longer operation with less maintenance expense."

Be careful to avoid suggesting the prospect should have understood the advantage. Give him credit for understanding it all along.

*Stated* objections often hide *real* objections. "Your price is too high" usually means "my desire is too low." When this occurs, present more benefits rather than argue the price. Look behind each objection. Until you locate the real objection, you cannot complete the sale.

Avoid coming to verbal blows. It settles nothing and often antagonizes the prospect. Bring in a neutral third party to give the answer. It softens the reply, makes it impersonal:

"Understand how you feel, Mr. Kelso. Bill Jones over at National Foods at first felt the system might not work for him. But let me show you a letter he wrote after using our system for a year." Bill Jones is answering the objection, not you. After all the prospect expects you to carry a healthy bias in favor of your product.

Keep a supply of references on tap.

Sometimes the objection doesn't give you enough information to frame an intelligent answer. When this happens, use the echo. Repeat the key words: "Price too high?" to stimulate more feedback like: "Yes, more than we budgeted." Or you may say: "Why do you *say* that?"

Or break down the objective to make it more palatable.

Prospect: "$250 for a chair is more than I wanted to pay."

Closer: "How long will you enjoy this designer chair? At least 20 years, I'm sure. But let's be conservative and say 10 years. That means it will cost you less than 25 cents a week to experience this beautiful styling and comfort. Just pride alone is worth more than that, don't you agree? That means the comfort and utility is a bonus!"

Prospect: "But this car gets only 27 miles per gallon and the other gets 30."

Closer: "Yes, the ratings do make this difference. You said you drive about 15,000 miles a year. That is about a gallon extra a week. You have to decide. Do you want the (name the additional benefits) for the week or to save a gallon of gas?"

A philosopher once said: "Nothing is difficult if divided into small enough parts." So true in negotiating the close!

# *T*HE LONG AND SHORT OF NEGOTIATING

All too often we think of negotiation as a long process. Peace talks on the Vietnam war come to mind. But it's all relative. Negotiations that finally concluded the 100 Years' War make the Vietnam settlement look speedy indeed.

Closing negotiations *are* sometimes long. Carrier Corporation once negotiated 10 years to place air-conditioning equipment in a major Chicago office building. ("Keep many pots boiling—work the averages.") But often a successful closing can be negotiated in one meeting. Manner and style often win right away. To wit:

- "If we can get you a higher trade-in, can you commit today?"
- "If I can arrange financing with no negative effects on your cash flow, can you give me an okay today?"
- "If my boss can see his way to enter your order at the old price, will you approve this today?"
- "If we can up-front this into our production schedule for next week, will you give us the go-ahead to build a prototype?"
- "If we advance our guarantee to include parts replacement, will you approve this order?"

Note how often the word *if* wins the day. Again, take a bow, Bob Baxter!

Another workhorse word is *suppose*—since negotiations often revolve around conditions. Control the conditions to close the sale.

- "Suppose my head office okays your proposed terms. Will you be able to provide the down payment today?"
- "Suppose we train your operator at our expense and pick up the shipping costs. Can we get this started?"
- "Are you saying we delay billing for 60 days and we've got an agreement?"
- "If we ship the first order at these unusually low rates, you'll order from us every month at our regular low prices—right?"

## *J*OUSTING WITH YOUR BRAND-NAME COMPETITOR

Gayle Freeland, a negotiating-oriented *World Book* sales manager in Memphis, loves to hear prospects ask how her product compares with her famous competitor, *Encyclopaedia Britannica.* Her strategy: *never* knock her competitor's authority.

One prominent businessman asked Freeland to come explain why her product was better than *Britannica*: "Mr. Dixon," she said. "*World Book* is widely known for its value in educating children. On that point, it has no peer. So I assume your concern is why *World Book* is better for *adults*." Dixon nodded.

"Well, Mr. Dixon," she said, "when you want to look up something in *Britannica*, it's there all right. I wouldn't pretend otherwise. But it's not easy to find. Why should you have to work that hard to get it? After all, your time is valuable. *World Book* makes it easy. That's why *World Book* is better.

"After all, *World Book* has 60 percent of the global encyclopedia market. The other 40 percent is divided among all the others. There must be a reason.

"There's also a reason why I sell *World Book*. I could be selling *Britannica*. But we always had *World Book* when I was small. There's no way we could have done without it. I believe in *World Book*."

Thus you have it. A powerful side-by-side summary. Sure the competitor is famous. Sure, it's authoritative. But there are people who believe in *World Book*. Maybe ease of access has something to do with it.

Dixon bought. Closing depends on the closer—not the fame of the product. Gayle Freeland proved it.

P.S. She closed *without* once mentioning price, yet her product is half the cost of her competitor's. And she was talking to a prospect who could easily afford any product he wanted! Does her lack of emphasis on price give you a clue? It should!

# $N$EGOTIATING BASED ON BUYING SIGNALS

A real objection is a strong buying signal. So naturally you return the volley: ask the prospect to clarify, explain, justify. Accept whatever rationale you get back and ask: "If I can solve this problem, will you buy?" This places you in the negotiation.

*All* life is negotiable. Sooner or later even fixed prices must change. With enough power (or pull or authority), fixed rules and prices can bend. But timing the negotiation is crucial. Everyone buying from you wants to feel he or she is dealing at exactly the *right* time to get the *best* deal from the *right* authority to *bend* rules in their favor. As you've seen, two elements, *time* and *power*, coupled with a third—*information*—make or break negotiations. Formal negotiations often revolve around which side controls more of these elements.

Georgia Bates does not try to close until she's sure desire has built up. She's never in a hurry. She lets pressure accrue to the prospect, not herself. She simply keeps sounding prospects out on how do you feel about A or B or C. Once she's sure all the motivational information is available, she reviews it with the prospect and asks for the order. She gets it more times than most.

Good negotiating means tapping into the *urgency* customers already feel. Part of your negotiation: dramatize for customers what will happen if they do *nothing*. Then switch to benefits from immediate use of their new purchase. Impatience is a common motivator. Why are most cars sold off the lot and not ordered on a custom basis from the factory? Buyer desire for instant gratification!

Information and lock-in questions are keys. Use the classic "If I can show you a way to . . . would you make a decision today?" It seeks more information, asks for commitment, and directs the interview toward your objective.

Prospect: I'm not interested.

Closer: Of course not. But can you foresee a time when XYZ might occur?

You then proceed to ask questions. Your mission: to find out more and lock in on the buying cycle.

The prospect says: "It's not right." Answer this way:

"I can see your applications would certainly be unusual. But perhaps you could clarify for me ways my product is not right." Don't let this question suck you into a tirade of defensive nonsense. Get the prospect to define *what* she doesn't like. Only by gathering information and applying it to prospect commitment do you work toward: "If I can solve *that*, will you buy?"

# *E*IGHT WAYS TO OVERCOME PRICE OBJECTIONS

Price is the biggest and most recurring objection. Even in buying a commodity set by a futures market 1,000 miles away, people still get hung up on price. Buyers know usually several prices exist. Since people are suspicious of being cheated, self-esteem and ego drive price objections. Knowing (as you do) what prompts the objection, you can frame an appropriate counter. Choose:

**1. Enhance the customer's sense of security by providing a time frame.** Some offer 30-day free trials. American Express offers a full year "no questions asked" warranty on everything purchased with its card. What can you do to create trust? Allow customers to say: "If I don't like it or it doesn't work, I can always take it back. How can we go wrong?" Price is not always the issue. Sometimes is purchase-money risk.

**2. Remove the price issue by linking cost to customer's prime needs.** When prospect says "$10,000 is just too much," your answer is: "Of course, no problem. Here is the list you asked us to provide. Which can we eliminate to reduce the budget?" This is an excellent approach when objections are tied to desire to save face or to appear as competent skilled negotiator.

Those responses redefine the issue. You remove the customer's definition of price (frequently a knee-jerk reaction). You spotlight instead the customer's real needs. Here are other ways to flank the headlong charge of "price too high":

**3. Take blame away from the prospect.** "I'm sorry I failed to make the point clear." Or "you're quite right in feeling the way you do now. But let me show you how another company found they could save many hours of labor with this equipment."

**4. Make a conversational concession.** "Yes, the price is higher than you're paying now. But when you consider you're getting additional (cite benefits)." Or: "Normally what you say is quite true, but with our service we have eliminated that problem."

**5. Agree that others felt the same way.** "The superintendent at Universal Plumbing said the same thing—at first. But let me show you a photo of his present installation. It saved 70 hours of labor the first week."

**6. Compliment the prospect's idea.** "I admire your concern with safety, and I agree that's an important factor. Let's see how our service can speed up your operation and continue to be safe for the employees."

**7. Blame insufficient information.** "I can understand how you might feel that way from your experience with similar products, but our service people may not have given you all the facts."

**8. Get on her side of the desk.** "I see what you mean. That *does* appear to be a problem. Let's see how we can work this out." When you show you are fair-minded and helpful, she'll be more willing to hear more about how you can resolve the problem. (P.S. You need to suggest a *really* solid solution.)

As a lawyer, Abraham Lincoln listened carefully to everything his opponent said. He then began telling the jury what a fine and brilliant person his opponent was—and how he had made valid points.

"However," he gently added, "There are other facts that need to be considered before you make a decision." Then he skillfully listed all the reasons the jury should decide in his client's favor. Jurors felt old Abe was helping them to reach an honest verdict, as if they were on the same side of the issue.

Your prospect will trust you when she sees you're helping her get what she wants.

# *H*OW TO WIN WITH TOP-DOWN NEGOTIATING

Retail negotiators often find the best place to start negotiating: at the top. To wit: "To appreciate the benefits of a quality mattress, let me start out by showing you *the very best.*"

Every shopper is interested in seeing the best, perhaps considering the best. It flatters the customer. You set the stage for selling the best or at least something better than what you'd get otherwise.

By using "the very best" phrase, you neither state nor infer that this is the only one to buy. Or that if the customer doesn't buy the best, she is making a mistake (with that approach, you'll either sell her the best—or nothing).

Instead, your message is: "You are a discriminating buyer. This product plays an important role in your life. It pays to take a few minutes to consider the very best. It will help you determine which quality is most suitable for you."

After demonstrating the best, quote the price in a positive and forthright manner. Never be afraid to quote the price. The customer is not going to fall through the floor or walk out. You've already established the value. Say: "You get all this for only $_____."

At this point, close. If you cannot, step down to the next product. Quote a lower price for reduced benefits. Having shown the best, everything down sells for less. You are saving the customer money as you step down.

The customer may feel: "True, I am paying less, but I am also getting less. Can I afford to give up benefits of the very best?" Many initiate the climb back up!

On the other hand, in starting at the bottom and moving up, you keep asking the customer to spend more money for something better. This creates a gnawing question in the customer's mind: "Are the *extra* features really worth the *added* cost?"

*Spending* the customer's money while *adding* value is much more difficult than *saving* the customer's money by *reducing* benefits. When you start at the top, you can easily move back to the top without confusing the customer.

# Negotiating Step by Step

The most powerful time to open formal negotiations: right after your prospect has expressed approval of a feature. When you hear the prospect express delight, simply ask: "Is there anything that would keep you from going ahead with this?"

Then stop!

That question opens negotiations. Sincere and honest, it cuts right to the chase. It is not in any way offensive. Wait for the prospect to respond (silence works *for* you!); then listen attentively. If the answer is "I do not see any reason not to go ahead," you've just entered the Tie-It-Up phase. Start writing.

What if prospects still show hesitancy?

- "I don't know! That's a lot of money!"
- "I wish you had a more advanced model."

Don't begin hammering away at reasons why the prospect's objection should not veto the sale. This is rude, inconsiderate, insulting to her intelligence. Realize instead that objections are often smokescreens to cover deeper feelings of uncertainty. You cannot negotiate with a smokescreen. Probe again to get conditions on the table:

- "Is that the only reason you'd be hesitant to go ahead?"
- If I could show you how to resolve that problem, would you be ready to go ahead?"

Bring true conditions out into the open. Then restate:

"Let me see if I understand. You feel uncertain about an expenditure of this size right now, and you'd prefer a lesser schedule. Is that right?"

## $K$*EEP A TRADE-OFF LIST HANDY*

When negotiation is cut-and-parry followed by side-to-side volley, throw a trade-off list into the fray. Consider these thought-starters:

- *Increased volume:* "I can reduce the price 1 cent a pound if you will increase your order to a million pounds. Will you do that?"
- *Change specs.* Ask permission to omit something in the specifications. "If you're willing to print the cover in two colors instead of four, we can reduce the price $325."
- *Ask the buyer to increase the total sale.* "If you agree to take the service contract for two years, I can reduce the price 5 percent."
- *Lengthen the contract period.* "If you agree to the maintenance contract for two years instead of one, I can give you an extra month of service free."

- *Offer less costly packaging.* "Since you sell this item in large quantities in your store, perhaps you don't need individual packages. If we can ship you cartons of 25 units, we can cut the price 5 cents a unit."
- *Ask buyer to absorb shipping costs.* "If you can pick up the furniture at our warehouse, I will drop the price by $75."
- *Ask buyer to set up merchandise.* "Let us deliver in the original cartons, you unpack, and we take 5 percent off the price."
- *Arrange for early payment.* Money that comes in ahead of the anticipated date is money that doesn't have to be borrowed.

Being a good sales negotiator takes time and effort. Whether your product is short term or requires months of negotiation, negotiating the close can double your income. Effective negotiation also gives you the recognition and personal gratification due a closer well versed in the diplomatic sell.

# CHAPTER TWENTY-FIVE

# Closing Sales to Groups

The distinguished board was considering James Hyatt's proposal. It required an investment of $100,000.

There were conflicts. One member wanted it. Another said no. One said wait. So it went on for half an hour, until Hyatt decided it was time to close.

"Gentlemen, you've all had your say," he said. "We've enjoyed much articulate talk. Now it's time for action. I want your approval for this service and I want it now. Will you OK the start-up?" Said the chairman: "Yes." Hyatt asked for an order and got it.

How rare! It will happen at times. So ask. But on the occasions when it doesn't, you need good ammunition for group selling follow-through—then and there.

Psychologically, when facing several buyers, the closer often fears (1) being outnumbered, (2) lacking feedback (you tend to get less response from a group), and (3) risking being cross-examined and thus losing initiative.

This unfavorable setting must be changed, if you want to control the meeting. Eliminate formal seating, parliamentary procedures, directive approach, and speeches. Instead, integrate yourself with the group. Outsider must become insider, and, as far as possible, the leader.

In advance, appraise results you *want* and results you can *get* via meeting. What arguments and appeals will help? How can they be used? More important: How can you integrate yourself into the group and become its leader?

Analyze participants:

- Who will be there?
- Who could be influenced to participate or stay away?
- What do these people think? Know? Expect?
- Who is a likely ally? Opponent: Neutral or indifferent?
- How can these people be influenced or guided. Every participant expects—by virtue of status, position, or personality—to play a certain role. Be aware of these role expectations and use the information accordingly.
- Individual contacts before the meeting often decide the sale. Premeeting tactics: Who must be influenced? How?
- Who's most at home there?
- Who won't open his or her mouth at the meeting?
- What's the physical setting?
- Can the meeting be moved to a better locale?
- Can the seating order be improved?
- How can you transform the meeting to a shirtsleeve gathering, thus making it easier for you to integrate?

Once the meeting gets underway, concentrate on keeping the initiative: disarm objections, neutralize conflicts, demonstrate empathy and knowledge, forestall objections. Then summarize decisions reached, push solutions forward for action, plan follow-up to ensure results gained.

## *A*SK YOUR PROSPECT TO HELP PRESENT

One smart ad agency developed the prospect's sales manager, John Beatty, in preliminary contacts, and asked him to help in the presentation. The agency got everything in complete rough form and invited Beatty to a rehearsal "so nothing in the presentation will run counter to your policies."

A daring move, possible only when the contact was already quite close. But under these conditions Beatty was greatly flattered, gave generously of his experience, commented in the final presentation on how all his suggested changes had been incorporated, and solidly supported the closer group.

Not only smart strategy, but sound procedure. You can sometimes enlist such priceless help if the client representative is convinced you're honestly asking for opinion and not just spooning out molasses. Sincerity pays. If you are just being slick, forget it. Backfire is worse than no fire.

Enlisting prospective client aid in presenting requires expert public speaking, conference control techniques, and group psychology. But it can relieve you of the frustrating role of outsider being grilled.

## GETTING INTO YOUR PROSPECT'S SHOES—LITERALLY!

In working with a genius/character, be prepared for sudden shifts in group closing—and learn to recover quickly. Walter H. Johnson, Jr., found this out working for the legendary Marion Harper.

Harper blazed across the corporate skyline as CEO of Interpublic, the advertising conglomerate. He had hired Walter Johnson away from airline sales management as executive vice president. ("The under-boss in Mafia terms," Johnson recalls wryly.)

One day Harper tooled into Walter's office on the 44th floor of the Time Life Building: "I'm making a presentation to American Cyanamid tomorrow morning in New Jersey. Can you stay in town tonight and help on the presentation?"

No one ever said no to Harper. Walter phoned his wife to tell her he wouldn't be home that evening. Then Walter discovered Marion hadn't even *started* on the Cyanamid presentation. At 9:00 P.M. the two men went to work. Data from computers flowed in, and rough charts rolled in from the graphics studio, on all-night alert.

By 4:00 A.M., the proposal was finished. The two men departed to nearby hotels. They met at 8:30 A.M. with the presentation. As the limousine hummed through the Lincoln Tunnel, Harper said: "I've changed my mind. You're going to make the presentation."

"Okay," Johnson replied, wondering about the last-minute change.

At Cyanamid, they went directly to the conference room. Six corporate people filed in and took seats at the other end. Instead of sitting beside Johnson, Harper sat with the Cyanamid people and talked about New Jersey politics. Once everyone assembled, he nodded for Walter to begin.

As the presentation moved along, questions arose—some critical and hard to answer. Marion, too, asked questions—some of the toughest.

"Son of a gun," thought Walter. "He has joined the client!"

The presentation lasted less than an hour. After a brief silence the chairman said: "Would you mind leaving us alone for a few minutes, Mr. Johnson, so we can discuss your proposal among ourselves?"

Johnson left the room, but Harper didn't move. After 15 minutes Johnson was recalled. They had signed the business. Harper had, in effect, joined the client and helped make the decision.

That's *really* getting into your prospect's shoes!

# USING PRESENCE IN CLOSING GROUPS

Presence, valuable in one-on-one selling, is much more of an issue in selling a group. Facing a *group* bedevils some presenters. They conclude, often subconsciously, that the group requires the presenter to be someone other than his or her normal self.

Actually, *just the opposite is true,* once the closer understands *presence. Selling presence is being comfortable and confident with prospectives and making them comfortable with and confident in you.* Client comfort *is particularly vital* for big-ticket items, since decision makers are not choosing a supplier, they're seeking a partner. They're placing their trust in you.

The key to *presence,* like so many other selling needs, is *knowledge.* You're meeting with directors of a company to sell a costly installation. Find out beforehand the dominant personality in the decision-making group. It may be the chairman or president, but not always. The president and chairman may be observers on this issue. When you make your presentation, pay a little more attention to that dominant person. She will expect that attention. If you do not give it, you won't make the sale.

On the other hand, do not ignore any group member, even the secretary who keeps the minutes. One enemy in a group can kill the sale. Keep each member in the picture. Glance around the room. Catch each person's eye momentarily as you talk. Then shift to another.

Never ignore "look-compliments." Look slightly longer and more often at Ms. Dominant. Mention each member's name at least once during the presentation (Ms. Dominant *more* than once). "This is a field Ms. Jerery has done much study in."

By all means, realize the first step in communicating *presence* to the group: be your own self. Just make that *self* larger than life the way an actor does in the theater. Your group is your audience.

One salesperson, who needed to improve his presence, *thought* he needed better *organization*. But when he audited a videotape of his practice presentation, he saw himself looking more at the floor and walls than at the group. His voice was lifeless. He tended to get as *far*—horrors!—from the group as possible. Once he started working on presence, his group selling improved drastically.

In communicating confidence and openness, videotape is most helpful to check eye contact, appearance, voice, body language. Review your practice tapes with a coach. Remember: you're not seeking praise. You need objectivity on weak spots.

Presence (sometimes called charisma) is difficult to define, but powerful in effect. John F. Kennedy had it. So did Martin Luther King and Franklin D. Roosevelt. Bill Clinton favors the town meeting format that enhances his presence. All instinctively knew how to communicate to a group via one-on-one intimacy. Each person in the audience felt like number one—and the only one. Power presenters bring the audience into *their presence.*

Fortunately, the degree of presence needed to be a powerful speaker to hundreds far exceeds what you need to sell to a group of 2 to 30 prospects. If you're good at one-on-one closing, just expand that persona to a broader audience. In the theater, this is called "playing to the cheap seats"—meaning to the last row in the balcony.

# Sharpening Your Eye Contact

Looking at a prospect encourages that person to look at *you*. It says you are *confident*, in *control, interested*. Here are ways to sharpen your eye contact:

- Begin by looking at one person in the group—not at the floor, ceiling, a sea of faces, or your nails.
- Pay slightly more attention to the senior decision makers, but do *not* exclude, ignore, or offend others.
- Look at people to your immediate right and left (often out of your normal direct vision).
- Keep your head and eyes moving around the room.
- If you are sitting, inch up your chair when you talk about price—to show you're confident. But sit back slightly when a client objects, indicating you're open to feedback.

# Guidelines on Presenting to Groups

Putting *life* in your voice keeps the presentation interesting. It projects credibility. *Do not read to the group.* Don't memorize word for word (sounds wooden). Refer to your key-word outline. Better: use a pictograf outline that *cannot* be read.

At worst, your voice should be a nonissue. At best, persuasive. A high-pitched voice—male or female—can annoy listeners. Regional accents are distracting. Native New Yorkers often score minus points by not knowing they sound regional.

How you pronounce place names also matters. If you are selling in Des Moines and you pronounce the *s*, the group will think: "Moron." But you'll goof in Des Plaines, *unless* you pronounce the *s*.

To evaluate the expressiveness of your voice, tape yourself, then listen objectively. Keep your *voice* lively. Research shows people who speak quickly (not rapid fire) are often viewed as more intelligent than slow speakers. *Nothing* is worse than a plodding presentation.

Vary your pace. Use pauses to show significance. Cover a main point, look at the group and wait 10 seconds. This pause gives listeners a chance to react, nod, or speak up (giving you an opening to respond).

In your group presentation, when you put words and action together, remember:

- *Be enthusiastic.* Your prospects take enthusiasm cues from you. Lukewarm presentation? Tepid prospect! Enthusiasm—or its lack—is catching.

- *Use conversational tone.* Draw out prospects with questions. Their reactions will clear up misunderstandings and help you spotlight important benefits.

- *Be detailed.* Without realizing it, you talk faster and faster as you become more familiar with a subject. Result: you leave out "insignificant details." Assume the prospect knows *nothing* until proved otherwise. The very points you omit may be sales-clinchers.

- *Key words to actions.* Make sure prospects focus attention on what you are doing. The office machine salesperson says: "Watch how easy it is to reduce or enlarge copies. First you press this button. . . ."

When you're addressing group prospects, start with undivided attention—both an advantage and a responsibility. Comport yourself accordingly:

- *Know your audience.* Ask in advance about the organization's history, membership, and expected attendance.

- *Grab them in the opening.* A bold statement, such as "I'm going to tell you why I think 'X' is the right thing to do" is more provocative than is "it's a pleasure to be here." Personal anecdotes, sports references, and current events also work well—but only *if* they're interesting and *tied* to your main theme.

- *Refine your message.* For a presentation of 20 minutes, establish a theme and support it with no more than four key points. Remember your allotted time. Be clear and direct.

- *Don't converse in long ponderous sentences.* The ear needs brevity and simplicity. Use the nickel word even if you think the dollar word is more impressive (it probably isn't).

- *If you enjoy humor, use it.* But if you're not funny, don't try to be. You can't refine a sense of humor that's not there in the first place.

- *Use numbers sparingly.* Consolidate and round them off.

- *Strive for varied pace.* A good presentation is much like a music conductor playing upon the moods of the people. Vibrate with energy, soften, grow to resounding crescendo, pause, and even rest.

- *Watch double-meaning words.* If you say, "Everyone in this room has something special in their genes," the audience may hear "jeans." At times you want laughs. But never titters.

- *Avoid "that reminds me of the story . . ." and "in conclusion . . ."* If you want to tell the story, tell it. If it's time to conclude the speech, conclude it. Period.

The American language is rich in words that appeal to senses, stir imagination, unlock the mind. Offer your audience the unexpected.

- *Close on a high note.* Tell them what you told them in a different way. Consider a concise but memorable quote. Slow the pace a little to signal the final statement. Make your ending swift, vigorous, positive.

- *A group presentation is more than a transfer of thought.* It's a performance. The message is the vehicle. Organize it well. Keep it simple and honest.

- *Practice, practice, practice.* The best text in the world won't work well without rehearsal. Practice aloud. Read it to your companion or friend. Get candid reaction, not soft-soap. One group closer recorded and played his presentation on his car tape deck for five days. He delivered it smoothly and convincingly.

- *Throw the script away.* Work from a key-word or pictograf outline.

- *But start with a script.* It helps you control time and stay on track. It also offers points of reference in the question-and-answer period.

- *Tell audience members you like them.* Say it with eyes, voice, gestures. This isn't a federal grand jury. They're friendly faces and eager ears. The better you rehearse, the more confident you will feel, look, sound.

- *Stopping on time is as important as starting on time.* If the group is about to lunch, you lose points by running over. If active discussion is underway, you may ask for an additional 15 minutes. But never run over allotted time without group agreement. One telecommunications saleswoman lost a major contract because cutoff time was 11:00 A.M. and she didn't finish until 11:30. Said the senior decision maker: "She knew we had to leave by 11:30 A.M. She wasn't sensitive to our needs!"

# SURPRISE! IT'S A GROUP PRESENTATION

Ever expected a one-on-one presentation only to walk in and find a group of strangers? It happens. Do not show your surprise. Begin by writing down the names and titles of those present. Don't feel uncomfortable about asking. After all, you need to know their areas of responsibility.

Act as if you came fully prepared for a group. If *you* don't indicate surprise, they'll never know. Remember, it is the first time they've heard it.

If you leave something out, say to yourself: "I'm the only one who will ever know."

Do not assume every member of the group knows why you're there. Many times people are invited with no notice. ("Harry, got a minute? You might want to hear this.") So start from the beginning. Reexplain everything as if a first call.

If you came to the presentation to ask for the order, proceed to do so with the group. How? With five people sitting around the table staring? Assume you already have the sale, hand your order form to the decision maker, and say matter-of-factly: "I just need your okay on this." Often he or she will sign it!

If they want to discuss it further, do everything in your power to stimulate discussion, such as asking prepared questions: "At this point, most people want to know how our company can deliver such a product at this price and still offer excellent service. Good question!" Then answer it.

Stimulate the group into a realistic open exchange. Once they jump into discussion, sit like an invisible person. Let them talk, even if you don't like what they are saying! If the group feels decision is partly theirs, chances of success are far greater.

If they clam up, leave your materials exactly where they are and head for the door. "It's obvious you need to discuss this privately. I need a break anyhow. I'll be outside when you're through."

Do not wait for a response. Simply close the door on your way out. The group will sit stunned! You are forcing a discussion without giving them the chance to say: "Why don't we give you a call when we've hashed it all out?"

It works!

# *H*OW TO FIELD GROUP QUESTIONS

But more likely you'll move into group questions—either their own or questions you use to prime the pump. How you answer is vital. Here is food for thought:

- *Avoid defensiveness!* Even more important in group selling. If you make a member uncomfortable in front of colleagues, you may win the battle but lose the war.

- *Don't devalue questions with a response like:* "No, that's really not valid because..." or "Well, you *may* have a point there, *but*..." or "No, that's not correct." Such comments diminish the question and the questioner. Putdowns do not stimulate signups.

- *Address the specific question.* Avoid the temptation to give additional information. A long contorted answer loses other players. Remember, the questioner is only one of a group.

- *Don't repeat negative words.* If the question contains inflammatory or hostile words such as "churning" or "unethical,"
  *do not* repeat the word to reinforce it. Instead, say, "I can
  understand your concern. What specifically...?"

  Once you answer a question ask: "Does that answer your
  concern?" This way you avoid overanswering and still make
  sure you satisfy.

- *Be fully grounded in your subject.* If you lack depth in a particular area, take along a specialist with expertise. One U.S.
  sales team needing up-to-the-minute Euromart market information took along a Swiss specialist to a multimillion dollar
  presentation. It worked.

- *Table it.* Sometimes you get a question better addressed later.
  Say: "If it's all right with you, I'd like to hold that for a few
  minutes. It is important and I want to cover it in the context
  of . . . ." This is perfectly acceptable in most situations.

# GROUP SELLING WHEN YOU'RE THE GROUP

Manufacturer's agents are often experts in group selling—particularly when the group is on the *selling* side of the desk. This occurs
when the manufacturer is visiting the agent's territory to "make a
few calls," says Max Robinson of Maximum Marketing, Inc.,
Bloomington, Minnesota.

"Some buyers are complimented when the manufacturer takes
time to make the visit. It gives evidence of full commitment. There-
after, he will have deeper understanding of customer needs," says
Robinson.

Bill Alexander of Southeast Sales, Bryson City, North Carolina,
loves joint calls: "Plan your call and share speaking time equally—
like you're partners," he says. "Too many principals want to sound
important and give the impression they brought along 'the fellow
who covers the territory.'"

Do Dobesh of Productivity Development Associates, Inc., Sioux
Falls, South Dakota, wants only joint calls "when the principal can

help me make a sale. Specific objectives should be established, and the principal should be well prepared for the call."

Walter Brown, Brown Sales Associates, Inc., Southampton, Massachusetts, says: "When a manufacturer wishes to make joint calls with me, I welcome the help. I especially welcome technical people who teach new technology, I learn when he teaches customers."

Edward McKeown of Costec, Inc., Palatine, Illinois, says: "We represent five principals and make many joint calls." McKeown sees these benefits of joint calls as a way to:

- Communicate sales support to buyer that cannot be conveyed in another way.
- Educate both salesperson and customer.
- Create opportunities that simply wouldn't happen otherwise.
- Stimulate information that often isn't provided one-on-one.

## *T*HE TIER-MARKETING GROUP CLOSE

Joyce M. Ross, Vancouver, Canada-based group selling expert, is cofounder of Camelion Hosiery. She organizes tier-marketing party demos in homes. Earlier she worked for Tupperware and Mary Kay cosmetics. In direct selling to groups, Joyce Ross's advice is (1) valuable as insight into tier-marketing, and (2) applicable to closing group sales in general.

Ross says tier-marketing group demonstrations should include a thank-you to your hostess and a warm welcome to guests, prizes the hostess can earn, an outline of the presentation to come, a *brief* company history, a team-building talk, and a demonstration of benefits of your products and services. Then follow with a question and answer period, a group close, and an individual close with each guest.

Greet each guest with the hostess. At the door, shake hands and get first names. If you are uncertain about a name ask: "Marian or Mary Ann?" It's flattering to ask now, embarrassing later.

"There are tricks for committing names to your short-term memory," Ross says. "If you have personally invited the guests to your hostess's group showing, memorize their names ahead of time. Then, at the showing, attach the names you already know to the faces you're meeting."

Next follow these steps, Ross suggests:

> "The first thing I would like to do is thank our hostess, Susanne, for allowing me to come into her home and introduce all of you to Camelion's sheer nonrun hosiery and our brand-new sterling silver jewelry line. I would also like to extend a warm welcome to all the guests here tonight.
>
> "As a thank-you for having me in her home, I've brought along a small gift for Susanne. Susanne also has an opportunity to earn $50 worth of free products when two of you book showings of your own and when group sales are over $200. As her gift for tonight, Susanne has chosen a Gold Scroll necklace and matching bracelet."

Stating what your hostess can earn is not being pushy. It is a way of letting everyone know you appreciate her. Guests want their hostess to earn a gift. Make certain the gift is tastefully wrapped. Present it with a smile and thank you!

> "Tonight following a brief history of our company, I will teach you how to use hosiery as an accessory. And what shapes of earrings and lengths of necklaces to wear to enhance your unique face shape and neck length. I will need our hostess and some volunteers for that. Of course, we will have a question and answer period. Then I'd like to meet with each of you to answer any personal questions. Susanne will be serving refreshments at that point too."

Tell your audience why you started your own direct selling business. Stress your belief in your company. Praise the benefits of your own business such as control over your time, ability to set your own income level, tax advantages, high earning potential, on a part- or full-time business. To young moms: talk about scheduling your business around your family. To career women: stress your company's management opportunities.

"I dedicate one to two nights per week to my Camelion business. Over the past six months, I've bought a new entertainment center for my apartment and started a savings account to buy a condominium. I have more than 150 happy clients. When I have 300 clients, I intend to quit my secretarial job and conduct my Camelion business full time. The only employer who will pay what you are worth is you!"

"So far, I've helped five ladies to start their own businesses and I am now a manager."

In the group demonstration, encourage participation from the audience. Ross often asks guests if they ever had an embarrassing hosiery run spoil the look of their outfit.

"Every woman nods her head," Ross reports.

Request questions.

Always repeat the question to be sure you and the audience understand it. Then, completely answer it before you move forward. Make certain your answer satisfies the questioner.

In your group close, your mission is to:

- Reinforce your company guarantee and why you think everyone should be using your products and services.

- Suggest that if anyone needs to leave early, she meet with you first.

- State amounts most of your new clients purchase (people usually do whatever they feel is *normal*).

- Inform the guests when you'll deliver their products and matter-of-factly include the cost.

# *H*OW TO CLOSE INDIVIDUALS AT GROUP MEETS

The guests who must leave early meet with you first. Ask:

- "Phyllis, would you like to begin by selecting your favorite sterling silver jewelry pieces or hosiery shades?"

- "Charlotte, I hope you enjoyed yourself. What have you decided to take home with you tonight?"
- "Lorelei, can you take advantage of our hosiery value package of six or twelve pairs?"
- "Marian, for an additional $8, you can take home two extra pairs. Is there any reason why you couldn't take home all six pairs to get these savings?"
- "Great! Write your full name, address, and phone number on the top portion of this receipt."

# *B*OOKING MORE SHOWINGS

Joyce: I'll phone in about two days to make certain you truly love the luxury of wearing nonrun hosiery. At each group showing I select one or two people I see as future hostesses. You would be great! Everyone admires you. As a hostess, you can earn $50 in free products! Is there any reason why you couldn't have a few friends over and hostess a showing of your own? I know you'd be terrific!

Jolee: I would love to be a hostess, but everyone I know is here tonight.

Joyce: Most of them weren't able to pick up everything they wanted today and would appreciate another opportunity. And we could ask your friends to bring someone with them who wasn't here today. Which would be better for you, two or three weeks from now?

Jolee: Three weeks from now would be better.

Joyce: Tuesday or Wednesday evening?

Jolee: Wednesday.

Joyce: Wednesday night it is then. 7:30 or 8:00?

Jolee: Eight o'clock.

So the close is complete. And the tier-marketing cycle starts over.

# CHAPTER TWENTY-SIX

# The Master Closer in Top Form

Effective performers draw on tested techniques to play the audience like an instrument. Master closers, like performers, use classic techniques again and again. Learn the keys in this book until they become second nature. Soon closing will become reflex. In time, as you move into closing, the correct techniques will pop up almost automatically. (One ace calls it "putting yourself in overdrive.") When the closing keys become part of your business personality, they emerge at the right time, with the right impact.

Bruce Alexander, the Tennessee real estate expert, believes the ace closer melds many major and minor keys into an *overall attitude.* Closing makes the critical difference between the trained professional and the order taker, he says. A seasoned closer plans ahead to control the sale.

"In closing on a house, save something that *they* can sell to *you*," he says. "When they start selling you, start writing up the sale. Do it in the living room if the seller isn't home. Or write it up on your car fender, or wherever you can. Don't drive all the way back to the office—only to find out somebody sold the property ten minutes earlier."

The contract close is the most basic of all. Simply ask questions and start filling out the contract. When it's complete, get the prospect to okay it, and you've closed the sale.

If the buyer has not sold enough to go right to contract, use the balance sheet close. They like the property, but you just can't nail them down. Say: "Tom and Mary, I want you to do something smart investors do before they make decisions."

Your prospects think: "Smart buyers do it. We want to be smart buyers. We'll do it."

Take a piece of paper and draw a line right down the middle. Say: "Let's write on this half of the paper all the reasons for *owning* this property. On this side, we'll write down the reasons you should *not* own this property." Help the prospect fill out the sheet.

"The property certainly suits your needs, doesn't it?"

"Gee, I like it." Write that down. *Property suits needs.*

When you finish, the positives should outweigh negatives three or four to one. Then ask the prospect where the weight of the evidence lies. That's impressive, the preponderance of the evidence. He or she is going to judge the evidence.

Convert all *general* objections to *specifics*. General: "I want to think it over." Ask: "What parts concern you?" Get the prospect to say: "I'm concerned about the lack of a second bedroom." Now that's an objection you can work on.

# *K*EEP YOUR ASSET FROZEN

Now suppose you cannot close on the house today. The buyer has a legitimate question. You can answer it tomorrow but not today. It's 2 o'clock in the afternoon. You don't want Tom and Mary to look at any other property today. Somebody may sell them. You want them to go right home.

If you go back to the office, and your prospects are parked in back, you park in *front* so they must come through the office. Get them in and go into the closing again. If you drive up near their car, they'll get in and blast off. Plan ahead like a closer.

On the way back, stop and get ice cream. Say: "I'd like you to take this little gift home. The kids have been great. They'll enjoy it."

Now there's ice cream in the car. They *must* go home before it melts. When they get home and give the kids the ice cream, they're not going to feel like going out again. They're off the market until the next day. Frozen assets may be a problem in finance. In closing: it's the way to outfox your competitor.

# *T*HE CLOSING ATTITUDE UNDER GLASS

Good closers are not born, they develop themselves. That's what makes a professional: perfecting your craft. But no matter what you sell, you benefit from exposure to expert closing. Convert it to your product or service. Put closing advice under a microscope, and you'll begin to see the keys emerge. Take apart the case you've just seen. Notice how the closing keys are so integrated they're almost invisible—but all the more effective.

- The *Little Question* appears several times, not overt, but interwoven.

- *Do Something*. He gets the prospect to write advantages and disadvantages and then make the final judgment.

- *Third Party Endorsement*. Who better than the prospects themselves? Let *them* tell *you* how wonderful it is.

- *Something for Nothing*. The ice cream. But it comes with a double-whammy: they must get it home quickly and cannot see a competitive property.

Closing keys, stitched in place, are all the more powerful because the seams don't show. They're closing keys to you, but to the buyer, they're reassuring advice, or helpful information, or a real solution to a problem. When your closing keys become second nature they'll be interwoven in the same manner, no matter what your product or service.

Of course, in some situations, the keys are more overt, as David Boue's classic close illustrates.

# *D*AVE BOUE'S VISIBLE CLOSING KEYS

Dave Boue arrives at the sale fully prepared to use any (or all) of his carefully orchestrated closers.

"What I use depends on what the prospect says or does," Boue says.

Does this mean Boue eschews homework and plays it by ear? Absolutely not. He sells a complicated business service in a volume of $500,000 a year. This requires intensive preparation. He must know his service inside-out, know the client's business, and know his closing keys.

"I'm prepared to draw on any of 25 responses," Boue says. "I don't know which I'll need, but whatever it is I'm ready."

Does that sound like an enormous amount of work? Yes. But it pays off in spades or, more properly, dollars. Watch Dave Boue call on Whitlaw Chambers, general manager of a company that makes solar products for the home. Boue sells a seminar service that dramatizes product benefits to the public. It's intangible, new to many prospects, and hard to grasp.

This is Boue's second call. On his first call, he left Chambers a plan and budget.

Boue arrives at Chambers' office at 8:45 A.M.—"the day gets complicated as it wears on at that company." (Before meeting Chambers, Boue stopped in to see Chambers' boss, Vickors Reilly, to make a valuable suggestion on a *completely unrelated* matter.) He's now seated with Chambers.

"Coffee?" Chambers asks.

"No, thanks," Boue says. "I brought my own." From his briefcase, he takes a small compact coffeemaker and small silver cup. "I have a special blend made in Brazil. Want to try mine?"

In wonder, Chambers does.

"Very appropriate we should be talking about solar products today, Whit," Boue says. "I was just reading this article from *The New York Times* last Sunday. It relates directly to the future of your business."

Naturally, Chambers is interested. ("It's amazing how many business executives have *not* read key articles," Boue says. "I use this to advantage.")

Boue summarizes the *Times* comments. Solar products, once considered a novelty, are now a necessity to many customers. When it comes to saving energy, people don't worry about whether to install a solar device—they concentrate on *how* to get it.

"So this is the solar era," Boue says. "But as you know better than I, you're in an ease-of-entry business. Almost anyone can set up in a garage and call himself a solar products manufacturer. The number of companies in the field has grown by 500 percent in the past year, according to the Solar Products Association. There's a power struggle going on right now for leadership. A few will emerge as leaders in the public mind. Many more will be left by the wayside and go out of business."

Chambers nods. What Boue is saying is certainly provocative.

"To establish leadership, your company must make a dramatic but legitimate gesture," Boue says. "Now it's true you put on a public demonstration about 18 months ago when the industry was much younger. And you've benefitted from that. But you must decide when you can be on the *give* and when you can be on the *take*."

Give? Take? How does that work, Chambers wants to know.

Here Boue stops the action (seemingly) to tell Chambers a story. When Nelson Rockefeller was running for reelection as governor of New York, his political enemies circulated rumors that Rockefeller was on the *give*—that he was giving money to certain groups to swing votes his way come election day.

"This contrasts with the usual political charge of being on the *take*," Boue says. "Naturally it wouldn't be credible to accuse a Rockefeller of being on the *take*. Who could offer him money that he doesn't already have? So they accused him of being on the *give*."

Chambers, who follows politics closely, is amused by the story.

"On the *give*," he says. "That's pretty good."

But there's a moral here, Boue says, that applies to the solar industry (in one deft stroke, he shifts back to closing).

"When you made that public demonstration 18 months ago," Boue says, "you were on the *give*—giving the public information and instruction to help buyers make decisions about solarizing homes. People appreciate that. When they get ready to buy, they turn—in many cases—to that helpful company that put on the demonstration."

Since that time, Boue tells Chambers, your company has been on the *take*.

"You've been reaping the benefits of that early demonstration," Boue says. "But you cannot go on being on the take forever. Now you've got to go on the *give* again. This public demonstration is the most dramatic legitimate way to go on the *give*."

Chambers is nearly convinced. However, there's the matter of cost.

"Let me pour you another cup of coffee," Boue says, "and I'll tell you how we can plan to save you money over the previous quote."

Boue then details a plan whereby Chambers can rent a meeting site at less cash outlay by bartering some of his solar products for seminar space.

"This will reduce your cash outlay by $2,000," Boue says.

Just then, Reilly comes into Chambers' office.

"Sorry to interrupt," Reilly says. "Just wanted to catch Dave before he left. Dave, that's a good suggestion you made today. We're moving out on it. Thanks a lot."

Naturally, Dave says he's glad to help.

"By the way, Vickors," Chambers says. "I want to see you a little later about a new plan for a public demonstration. We want to make a decision on this right away."

Vickors agrees and leaves. Boue asks Chambers to decide *which* products he wants to barter. He then gets Chambers to initial the contract. The sale is closed.

# *H*OW BOUE CLOSED THROUGHOUT

Off the cuff? Far from it. Dave Boue went in loaded for bear. Canned presentation? No. Boue stored a number of *prepared elements* in his mind, but the presentation moved like a skilled performer on a talk show. Boue drew on rehearsed components. He filled in between the bricks with pleasing and convincing conversational mortar.

Are you willing to prepare to that extent? Do you know your closing keys so well they pop up as needed—almost (but not quite) by reflex? Well, master closers *do*. Examine the closing keys Dave Boue drew from mental inventory.

First, he set the time to suit buyer mood (in this case in the morning) to close in the right psychological climate. He brought along a distinctive coffee pot and offered his customer a drink from a silver cup (the *do something* key). This ensured customer interest. It set Dave aside from 999 other salespeople Chambers may have known.

Dave was selling an event, so his *coming event* key was built-in. His well-prepared manner assumed he'd get the order (*beyond any doubt* key). He used Chambers' own boss to get his *third party endorsement*. Of course, Reilly coming in to Chambers' office was a stroke of luck. (Or was it? Good closers make their own luck!)

Boue also used the *coming event* key in talking about the industry shakeout and how some companies will be left by the wayside.

Because he had investigated a less expensive way for Chambers to buy, he was really offering *Something for Nothing*.

Boue even worked in *The Little Question* key by asking Chambers which products he wanted to barter. Not *if* but *which*—a much easier decision to make.

Of course at the end Boue trotted out *Ask and Get*—time for Chambers to sign. He signed.

Clearly, Boue's most important move was stopping the sale to tell a related story about Nelson Rockefeller. Storytelling is part of the *Third Party Endorsement* key. But once he told his story, Boue immediately moved back into the close.

He opened with a true story from *The New York Times* about Chambers' industry. You can't hit them harder than that.

In this one close, Boue wove all seven major keys into his presentation. He used a number of special keys—plus much good common sense and good closemanship. He was *prepared* totally—a true professional at work.

## CLOSING ARSENAL AVAILABLE TO YOU

The seven major keys and dozens of special keys to closing are now yours. Scale them up and down. Adapt and adopt. Rejigger and rebore. Polish and sand. By the time you finish, they won't look like these keys at all. No matter. Use these principles as your launching pad. Where you go beyond that is as wide open as outerspace.

Review what you have learned in this book. You started with the importance of closing—quite simply, if you cannot close, you cannot sell. There are no born closers. Closing can be learned. Take your instruction from the world's champion closers.

You learned the importance of building a foundation. Dave Boue started working on his close when he read *The New York Times* article and decided to use it as ammunition. (Correction. He started his close by keeping informed in the first place!)

Your foundation includes being able to speak clearly, colorfully, and persuasively—the closer's *fundamental* tools. If you're not an expert speaker, start studying. You must master the language before doing anything else.

Classics *are* classic because they can be experienced time and again with increasing value. H. L. Mencken said: "Everyone who loves music should hear Bach's Mass in B Minor at least once a year." So it is with this collection of closing techniques.

Use this book as a reference whenever you face a knotty problem. No matter what you need, there's advice or experience here that will help you. Reread this book once a year to reinforce your closing knowledge.

Once you make the closing keys part of your nature, you'll close the easy sales easily and medium-hard sales automatically.

The purpose of *Secrets of Closing Sales* is to make your work easier, more productive, more profitable, and—perhaps most important of all—more fun. You now have the tools to do just that. Good selling! And remember: good closers make their own luck.

## CLOSING LAB

*KAT:* In visiting with master closers, we've seen minor keys employed to *complement* major keys.

*CRAY:* Also to crack unusual cases. Take the *whadeye hafta key*, for example. That usually comes to play at the end of a seemingly successful conversation. Everything has gone swimmingly—except that the prospect just sits there.

*KAT:* Then the closer says *whadeye hafta* do to get you to make your decision today? Often it smokes out objections that haven't come out earlier.

*CRAY:* And expert closers *love* objections! When they get an objection on the operating table, they go at it with a rapier, a scalpel, or a baseball bat.

*KAT:* Tell me about the *Ben Franklin key,* named for that great American sage.

*CRAY:* To use the *Ben Franklin,* you ask the prospect to compare features of Product A and Product B—on paper. On your left list all the reasons *for.* On the right, all reasons *against.*

*KAT:* Must the prospect do this all by himself?

*CRAY:* Not a bit of it. You're more acquainted with the facts. Don't deprive him of your assistance.

*KAT:* Are we looking for a complete whitewash?

*CRAY:* No. Find a few points on the other side. But fix it so *your* side outweighs *his* side 4 to 1. This is war—business war. Then the document becomes the closer! No one can argue with the facts!

*KAT:* So the best closers often use major keys throughout and wheel in minor keys when they need a change of-pace! To me, Cray, we're saying the seller must "do something even if it's wrong."

*CRAY:* Closing favors the activist, all right. When in doubt, take action—you won't be wrong often.

*KAT:* But the *right* action at the right time! Draw on the combined experience of seasoned closers. What are do's and don'ts from inventory?

*CRAY:* In the theatre, seasoned directors, train casts to "give the illusion of the first time." The problem: the more you give your presentation, the better you know it. But knowledge often attacks freshness. You still need to make it sound like the first time.

## CLOSING LAB

CRAY: Selling and performing are closely related in other ways too. A top salesperson is a business actor. The customer is both *audience* and *critic*.

KAT: But, in this case, the audience pays at the *end* of the show—*only* if they like the performance.

CRAY: Right. One show biz key is called the *Marcel Marceau.* Johnny Chapman sells toiletries to retailers. He's very chary with words. He displays his products lovingly. He points out key phrases in the point-of-sale material. He shows merchandise. He points to this feature and that. He demonstrates. He lets the products speak. Then he starts writing and asks: "How many?" Or takes out an order blank, marks an x and says: "Here." It works. Silence can be powerful. *The Marcel Marceau.* Now are you ready for the Lauren Bacall close?

KAT: Does this close have anything to do with her throaty comment to Humphrey Bogart? "You know how to whistle, don't cha, Steve? Just put your lips together and (pause) *blow.*

CRAY: Listen to this from the buyer side. Here's my tape of Jackson Reich, a department store buyer.

REICH: I buy from this nutty saleswoman, Janice Bothwell. She has this husky voice like what's-her-name, the movie star. As Janice gets closer to wrapping up the sale, she gets more and more intimate. And that basso voice gets low enough to break glass in the basement. So I lean forward to make sure I hear it all. She continues to whisper. I continue to listen. Before I know it, she asks me to buy. I whisper: "Yes." I tell you it's uncanny.

KAT: Janice Bothwell could have pursued a successful career on stage or screen. But the selling profession became richer when she decided to join us.

But a closer cannot use the Marcel Marceau very often. He also needs power words for power closes!

CRAY: Yes, use viewpoint words to present your industry in fine light. *Old-fashioned* is a wonderful word if you're selling *lace, ice cream* or *hotel service*. But if your product is *computers, airplanes,* or *copying machines,* old-fashioned is the last phrase you need.

KAT: Agreed! In presenting West Virginia coal, we used *surface* mining—never *strip* mining. For Renault, *imported* cars. But in talking about American coal, we also stressed *foreign* oil. For Lincoln Logs, we say log *homes*—never *cabins*. For National Pest Control Association, we valued the *pest control specialist*—never, God save us, the *exterminator*.

CRAY: Collect workhorse words that motivate. The right words rule the world. Power words that make your speech golden and your pocket green. Power words motivate, captivate, and titillate your prospect. Power words place your prospect in a Yes mood.

Most closer words are simple including *which* (something or something), *why* (the favorite of all great closers), *what if* (the fantasy spinner's workhorse), *let's* (remember Lyndon Johnson's "Come, let us reason together"), *here's how* (this will save you money or time), *right* (everyone wants to do what is right), and many more.

# Bibliography

Bennis, Warren. *On Becoming A Leader*. Reading, MA: Addison-Wesley, 1989.

Bliss, Edwin C. *Getting Things Done: The ABC's of Time Management*. Charles Scribner & Sons, 1986.

Collins, James and William Lazier. *Beyond Entrepreneurship: Turning Your Business into an Enduring Great Company*. Prentice Hall, 1992.

Coney, Stephen. *Principle Centered Leadership*.

DePree, Max. *Leadership is an Art*. Doubleday, 1989.

Dickson, A. *A Woman in Your Own Right*. New York: Quartet Books, 1982.

Godfrey, Joline. *Our Wildest Dreams: Women Entrepreneurs Making Money, Having Fun, Doing Good*. Harper Collins, 1992.

Hanan, Mack. *Fast-Growth Strategies: How to Maximize Profits from Start-Up Through Maturity*. McGraw-Hill, 1987.

Larkin, Geraldine A. *Twelve Simple Steps to a Winning Marketing Plan*. Probus Publishing, 1992.

McConkey, Dale D. *No Nonsense Delegation*. New York, NY. Amacom, 1986.

McCormack, Mark H. *What They Don't Teach You at Harvard Business School: Notes From a Street-Smart Executive.* Bantam Books, 1984.

Popcorn, Faith. *The Popcorn Report.*

Resnik, Paul. *The Small Business Bible.* John Wiley & Sons, 1988.

Sherman, Andrew. *One Step Ahead: The Legal Aspects of Business Growth.* Amacom Books, 1989.

Snyder, E. Kenneth. *Employee Matters: A Legal Guide to Hiring, Firing and Setting Employee Policies.* Probus Publishing, 1991.

Spraguis, Ellyn. "How to Fire." *Inc.* May, 1992.

Ury, William. *Getting Past No: Negotiating with Difficult People.*

*Bits & Pieces*, Vol. N/No. 3. Fairfield, NJ: The Economics Press, Inc.

# Index

## A

Adams, William W., 20
Ad-libbing, 258
Affirmation, 50, 59, 246
Alertness training, 37, 39, 86
Alexander, Bill, 345
Alexander, Bruce, 159, 351
Allaire, Lloyd, 23-24
Allaire, Paul, 16-17
Allard, Lloyd, 184-85, 237-38
Antiquo, Robin, 47
Appeal to pride close, 212
Approach, 39
Armstrong, Warren, 98-99
Ash, Mary Kay, 53-54
Ask and Get key, 130, 193-208
    basics of, 193-95
    chief benefit of, 197
    cold calls, 200-201
    direct requests, 195-96

presentation step, when to
    skip, 198
when to use, 202
Assumptive closing technique,
    148-49
Attitude:
    coping with shifts in, 62-64
    and customer reassurance,
      64
Authority Close, 179-80
Autoconditioning, 37-38
Avoidance of worry, as human
    motivator, 67, 68
Ayers, Richard H., 20

## B

Backsliding, 287-88
Backup plan, holding in
    reserve, 227-28
Balking, 204-5, 227

# C

# H

Hahn, Marshall, Jr., 20
Half nelson close, 211
Halyard, O. C., 50, 105-7, 319-20
Handler, George, 37
Harper, Marion, 337-38
Harris, Art, 96-98
Harris, Sonny, 264
Harrow, Bryce, 145-46
Hawkins, Old Amos, 137-38
Hawkins, Robert, 221-22
Hay, Louise L., 50
Helms, Ben, 240
Herd complex, 58
Hesitators, motivating, 150
Heston, Charlton, 249
Hidden needs, uncovering,
    44-45, 67-68
Hill, John, 27
Hobbson, Ellerbe, 224
Hockstein, Peter, 281
Hodge, Georgeson, 201-2
Holbrook, Hal, 249
Honorary sales manager, use of,
    218
Hopkins, Barclay, 48-49
Hopkins, Claude, 187-88, 236
Horowitz, Samuel, 137
Hughes, Charles C., 60
Human motivators, 67
    in buying situations, 68
Hunt, H. L., 101-2

# I

Iden, Jay B., 115
If-by-whiskey straddle, 253-54

"If the Office Approves, Do We
    Have an Agreement?" close,
    214
"I'll think if over" close, 215, 225
Inflammatory words, replacing,
    285
Information, as negotiating
    tool, 324
Intuitor, as buyer type, 89, 90, 91
"I want to think it over" close,
    217

# J

Jaworowski, Gregory, 222-23
Johnson, Walter H. Jr., 13, 246,
    337-38
Jordahl, Ellery, 205, 292-93
Jordan, Harold, 155-57
Journalistic presentation, 257
Just-suppose questions, 188-89

# K

Kahn, George N., 34-35
Kellar, Robert E., 318-19
Kelly, Fred C., 185-86
Kempner, Dr. Walker, 255-56
Knowledge, as power, 51, 246
Kroc, Ray A., 11

# L

Laird, Dr. Donald, 58-59
Language, as a weapon, 313-14
Language skills, 271-73